ISADORE'S SECRET

~Isadore's Secret

SIN, MURDER, AND CONFESSION

IN A NORTHERN MICHIGAN TOWN

Mardi Link

The University of Michigan Press

Ann Arbor

Copyright © by the University of Michigan 2009
All rights reserved
Published in the United States of America by
The University of Michigan Press
Manufactured in the United States of America
⊚ Printed on acid-free paper

2012   2011   2010   2009   4   3   2   1

A CIP catalog record for this book is available from the British Library.

Library of Congress Cataloging-in-Publication Data

Link, Mardi.
    Isadore's secret : sin, murder, and confession in a northern
Michigan town / Mardi Link.
       p.   cm.
    ISBN 978-0-472-07079-4 (cloth : alk. paper) — ISBN 978-0-472-
05079-6 (pbk. : alk. paper)
       1. Murder—Michigan—Isadore.   2. Convents—Michigan—Isadore.
3. Isadore (Mich.)—History.   I. Title.
HV6534.I8L56   2008
364.152′3092—dc22   2009020597

TO BEVELCHA CYNTHIA MARY MARSHA WOJCIECHOWSKI,

POLISH PRINCESS AND BEST FRIEND FOREVER

If you reveal your secrets to the wind,
you should not blame the wind for
revealing them to the trees.

—KAHLIL GIBRAN

ACKNOWLEDGMENTS

FIRST, HERE'S TO THE PACK RATS. To the researchers, collectors, history buffs, hoarders, genealogists, and trash-pickers who think enough of their paper loot to pass it on. They are the primary sources of the pieces of this story that I uncovered at the University of Notre Dame archives, Archives of Michigan, the Leelanau Historical Museum, the Traverse Area Historical Society, and umpteen libraries. People, save your diaries and your letters, because someday some writer may come looking for them.

Ruth Tucker provided an opportunity to spend a weekend in Isadore, watching the comings and goings at Holy Rosary in the present day. Isadore native Paul Brzezinski provided both a friendly ear and his expert Polish/English translation services. His niece, Kathy Britton, got me started, as did Professor Marty Trapp. Connie Walters also helped with translations. Leelanau County Clerk Michelle Crocker and her entire staff were efficient and welcoming. George Meredith offered up a few historic gems; Jack Sweeney has a unique understanding of the many ways this case invites obsession, and shared his precious notebook with me. Bonnie Hain, Marylyn Link, Deb Schepperley, Julie Schopieray, and Beverly Wojciechowski each read an early version of the manuscript and offered many helpful suggestions. Author and attorney Steve Lehto is a thorough, careful, intuitive reader and helped a great deal with legal and trial aspects. Aimé Merizon and Ceil Jensen provided some helpful long-distance research.

The University of Michigan Press, editor Ellen McCarthy, sales manager Mike Kehoe, jack-of-all-trades Scott Ham, digital mastermind Melissa Baker-Young, and banker Karyn McIntire all continue to be friends and advocates for regional authors who find stories in their own backyards but still have designs on areas far beyond their own neighborhoods.

Owen, Luke, and Will did an admirable job of tolerating their mother's latest endeavor. Bravo, boys. Pete Morton expressed just the right amount of angst and wonder at all the proper plot points.

CONTENTS

AUTHOR'S NOTE

A NUMBER OF NORMALLY UNRELATED factors worked together quite effectively to isolate Isadore, Michigan, from the outside world at the turn of the previous century. Geography was the first of these. We Michiganders love to hold up our right hand, palm out, to anchor some specific locale in the lower peninsula of our state. Using this time-honored system, Leelanau County is the pinkie fingernail, slipping away slightly from the hand's other digits into the vastness of Lake Michigan. The West Arm of Grand Traverse Bay divides this little finger further. Though Isadore is located inland, uncharted swampland, acres of farmland, and finally what amounted to a three-sided moat separated the village from the rest of the state, the country, and the world beyond.

Working alongside geography were two other random isolators, religion and nationality, which, at the time this story takes place, amounted to one and the same. Virtually everyone who lived in Isadore in the decades before the murder until long after the trial was Catholic and of Polish descent. They spoke and wrote in Polish not only at home but also in school and in church. They conducted business, whenever possible, with other Polish speakers; even today, if you attend a gathering in Isadore—an auction say, or Holy Rosary's annual Summer Festival for a plate of their *smaczne* (which means delicious) fried chicken—you will hear Polish and English spoken in equal measure, with few offers to translate the former for a visitor.

And finally, the weather worked to set the tiny village apart. In an

average winter, more than ten feet of snow falls on this region from November to April; a hard winter could bring as much as fifteen feet, along
with a near constant arctic wind and weeks of ice. In the early 1900s,
roads were crude and cars still a novelty; even going short distances required skis, snowshoes, or a sleigh; traveling in or out of the region from
late fall to early spring was a suicide mission. "It keeps out the riffraff,"
today's residents say proudly, of the northern Michigan winters. In
Isadore at the time of this story, anyone not local was riffraff.

Into this remote northern village came two unmarried women who
couldn't have been more different: one a gregarious and naive Catholic
nun, and the other an uncompromising and joyless housekeeper. Within
the isolation of Isadore, they separated themselves even further. The
tiny church, school, convent, and rectory were yet their own island, and
it was there that these two women found themselves living in the same
household. The result would be sorrow of the worst sort.

Today in Isadore they refer to the crime as "the tragedy"—if, that is,
they refer to it at all. Though the same last names that began appearing
on headstones in the cemetery as early as the 1860s can be found on
mailboxes of the living all along the roads leading in and out of Isadore,
very few members of these pioneer families will talk openly about the
event, even though it happened more than a century ago. One elderly
woman pointed a bony finger at me and rasped, "You should be afraid
of the evil eye." A force still feared in Isadore.

As a side note, it's worth mentioning that, for clarity's sake, I committed to a single spelling of the Polish surnames belonging to the
people in this story. During my research I found multiple spellings of
each last name on everything from gravestones to immigration papers
to newspaper articles and even court documents. An early settled America dominated by English speakers had a difficult time with the conso-
nant-heavy and lengthy Polish last names and often misspelled them.

So as not to confuse the reader, here Stella's full name is always
spelled "Stanislawa Lipczynska," even though historical records document her name in a variety of incarnations including "Lypchinski,"
"Lypcrynska," "Lipinski," "Lipinska," etc. Likewise for the surname
"Flees"; it has been spelled "Fleis," "Fleece," and even "Flies." To further confuse things, in the Polish language the suffix "ski" generally
refers to a man, and "ska" to a woman, sometimes to a woman unat-

tached to a man either because of youth, free choice, divorce, or widow-hood, as was Stella's case. And, finally, the *J* in Sister Janina's name is pronounced like a *Y:* "Ya-nina."

The story I tell here is entirely nonfiction, pieced together from anonymous and attributed personal interviews, historic newspaper accounts, magazine articles, court documents, prison documents, police records, personal letters, family memoirs, priests' notes, sacramental records, church correspondence, and local histories; everything in quotation marks was spoken aloud and came from one or more of these sources.

While this story centers around a murder of the most ghastly sort, there is love here, too, and devotion, and religious fervor. There is sin, sex, torture, confession, and secrets. Every device imaginable for the darkest gothic novel appears in these pages, and yet this drama was not drawn from the imagination, but from tattered bits of fact confined, for more than a century, to local gossip and legend, and scattered historical records. This story is true, and yet somehow had escaped a thorough retelling until now.

The quotes that begin the sections (and can be found sparingly in the text) are taken from a battered copy of *The Nun's Rule,* by Bishop Richard Poore, Rev. James Morton, and Rev. Francis Aiden Gasquet, published in 1905 as part of The King's Classics series. I found it for $1 at Holy Rosary's annual Attic Treasures sale.

Prologue: A Grave
November, 1918

> They are the devil's dirt-men, and
> wait continually in his privy. Thus,
> they are busy in this foul employment,
> and strive with each other about it.
> Such men stink in their stinking trade,
> and make every place stink that they
> come to.
>
> —*The Nun's Rule*

SWINGING PLANKS OF LANTERN LIGHT shine through the musty air and onto the dirt floor of the church basement. The oddly glowing rectangles syncopate over the damp ground and illuminate even the darkest, stooped-down corners of the space beyond.

The shapes are out of place on this bright autumn afternoon. Outside, it is still daylight. Only an hour ago, the end-of-day voices of schoolchildren could be heard echoing over the grassy hillside as the students walked home together to neighboring farms. Down here in the dank, the only human sound is the ragged breathing of two men.

If not for this gruesome errand and their shared spiritual faith, these men would have nothing in common at all. They are separated from each other by class, motive, age, and vocation, and yet have been made temporary equals by the dread they now share.

One of the men, the young parish priest, holds a malignant rumor in his heart and the lantern handle in his hand. A hand that shakes without ceasing, causing the kerosene glow behind the light's glass chimney to illuminate its earthbound quarry unevenly. The other man, a laborer, is much older and has only recently been promoted to church sexton. He grips a hand-forged farm implement and slides it gingerly into the dirt. His tool is a potato fork; a shorter, squatter, less savage-looking cousin of the pitchfork. It is commonly used for bringing potatoes up out of the ground at harvest time without damaging them, and not for authenticating church gossip. Leaning nearby, against the basement wall, are two shovels, just in case.

Despite their differences, above ground these men belong completely to this place, in both body and soul. A glimpse of their faces anywhere in the sanctuary, the rectory, the school, the barn, or the gardens would be a welcome sight. The priest is the religious and cultural leader of an insular flock of immigrant Polish farmers in northern Michigan. He is well liked and respected for his handsome good looks and obvious spiritual fire. The sexton is appreciated too, for his consistency and practical skills. And today, by the priest at least, for his loyalty.

But here below, these men of Isadore are interlopers. Only trespassers would sneak silently into the church's sloped underbelly without witness to carry out such a sinful and secret errand as this one. Despite their tools, and their lantern, and their resolve, neither is equipped for the task at hand or for what is to come.

Still, the younger man watches while the older man labors. The grave they seek isn't deep, and they don't have to wait long before it is found. The pile of lumber that hid it for more than a decade is gone. The tines of the sexton's fork strike something hard and smooth and almost porcelain-like. A bone. A human thighbone.

The men share a long look at one another but say nothing. They each must know what the other is thinking. That the rumors are true. That the missing nun, their spiritual sibling and fellow attendant of God, did not run away from the convent, after all. She didn't turn her back on her calling and flee with a lover. She wasn't kidnapped and neither did she slip into madness like her mother, and wander into the swamp at the edge of the meadow. Instead, she was taken from them. And yet, she was also here all along.

The shovels turn out to be necessary. The priest puts down the lantern to help his sexton dig. With first the potato fork, and then the shovels, and finally their bare hands, the men find many more bones—

nearly a full skeleton—laid to rest on her back as if bent in half, her arms flung over her raised knees. At one end of the grave they find a pair of low-heeled shoes with small foot bones still inside. At the other end, a human skull.

Rotting over these bones are remnants of the coarse brown wool traditionally used to fashion a nun's habit, as well as a piece of braided black waist cord. It was is if the Sister simply went to the basement, ducked her head under the small doorframe, walked to her shallow grave, and, without making a sound, lay down in this raw grittiness and died. Except for one thing.

The sexton digs up the skull with his shovel, then cradles it in the warm bowl of his dirt-smeared hands. The earth surrounding this spot has a darker color than anywhere else. The sexton caresses the brain cavity with his calloused thumbs, rubbing away years of dirt. He does not see or feel the crack a few inches above the skull's right temple, but it is there.

Yes, it was exactly as if the Sister just walked here of her own volition and lay down in her grave, except for that.

Lost Soul

Summary, 1907

> Surely our foe, the warrior of hell,
> shoots, as I ween, more bolts at one
> Sister than at seventy and seven
> secular ladies.
>
> —*The Nun's Rule*

THE THREE SISTERS stood shoulder to shoulder on the porch of the out-of-the-way church and waved good-bye. Despite the midday heat, they were each covered from their shoulders to their ankles in the heavy brown wool favored by their Felician Order. A black veil trimmed in white encased their heads, hiding their hair and flowing past their elbows. The only visible flesh was the skin of their plain faces and the palms of their waving hands.

From the seat of his fine buggy, the priest waved back. Father Andrew was not wearing his traditional black cassock. He, his younger sister, and the parish's chore boy were going fishing for the afternoon. Besides saying Mass, it was one of the priest's favorite activities, and one of the few, along with hunting, that he shared with the other men of Isadore. Out of earshot they questioned his ethnicity and called him a "ruthless Tartar"; in person they couldn't deny his prowess as an outdoorsman. Father Andrew hunted or fished several times a week and had been out on the lake just the day before. "God does not subtract the time I spend fishing from my allotted time on earth," he was fond of saying.

In town that morning, the men talked about how well the pike and walleye were biting on nearby Lake Leelanau. If there were a more peaceful place to pass an afternoon, it would be difficult to conjure. It had been described by a traveling publisher as "a beautiful sheet of pure water, resting in the bosom of the hills, which, with their rounded, forest-covered forms, furnish a setting of surpassing loveliness." Rain was in the forecast for this enviable setting over next few days, and the fishing was always best just before inclement weather. The parish housekeeper, Stella, made a good pike dinner, in the traditional Polish way with gray sauce, butter, and summer vegetables, and he was hungry for it.

Fishing rods, hooks and fishing line, a net, and a bait can were loaded into the buggy along with an afternoon snack. This time of year on northern Michigan's inland lakes the best fishing could be had only in the early morning or the early evening. Anglers could either launch their own boat from the Narrows, fish from shore, or buy a ticket on the steamer *Leelanau* for $1.50. The priest's fishing party had already missed their first chance of the day, and so Father Andrew told Stella not to plan for the group to be back until dusk at the earliest.

Tall and broad shouldered, clad in dungarees and a summer-weight camp shirt, despite his usually stern expression, today Father Andrew looked more like a man on summer holiday than a priest. Against his better judgment, the day's work would have to wait. Though he wanted to leave the chore boy behind to keep up with the daily labors, Stella encouraged him to invite the lad along.

"Let the boy go," she said.

"He has work to do," Father Andrew told her. "He should stay home."

Something must have changed his mind, because as the horses pulled the buggy down the dirt road, away from the four corners of Isadore and Holy Rosary Parish, the fishing party numbered three: Father Andrew, his younger sister Susan, and their live-in laborer, Theodore Gruba.

When the sound of horse hooves and harness tack and buggy wheels had faded away, the three Sisters walked together back to their quarters in the schoolhouse for their afternoon rest. The new brick building had three floors and an attic; the third floor functioned as a small convent with separate bedrooms for each of the nuns. Their own word for their private space was *cell*.

Sister Angelina, Sister Josephine, and Sister Janina were all in fragile health, and it was their practice to sleep for a few hours every afternoon to help restore their energy. All three were Felicians, members of a relatively new order, begun less than a century earlier in Poland by Blessed Mary Angela Truszkowska. Prior to this new order, nuns since the Middle Ages had been restricted to a cloistered existence of prayer and contemplation. The Felicians would spend some of their time in prayer but would also circulate out in the world as schoolteachers. Most women who found their place in this modern order were comparatively energetic as well as assertive, unafraid of the prospect of serving in the wilds of America.

Final approbation for the new order hadn't been received from the Vatican until 1899, just eight years prior. It would take another century, but Sister Mary Angela would be beatified for her works in the church.

"The Sisters are called to save their own souls and the souls of others, hence they should lead as perfect a life as the Savior preached," their founder explained in her private writings. "Their perfection should not consist in doing unusual things but in leading ordinary lives in an extraordinary way."

Answering the Felician call meant total surrender to God and to His less fortunate followers; to serve "the needy, the lowly, the poor, and the marginal, with joyful, compassionate hearts." Their charge was simple but limitless: cooperate with Christ in the spiritual renewal of the world.

Like the first followers of Sister Angela, the Isadore nuns divided their time between contemplation and teaching. All three taught at the convent school but had remained in Isadore for the summer, even though without students their duties were now quite light. The rigors of travel back to the Motherhouse in Detroit would surely tax whatever strength they had left.

Sister Janina, the convent's Sister Superior, had contracted tuberculosis and was installed here in the north because her elders thought the country climate might improve her health. This particular form of suffering she shared with her order's founder. The Blessed Angela had contracted tuberculosis at sixteen but found recovery in the Polish countryside. Sister Janina would do the same here in America, the elders back at the Motherhouse prayed. The Sisters tried to view their physical problems as an opportunity instead of an affliction. God, they were certain, was just as present in illness as He was in robust good health.

The disease was a common one, especially prevalent in the close quarters of convents; Sister Janina's two junior Sisters suffered from the same affliction. Their frequent naps during the hottest part of the day seemed to do them all good, though the practice had caused some jealousy among the two other women of the household. Stella and her daughter, Mary, had also come outside to bid the fishing party good-bye and watched now as the nuns moved off toward their cells to rest.

"Listen, Mother, the Sisters got here a pretty good time," Mary complained, in their native Polish. "They are going to take a rest, and we must always work so hard."

Stella considered her daughter's lament. The conduct of these nuns, especially that of Janina, the Sister Superior, was suspect, but she still hoped for an easier life like theirs someday for her only child.

"When you grow up and get to be a Sister, then you will have a good time, too," she answered.

From the Sisters' perspective, the naps were not an indulgence but a necessity. They needed to conserve their precious energy, especially now. Only two days remained before the Bishop would arrive to bless their new school. It had been built that summer after two previous school buildings had burned down under suspicious circumstances. Both fires had ignited at the midnight hour. There was anti-Catholic sentiment in the region, perhaps a backlash against the large influx of Polish immigrants who were almost exclusively Catholic. Rumors circulated that the fires were arson.

"A peculiar thing about the fire was that several years ago a new building, which had just been completed at a cost of $2,700, was also destroyed, the origin of the fire never being learned," the newspaper reported. No children had been harmed when the school burned, but Sister Josephine, just a postulant then, had broken her leg jumping out a second-story window. The cause of these fires was never determined, but a remedy had been: This new school and its crowning convent were to be built out of brick.

The Bishop's blessing, they prayed, would add another layer of protection to the building, and the Sisters and Stella still had much to do to prepare for his arrival. The grounds had to be tidied, food prepared, and, most important, the church sanctuary and school needed to be decorated. Over the past several weeks, Sister Janina had been sending away for packages of manufactured paper flowers for just that purpose. Five boxes of them had already arrived in the mail and were safely stored in the church basement. The decorating work was to begin after their rest.

The Sisters climbed the stairs to the quiet refuge of their cells. On their knees before their cots, they prayed: *Teach me to do your will, for you are my God. Show me the path to holiness that you desire of me.*

Windows were left open to let in whatever breeze might happen by while the Sisters rested. Stella watched from the yard as the shades in each of their windows were drawn down against the heat and glare of the afternoon sun. "Wherefore, my dear Sisters, love your windows as little as possible," admonished *The Nun's Rule,* the small guide to behavior and prayer each carried in the breast pocket of her habit, "and mind your eyes there, lest your heart escape and go out and your soul fall sick as soon as it is out."

The rest of the day's work spread out before Stella like a hard march toward a far-off horizon. Whatever the task, she would manage. That's what Stanislawa "Stella" Lipczynska did. She managed.

She managed to go on when she was barely out of her teens and her husband died, leaving her alone to raise their infant daughter. She granted the promise he asked for on his deathbed: She would never remarry. She managed to escape the increasingly bloody persecution of Poles under Prussian rule and find her way safely to the American heartland. She managed to settle among her own people in this Polish community and find work that sustained both her and her daughter. And, much to the consternation of the parishioners, this small and snappish spider of a woman managed the affairs of Holy Rosary.

Tiny but fierce, her own hard work and her neighbors' hard opinions only fueled her on. Behind her back, a few of these neighbors even suggested Stella might be one of the terrible *Wilas,* the vicious feminine spirits who haunted the woods of their native Poland. One of these spirits could have followed them all to America just to torment them in their new land, they said, sometimes in jest and sometimes not. At not even five feet tall, the fear Stella inspired in both her enemies and her friends dwarfed her physical being; children ran away, hearts pounding, at the sight of her.

No matter what her neighbors thought of her, there would be no leisurely fishing trip for Stella, or her daughter, or any chance for a rest, either. God had put her on this earth to work, she often grumbled; that was her lot and she embraced it, with a fervor both religious and rigid.

Friday was baking day in the church kitchen and in the kitchens of the surrounding Isadore households as well. These four corners in Michigan's remote Leelanau Peninsula were made up of farms, Polish farmers, farmer's wives, and their large broods of children spaced together as closely as Russian nesting dolls. Every woman for twenty miles in any direction did her baking on Friday.

In preparation for the Bishop's visit, Stella had loaves of dark rye bread and white yeast bread, mixed flour bread, and pans of biscuits to bake. The garden had to be seen to, and so did Father Andrew's menagerie of animals. Stella herself kept a large flock of free-ranging geese and a coop full of chickens. As if this weren't enough, Mary needed help fitting the sleeves on a new dress she was sewing to wear for Sunday's blessing. She was going to put her piano lessons to good use and play a song for the Bishop, and she wanted to look pretty for her important moment. Sister Janina had been helping Mary earlier with both the song and the sewing, but she was probably sleeping, dead to the world, and of no help to her now.

No, there would be no rest for the housekeeper.

"Have you seen Sister Janina?"

Groggy from their naps, only two of the three nuns appeared in the doorway to the rectory kitchen later that afternoon. The oddly discomforted pair wobbled in without their leader and found Stella at the stove alone, baking bread. She ignored them as usual—they were always after something from her—but this time they would not be put off.

"Have you seen her?" they asked the housekeeper again.

Stella shook her head no and kept on with her work. A few minutes passed and the nuns held their place at the door, staring at her silently. She finally stopped, wiped her hands on her apron, and returned their gaze.

"Mary," Stella called out to her daughter, working in the adjacent sewing room. "Mary, there are Sisters here and they're asking for the other Sister. For Sister Janina."

"I ain't seen her," Mary answered, turning her attention back to hand-stitching a sleeve into one of the armholes of her new dress.

"Maybe the dog got her," Stella joked.

A scraggly black neighbor dog was a regular visitor to the kitchen doorway, on the hunt for scraps. It was Sister Janina or Father Andrew, animal lovers both, who usually obliged the mutt. From Stella, he was more likely to get a swift kick in the hindquarters, and he had learned to avoid her. The nuns laughed nervously and looked around the yard. No dog, black or otherwise, was in sight.

"I'm worried," Sister Angelina said.

The pair told Stella that when they awoke, they looked for Sister Janina in her cell but found it empty. All that told them of her recent presence there was her long rosary, hanging abandoned on her doorknob. Unless she was sleeping, it should have been safely attached to her waist cord. The Sisters then went downstairs to the common room and boiled water on the hotplate for their urn of afternoon coffee. Something unusual captured their attention.

The door from the common room to the outdoors was open and swinging wide on its hinges. This door was usually kept locked, especially in the afternoons when the upstairs occupants were sleeping and vulnerable to thieving transients, anti-Catholic pranksters, or any other unwelcome disturbance. The women called out for the Sister but received no reply.

On the windowsill closest to the door was Sister Janina's *Nun's Rule*, its pages fluttering to and fro in the breeze from the open window. This tiny omen was even more worrisome, they said, than the swinging door. When they took their vows, Felician Sisters promised to keep their *Nun's Rule* and their prayerbooks with them always, tucked in a small pocket sewn inside their habits, next to their hearts. They were to read from these books, follow their directions, and pray at every opportunity. "Here say, 'Hail Mary,' fifty or a hundred times, more or less, as ye have leisure," read one such direction. Like their rosaries, the Sisters were to relinquish these books only at bedtime.

Sister Janina was lighthearted and lacked the seriousness of many of her peers, but she was also pious, and it was not like her, they said, to break any vow of prayer. Especially one as fundamental to their calling as this.

There were a few neighboring farms, but Holy Rosary was quite isolated from the world beyond the Polish enclave of Isadore, so the women could only believe that the Sister was probably somewhere nearby. The little church community had been built on the northwest corner of a crossroads, the convent and school less than fifty yards north of the church. Out the church's back door was the rectory and barn. Beyond that, the cedar swamp. A cemetery bordered the convent to the north. With its angular steeple and long windows, Holy Rosary fit at the junction of Gatzke and Schomberg roads as tightly as a carpenter's corner-square.

Before they came to the rectory's kitchen to bother her, the Sisters told Stella, they had already taken a quick walk through the rest of the convent floor, and then looked downstairs throughout the empty schoolrooms. Once outside, they had stood in the yard and scanned the surrounding cornfields and meadow. They looked down the road toward town. Nothing.

Like Stella's, Sister Janina's life had gotten off to a trying start. Born Josephine Mezek on January 24, 1874, in Prussia, she entered convent life when she was only nine years old. This was not by choice but by necessity—her mother had been committed to the Illinois Eastern Hospital for the Insane, and shortly after that her father, a stone mason, died suddenly in a traffic accident, making her an orphan. Josephine had three brothers, Frank, Joseph, and Emmanuel, "Emil," who somehow managed to fend for themselves and make their way in the bustle of their home city, but they could not care for their sister. The Felician Order of Detroit took her in, and the nuns there taught her to read and write, and spiritually groomed her in their own image.

As a girl, Josephine bent to their instruction, if not always obediently, and the nuns doted on their outgoing and vivacious young charge. In 1888 when she was fourteen, Josephine Mezek became a postulant—a young woman promised to God and to the Catholic Church. She went from the school uniform worn by the high school aspirants to the simple black dress marking her as a woman just beginning to embrace religious life. She began a program of study, work, prayer, daily Mass and communion, weekly confession, and a monthly day of recollection. As an answer to each of these requirements she prayed, *My spirit rejoices in God, my Savior.*

Josephine took her first vows in 1892 when she was eighteen, becoming a novitiate. Her superiors gave her a pair of sandals to wear to remind her that from this day forward the ground she walked on was holy, and a crucifix to be her source of comfort in the days ahead as she grew spiritually, in "kindness, humility, modesty, and patience."

This was also the year that Josephine was given the brown Felician habit, the white veil, and the white waist cord. Her constant companions were the *Book of Rule of St. Francis* and the *Chaplet of the Seven Joys of Our Lady.* A time of self-examination followed.

What Josephine learned about herself must have convinced her that she was on the proper path. In 1901, she took her formal vows. The ritual she participated in has been compared to both a christening and a wedding, but neither fully conveys the "death of self" nuns willingly enter. "I am espoused to Him Whom angels serve," they pledge, or words similar.

On August 25 of that year, when she was twenty-seven years old, she exchanged her white veil and her white waist cord for black ones, which each symbolized her detachment from the outside world. After a wooden crucifix was placed over her neck, she pressed her lips to the convent's relic of St. Francis and stood to receive the kiss of peace from her Mother Superior and congratulations from her fellow Sisters. Finally, a silver wedding band, engraved with the Polish words, "*Jezus Moj Wezystko D.M. 25801,*" which translated meant, "Jesus My All, August 25, 1901," was slipped onto her ring finger.

Her future was now decided by church doctrine: "The main objective of the professed Sister for the next six years—during which time she renews her vows annually—is to advance in personal holiness by fidelity to her vows, trying to live the Felician way of life where all are united by a common end: to further the work of Christ and His Church through the medium of Christian education and other forms of apostolic work."

All she knew of the outside world were the memories she had from the earliest years of her childhood. When Josephine put on the habit, she had never gone to a dance, never gone on a date, never had a boyfriend. Regimented religious life had not squelched her innate personality. She was fun loving and gregarious, a pet of many of the older nuns and more interested in socializing than studying. She graduated twenty-second in a class of twenty-two.

From that moment on, Josephine Mezek became Sister Mary Janina. "You shall no longer be known as Josephine but as Sister Mary Janina, your new name in religion," the presiding Bishop said to her, as he lit her proffered candle. The name change honored a similar sacrifice made in biblical times: Abram became Abraham, Jacob became Israel, Simon became Peter, and Saul became Paul when they gave themselves and their lives to God. Josephine and the twenty-one other women in her class would do the same.

"Mary" was the adopted first name of all the women who take the vows of the Felician Order, and she chose "Janina," a traditional Polish name pronounced "Ya-nina," in deference to a village in eastern Europe whose residents resisted religious persecution. Translated into English, it simply meant "John."

The ceremonial words she spoke, most likely in her native Polish, were these or a similar version of them:

> *At last Jesus will be mine and I will be His. What more can I desire? The whole world could not satisfy my heart, for it belongs to Him whom the angels adore and the moon and sun stand before in wonder. I will espouse Christ, my beloved, King of Heaven and earth and wish to remain His Bride forever.*
>
> *Therefore, I, Sister Mary Janina vow and promise Poverty, Chastity, and Obedience to Almighty God in the presence of the Blessed Virgin Mary, the angels and saints, the whole heavenly court, to all my superiors and their successors according to Our Holy Rule and Constitutions, and I hope with God's grace to persevere faithfully until death.*
>
> *Amen.*

Despite the tragedy of her parents, despite the tuberculosis bacteria that curdled her lungs and made even the most routine labor difficult, and despite being exiled to a remote parish in the country, far from the city life she was accustomed to, Sister Janina radiated an abiding happiness. She had a clear and pleasing singing voice and could be heard throughout the church grounds singing while she worked. She was accomplished on the piano and sometimes seemed to almost disappear into the keys while she played. Those who knew her best said her sacred melodies originated from a divine source, both internal and eternal.

The snippets of the lyrics of her favorite hymn, "Jesus, Lover of My

Soul," echoed in the garden and through the church sanctuary. The flock of geese Stella kept in the yard and the rows and rows of carrots, parsnips, and turnips were treated to these sacred words.

Jesus, lover of my soul, let me to thy bosom fly.
While the nearer waters roll, while the tempest still is high.
Hide me, O my Savior hide, till the storm of life is past.
Safe into the haven guide, O receive my soul at last.

The parishioners of Holy Rosary took to the extroverted nun much the way the Felician nuns of the Motherhouse in Detroit had taken to her when she was just a young girl. "Sister Janina had a great personality," wrote a descendant of one of the area's first settlers, "intelligent and an extrovert, speaking to all persons in the area in that era. This was very unusual for a nun to speak to everybody." The schoolchildren, Father Andrew, the farm wives, her fellow Sisters—everyone looked fondly upon Sister Janina. Everyone, that is, except for Stella. The two women could not have been more different in outlook if one were a songbird and one a crow, one a ladyslipper, one a pricker bush. The housekeeper was not fond of any of the nuns but reserved her harshest words for Janina.

"That one is no good as a nun," Stella said often, to anyone willing to listen. "Her duties go unfinished."

And so when Sister Angelina and Sister Josephine told Stella they were concerned about Sister Janina, that it wasn't like her to just disappear, especially without her rosary or her prayerbook, it wasn't surprising that Stella put them off at first. Sister Janina liked to walk in the woods and pick wildflowers more than she liked to do her work, and that's probably where she was, Stella said. Besides, there was still baking and cooking and sweeping to be done, and the housekeeper couldn't be bothered with a wild goose chase for a flighty nun.

Undaunted, the two worried Sisters launched the first of what would become many searches for their missing Sister. They retraced their steps, they looked in the church, the school, the barn. The parish wasn't that big—just a white wooden church, the brick building that housed the school and the convent, a barn, some small outbuildings, a garden, a cemetery, and the rectory where Stella and Mary were working. The Sisters searched everywhere and found not one sign of Sister Janina.

Three long hours later they were back at the kitchen door, begging for scraps of Stella's attention, but weren't received with much more welcome than if they'd been the neighbor's bedraggled dog. Still, they asked again. Would Stella please help them now?

"I need to ring the bell for six o'clock," she told them.

Like many rural churches of the day, Holy Rosary functioned as its community's timepiece. The steeple bell was rung every day at six o'-clock in the morning, at noon, and then again at six o'clock in the evening. Its tone traveled great distances, and farmers would set their daily schedules to the familiar sound. The constancy of the bell was also supposed to make the church's scattered congregation mull the wishes of their Creator at least three times between dawn and dusk.

Since her husband had died, Stella had dedicated her life to her daughter and to her church, and she was not about to be the mortal who stood between God and His flock, even if the fate of a nun was at stake. The bell would ring this evening, just like it had every other evening for the last twenty-some years when it was installed in the steeple. It was her duty to ring it, she told the Sisters, and she took that duty seriously in spite of whatever else was competing for her attention.

Let the Father attend to Janina when he returned. For reasons Stella tried not to fathom, she was his favorite. Let him find her.

The sound of wagon wheels grinding on the dirt road bearing the fishing party home was finally heard at eight o'clock that evening.

Whatever triumphant conversation about their day's catch had been emanating from the wagon was surely cut short by the dark sight of Stella, running across the yard. In the waning light, her skeletal-like form, clad in her perpetual black housedress, must have recalled for them a marionette swinging forward on eerie strings. Apparition-like, whenever she ran her quick and tiny feet looked like they were floating, somehow unconnected to the ground underneath.

The buggy slowed to a stop and Stella grabbed hold of its side. With the priest home, her indifference had changed into what appeared to be sincere concern.

"Father," she said, breathless, "have you seen Sister Janina anywhere? I do not know where she is."

Behind her, the two remaining Sisters walked up, and together they approached the wagon, too.

"We cannot find her," one of them said.

"Have you searched the premises?" Father Andrew asked.

"We have, Father," the Sisters replied in unison.

"Did you go into the church?"

"We did, Father."

"The school?"

"Yes, Father."

The afterglow of his pleasant afternoon of fishing was instantly erased, and anger took its place instead. The three women assembled here, and the entirety of Holy Rosary parish, were no strangers to the priest's legendary fury. Errant schoolboys went home with their ears red and swollen from Father Andrew's meaty fists. Outspoken parishioners were shunned. Women considered not devoted enough to church affairs for the Father's liking were treated rudely, even in public. Farmers out of favor were not allowed to sell their wares to the church, and neither were their sons or their daughters. His quick temper showed itself now.

"Why did you not rouse the neighborhood!" the priest demanded. When not one of the women had a satisfactory answer, he insisted that another search for the missing nun begin immediately.

Full dark had settled in by the time his team of horses was stabled and the lanterns lit. The searching party numbered either six or seven— the priest, his sister, the housekeeper's daughter, the chore boy, and the two nuns. Later, these witnesses would dispute whether or not Stella had been among them. But the supper the housekeeper had prepared sat untouched and was left to go cold on the stove. Everyone remembered that.

Father Andrew's first thought was that Sister Janina had gone to a nearby farm, with the promise of eggs, apples, or some other eatable. If that were the case, she was safe from harm, and so he decided to search the church grounds again, before they disturbed the neighbors.

For the next four hours the glow of lantern light, the footfalls of the searchers, and their looming shadows moved systematically over every patch of the church grounds and every corner of its infrastructure.

They began in Sister Janina's bedroom where Father Andrew was shown the rosary hanging from the doorknob. At any other time, it would be scandalous for a man, even a priest, to be inside a nun's private cell; that these conventions were set aside illustrates how dire they considered her situation to be.

The group moved on to the workroom, where Father Andrew took in the abandoned prayerbook and the outside door left ajar. They searched the rest of the convent, the attic, the basement, and all four classrooms in the school. They looked inside the school's small chapel and scanned the sleeping quarters used by students who boarded in the winter. They went into the church's sanctuary and searched under every pew. They peeked inside the three-quarter-sized door to the church basement, scanned the dirt-floored darkness, and then searched the barn, the outbuildings, and the rectory. They found nothing.

Outside, the searchers turned their attention to the cornfield. By late August, the aligned stalks were thickly tasseled, grew chest high to a man, all but dwarfed the women, and the group walked down each row, swinging their lanterns to cut through the darkness. They looked in the vegetable garden and around the corner shadows at the edge of each of the buildings. They searched the horse shed and the chicken coop. No one found any sign of Sister Janina. Not a footprint, not a depression in the earth where she rested, not a stray fiber of her wool habit, nothing. It was as if God Himself had reached down and plucked her from them.

Just before midnight, the bedeviled cluster returned to the rectory and ate their cold supper. No amount of conversation would solve this mystery tonight, and the wild imaginings of what could have happened to the missing Sister were allowed to multiply fiendishly in their minds.

She could have been kidnapped. She could be lying in the dark somewhere, unconscious from an unknown affliction. Some human harm could have come to her. Her mind could have faltered, much like her mother's had before her. She could have broken her vows of chastity and left of her own volition. At least one person in the household subscribed to this last possibility.

"She's an ungrateful nun," Stella said to the priest when the others had finished eating and turned in for the night. "If she intended to go, and told no one, and now caused all this disturbance? Ungrateful. And after all the care we've showed to her."

A storm was coming. The next morning, Saturday, began for Holy Rosary before the six o'clock bell, and even before dawn. Who among their small group could sleep when one of their own was ominously unaccounted for?

Father Andrew tried to calm his household. Perhaps the same gathering thunderclouds that made fish hungry had kept Sister Janina from coming home, wherever she was. Maybe she was making her way back, or planning to, right this minute.

The Sister failed to appear anytime throughout the morning, though, and Father Andrew grew increasingly alarmed. His only comfort came from his original thought that she might have gone to a neighbor's house—the Sister had a friendly nature and was chummy with many of Holy Rosary's parishioners, and even the closest of these were spread out over several miles. Maybe a neighbor came and picked her up in their wagon. Or, she could have walked a good distance to one of their houses while the other Sisters were napping, enjoyed a long visit, and then realized she had stayed too late to walk home alone in the dark and impending foul weather.

Or, perhaps she felt well enough to walk to one of the neighbors' but became sickly, and couldn't return, and the neighbor had called for the doctor. This was as good a possibility as any. Her health had been poor, and the local doctor was a frequent visitor. If her faltering health were the cause of her absence, she very well could have spent the night away from the convent.

Still, an occurrence such as either of these, Father Andrew knew, would be a first. Sister Janina was friendly with the neighbors but had not spent a single night away from the convent since she arrived there a year ago. The nuns were forbidden by their order to travel alone and always went with another Sister, a child from the school, or someone else from the household.

The priest refused to even consider that Sister Janina had left of her own volition. On the contrary, the Sister seemed to love her position at Holy Rosary. Earlier that spring she asked Father Andrew to make a special request of her Mother Superior so that she could stay in Isadore over the summer while the students of the convent school were on break, working their parents' farms.

Normally, she and the other nuns would have returned to their

Motherhouse 275 miles to the southeast in Detroit. Janina named her poor health and the difficulty of travel as her reason for staying on, and it was a valid one, but she also wanted to stay in Isadore simply because she liked it there. The beauty of the country held a novelty for her that only a girl raised in the city could know. Plus, the Motherhouse was overcrowded with nuns, and her schedule was so regimented there. Here in Isadore, she had her freedom. Especially during the summer vacation. A night spent away from the convent was an unacceptable way for her to show her gratitude and could have even been grounds to be sent back to Detroit and disciplined.

Though he had to know that the chances of finding the Sister happily chatting in a neighbor's parlor were slight, Father Andrew dressed quickly, skipped his breakfast, and spent the rest of the morning knocking on doors.

Behind the first of those was Jake Rosinski Jr., a native son of Isadore. His father, Jacob Rosinski Sr., had been one of the first pioneers in the area and the man who selected the site upon which Holy Rosary Church was built twenty years previous. Jake Jr. now owned the farm and small general store directly across the street from the church and was Holy Rosary's closest neighbor. He was also Isadore's postmaster and a duly commissioned justice of the peace. Though he was not fond of Father Andrew, and his wife was feuding with Stella, their children attended Holy Rosary School, and Jake's notarized signature appears on the official school census of Leelanau County's District No. 4 from 1907 to 1910.

Jake was well aware of the mailing habits of his neighbors and their legal needs. By proximity, he knew when the church garden was planted and when Father Andrew was preparing for Mass. He watched Gruba go about his chores and Stella go about hers. And he was also privy to the secret insults the housekeeper flung at the Isadore nuns from the safety of his very own kitchen. Jake was not Stella's intended audience, however; she would come to his house to use his postal services and then gossip with his wife. He just overheard their conversations.

When Father Andrew came knocking, though, Jacob kept this knowledge to himself. No, he told the priest truthfully, he hadn't seen the Sister.

The next door that Father Andrew knocked on belonged to Constantia and Michael Gatzke. There was bad blood here, too, but again it did not keep the priest away. Though Michael's daughter Mary Gatzke had once been friendly with Stella, the priest was vaguely aware of an ongoing feud between the two women. He couldn't remember the details of their disagreement, but truth be told, he didn't begrudge his housekeeper her foe—he didn't much care for the Gatzke clan, either. They were meddlers. Still, the Gatzkes were longtime supporters of the church, they lived within walking distance, and he knew that Sister Janina observed none of his, nor of Stella's, prejudices. She had been friendly to everyone. Sister Janina could be at the Gatzkes' right now, and a feud, no matter how justified, would not keep him from finding her. He walked up their front steps and knocked.

Mary Gatzke answered. When she and Stella were on friendly terms the pair would visit several times a week; she, too, had been a listening ear for the housekeeper's sharp words against the nuns. They didn't work hard enough. They didn't pray long enough. They were too soft on the schoolchildren and too friendly with the priest. Though she criticized nuns in general, Stella saved her harshest words for the one who was now missing. As far as the housekeeper was concerned, Sister Janina and her ilk were not sacred vessels but functioned more as "priests' wives."

But like Jake Rosinski, Mary Gatzke wasn't one to talk out of turn, even against someone she was feuding with, and so she, too, said nothing of Stella's gossip to the priest.

No, she told Father Andrew, she hadn't seen Sister Janina, either.

By Saturday afternoon twenty-four hours had passed since Sister Janina was last seen pulling down the shade in her cell's window. Word of the mystery had spread. The women of Isadore took off their aprons, put their babies down for their naps, came out of their houses, and searched through their yards and their gardens, their sheds and their barns. Their concern yielded not a single clue.

With nothing to go on, Father Andrew had no choice but to call for the help of professionals. He hated to expose church business to the secular world, but he had no choice. Father Andrew picked up the parish's telephone and summoned John Nolan, a deputy from the nearby town of Cedar, a few miles to the south, and then telephoned the Leelanau

County sheriff, Martin Brown, whose office was in Leland, a coastal town a few miles to the north.

"It might be that she has gone away, or she might have fainted away, or she might have been carried away," the priest speculated to the lawmen.

"It's my day off," said Nolan. "Who's going to be paying me then?"

Father Andrew was disgusted by the deputy's obvious lack of commitment to public safety. It had taken some amount of personal resolve to alert them in the first place, and this was the reaction to his plea for help? The priest knew from his own work that hardship did not take time off on weekends, and he, for one, always acted accordingly. Whenever his parishioners needed him, he made himself available, no matter the day or time. Unless of course he was out fishing or hunting, and couldn't be reached.

"*I* will, if it comes to that," he said.

The sheriff and his deputy both came to the parish and looked around, but even their trained eyes didn't see much. On horseback, with their badges and their guns and their suspicions, they found no more evidence of the missing woman than the Sisters and the priest had found on their midnight search, or the neighborhood farm wives found the next afternoon.

Stymied, their only suggestion to Father Andrew was for him to post sentries up and down the surrounding roads, and to keep them at their posts overnight. Perhaps the Sister was still in the area, they said. Perhaps other women were in danger too, from whatever dark force had spirited her away.

At dusk, five men from the neighborhood volunteered for the assignment and stood guard along Gatzke and Schomberg Roads, and also at the outlying edges where the cultivated fields met the wildness of the woods. With the involvement of the law, and now this group of neighbor men, news of the mystery had escaped the boundaries of Isadore.

Sister Janina's whereabouts were now of keen interest to the farm families in the surrounding area, to neighboring townsfolk whether they were Polish or not, and to the editors of the nearest daily newspaper, published in Traverse City. A reporter for the *Evening Record* was dispatched to observe the watchmen and write up what he saw.

When all traces of daylight had long faded, the five completed a search of the parish's perimeter and stationed themselves at the edge of an abutting oat field. Each was armed with an individual amount of bravery, understandable curiosity, and a rifle, if he owned one. A damp chill snuck in from nearby Lake Michigan and took the long hours of the day's August heat out of the air in minutes. The oat grasses brushed against each other rhythmically, making a sound that was almost words, but not quite.

Inside the sanctuary of the church, Sheriff Brown, the newspaper reporter, and reinforcements for the watchmen set up sleeping cots. The men would work in shifts. If something or someone was prowling amid their churchfolk, they would find it.

Before anyone could get to sleep, however, an eerie sound floated out over the tops of the whispering grain. A woman was singing, and the faint melody was coming from the direction of the cedar swamp far beyond the reach of the watchmen's lanterns. It took a careful ear to make out the tune, but it was a hymn. Sister Janina's favorite hymn.

The watchmen heard it first, and then the sound drifted in through the open door of the church, where Sheriff Brown said he could hear it, and so did the newspaper reporter. The plaintive lines of "Jesus, Lover of My Soul," in its entirety, wavered through the darkness.

Jesus, lover of my soul, let me to Thy bosom fly,
While the nearer waters roll, while the tempest still is high.
Hide me, O my Savior, hide, till the storm of life is past;
Safe into the haven guide; O receive my soul at last.

Other refuge have I none, hangs my helpless soul on Thee;
Leave, ah! leave me not alone, still support and comfort me.
All my trust on Thee is stayed, all my help from Thee I bring;
Cover my defenseless head with the shadow of Thy wing.

Wilt Thou not regard my call? Wilt Thou not accept my prayer?
Lo! I sink, I faint, I fall—Lo! on Thee I cast my care;
Reach me out Thy gracious hand! While I of Thy strength receive,
Hoping against hope I stand, dying, and behold, I live.

Thou, O Christ, art all I want, more than all in Thee I find;
Raise the fallen, cheer the faint, heal the sick, and lead the blind.
Just and holy is Thy Name, I am all unrighteousness;
False and full of sin I am; Thou art full of truth and grace.

Plenteous grace with Thee is found, grace to cover all my sin;
Let the healing streams abound; make and keep me pure within.
Thou of life the fountain art, freely let me take of Thee;
Spring Thou up within my heart; rise to all eternity.

The men held fast to their posts, and inside the church all was silent as every man there lay still and listened. Here was a clue, and yet no move was made to investigate the source of the singing. The sentries stood rigid, their feet planted on the road. The sheriff and the reporter looked out the church window but did not go outside. No one ventured into the dark woods.

Later, some would admit without shame that what they felt when they heard the sound of a woman singing was not relief, not curiosity, but terror. The voice was indeed singing, and yet it did not sound human. The melody was that of a religious hymn they all knew by heart and had sung themselves many times at Mass; how then could it sound like it had originated not from a nun's pure heart but from some ghostly hell?

"The sound of a woman's voice floated out upon the night air coming from somewhere way back in the depths of the morass," the newspaperman reported the next day. "The watchers were evidently frightened for they made no effort to look up the source of the sound. The nun was always singing about her work and was possessed of an exceptionally sweet voice."

The following day, the *Evening Record* ran his first-person account on the front page. A local woman corroborated the story with an image. She had seen an apparition dressed as a nun wandering in the swamp, its way lighted by a candle. The hymn, she said, came from it and when it walked the candle flame did not flicker.

When Father Andrew stepped out from the sacristy the next morning and stood before the altar to say Sunday Mass, he looked down upon the largest group of worshippers that had ever gathered inside this modest

country church. Two hundred, at least. If he was surprised by the attendance, he made no mention of it. He did, however, shorten the service
and, after only half an hour, turned to face his bulging congregation.

"One of the Sisters from this convent is not accounted for," Father
Andrew announced, though many of those present already knew about
the missing nun, and it was her very absence that had brought them into
a house of worship. "We don't know what happened to her, but each of
us here ought to help find Sister Janina. It might be that she's gone away
on her own. Her health isn't robust and she might have fainted."

"Or," he paused ominously and leveled his gaze slowly over the
crowd, "she might have been carried away by someone with the darkest
of motives. I am asking all men and boys here now to remain. We will go
through the woods and the cornfields. We will look for tracks or any
other sign that might lead to finding her."

Normally after Father Andrew concluded Mass, the Sisters would
stay in the sanctuary for several minutes and continue to pray. "After
the kiss of peace in the Mass, when the priest consecrates, forget all the
world, and be entirely out of the body," read the instructions from their
Rule. "There in glowing love embrace your beloved Savior who is come
down from heaven into your breast's bower, and hold him fast until he
shall have granted whatever you wish for." Today, however, there was-
n't time for glowing love; each would help in the search.

Within the hour, a throng of able-bodied men, boys as young as
twelve, and grandfathers walking only with the help of canes assembled
in the churchyard. A cacophony of male voices and European accents
mingled in the churchyard. Polish and English, French and German
blended with cuss words and superstitions.

In this insular outpost tucked away in the most rural portion of a remote northern county that only numbered some sixteen hundred residents, nearly four hundred souls assembled that Sunday morning to
look for Sister Janina. They were curiosity seekers and crackpots, politi-
cians and drunks, lumbermen out of work and lapsed Catholics looking
for redemption. Many others were members of Holy Rosary Parish who,
under normal circumstances, wouldn't associate with non-Poles, let
alone the likes of these heathen visitors. Today, though, they were simply four hundred sets of eyes multiplying the work of the parish's own,
and Father Andrew and his congregation were grateful for them.

The priest organized the mismatched group in lines thirty feet apart, and instructed them to search the woods to the west, working their way between the church grounds where they now stood and the railroad tracks a few miles off.

"Kick at the underbrush," he told them, "turn over logs and note anything out of the ordinary."

A current of excitement spread through the lines of men, almost as if they were lining up for a sack race or a treasure hunt. Who would find her? And what would be her condition? Perhaps crazed and raving, or weak and grateful. Maybe she was brutalized. Or dead.

Their motivation was strong, but the fortunes of the weather were not with the searchers that day as the human lines moved off into the countryside. After several hours on the hunt, the rainstorm that had been threatening all morning pummeled them all and brought them back to the church by early afternoon, dripping and dejected.

Despite Father Andrew's best hopes, their large number proved to be of no advantage at all, and they found not a single sign of the missing nun. Instead of returning with her in tow, they had only wet socks inside wet boots, and the increasingly wild notions of her imagined fate to show for their efforts.

Maybe, they grumbled, there was nothing to find. Maybe the nun wasn't pure at all but had left with a man to places outside the county.

"One theory was that as Sister [Janina] walked the halls of the convent, prayerbook in hand and with her heart open in supplication for humanity, the sound of a knock echoed through the building," the newspaper reporter wrote. "The nun might have stopped, placed her prayerbook on the window sill and unlocked the door to admit the caller. As the door swung open, a hundred things might have happened."

Of those one hundred possibilities, Father Andrew only wanted to consider the single truthful one, whatever it turned out to be. Though he was not well liked by this tiny Polish enclave, and though gossip had already begun to swirl that he was too intimate with the Sister and had somehow caused her disappearance, even his detractors agreed that the priest had done all he could to find her.

After searching with the five remaining members of his own household the evening she went missing, and then searching again with a few dozen of his neighbors, later searching a third time with a handful of lawmen, and finally with four hundred volunteers on foot and on horse-back, Father Andrew was crestfallen and exhausted.

"The priest has worked like a madman, sleeping and eating but a portion of the time," the newspaper reported. "After he had said his Masses Sunday, he tramped the woods with the rest of the searchers endeavoring to find some token by which he could locate Sister Mary Janina."

Would a guilty man, his neighbors wondered, go to such lengths?

Oblivious to gossip, whether it came down in his favor or against, Father Andrew now considered that the answer to what happened to Sister Janina might not lay in Isadore. That evening, he booked passage on the next train to Detroit.

"Well, I told you not to send her away," a nun said to Mother Mary Antonia, the Superior at the Motherhouse in Detroit. Father Andrew had just arrived and broken the news.

"I need more details," the priest demanded of these Detroit Felicians. "I need to find out whether she was dissatisfied. Whether she was planning to go off."

Until now he had refused to entertain such an idea, but the beginnings of panic were gnawing at his conscience, and he was willing to consider all theories, no matter how inconceivable. But no one at the Motherhouse could say what had happened to Sister Janina. Nor did anyone confess to having any womanly knowledge of her state of mind before she disappeared. As far as any of the Sisters there knew, Sister Janina was as committed to the church on the day she disappeared as she was on the day she took her final vows. This matched the priest's own private opinion, though it was of no comfort to him now.

"I'm worried that you are right," he told them. "She would no more take off her habit than I would remove my cassock."

Father Andrew was not a wealthy man, but he did have resources. According to an amateur Catholic historian Father Stanley Bur, Father Andrew was the last priest of the diocese who still ran his parish "from his pants pocket." This meant that rather than a set annual amount, Father Andrew believed that a fair salary for a man of God such as himself was the take from the collection plate on the third Sunday of every month.

From this personal income he had purchased the fancy buggy and team of horses many of the neighbors thought too ostentatious for a country priest. On Saturdays when he traveled to the neighboring town of Maple City, to say Mass at St. Rita's, he came thundering into the village, driving his team at a full gallop. The previous priest had walked in on a geriatric pony; people were not used to flamboyance and distrusted it.

In Isadore Father Andrew had also populated the barnyard with creatures not usually found living together on a farm in the northern Michigan countryside: two foxes and a badger; large flocks of pheasants, ducks, geese, and chickens; a pet crow that would sit on his shoulder and take food from his hand; hutches filled with rabbits; hives of bees; a tame squirrel; and most unusual of all, a pet alligator.

This big lizard roamed the parish grounds at will in the summer months, frightening neighbor children and dispatching unsuspecting barnyard fowl. The neighbors soon tired of losing their winged livestock to Father Andrew's exotic novelty and someone left the carcass of a duck laced with poison out in their yard. The alligator found it, and swallowed it down. When the beast died a day later, the priest was both mystified and disappointed; the alligator had been expensive, and Father Andrew was known to be a bit of a miser, saving up for flashy purchases like the buggy and the two handsome horses to pull it, and his exotic pet.

The priest never did find out who had poisoned the beast, though he had his suspicions. To solve the bigger and much more dire mystery of Sister Janina's whereabouts, though, Father Andrew was even willing to spend some of his own money.

From the Detroit Motherhouse, he went directly to the offices of the Murphy-McDonnell Secret Service Company, a downtown detective agency affiliated with the Pinkertons. There he secured the services of one Detective J. R. Castle. Father Andrew told the man all he knew of the Sister who had been in his care, and the detective assured the priest he could find her or at the very least find out what had become of her.

Later that night two very different men—one with a Bible and one with a sidearm—sharing a common mission boarded the last train out of Detroit heading north.

Monday morning, this unlikely pair emerged blearily from their passenger car at a stopover in Traverse City. They had traveled all night, thor-

oughly discussing the case and sleeping little. The train would not de-
part for its short run to Isadore until later that afternoon, and so they got
out to stretch their legs. Father Andrew, a tragic local celebrity now, was
recognized by several townspeople as he and the stranger from Detroit
walked along the street outside the train station.

"We heard about your missing nun," one of the townspeople said.

"Yes, and we have an idea to help find her," said another.

"Well, then," said the priest, "let's have it."

Their idea was not another man-powered search but a canine-pow-
ered one. They said they knew of a lawman in a nearby county, a sheriff
in fact, who owned a trained bloodhound whose ability to track a human scent over any topography was becoming legendary: Sheriff
William Kittle of Antrim County and his young bloodhound named
Tom. The dog came straight from a kennel in Kentucky, where people
knew how to raise hounds and train them, too. This dog had found wandering children, lost hunters, and escaped convicts. Maybe Tom could
find Sister Janina, the men said.

Animal lover that he was, Father Andrew liked the idea and inquired about the cost.

"The price for the services of the dog is fifteen dollars a day," the first
man said.

This at a time when a toothbrush cost a quarter, men's flannel night-
shirts could be had for seventy-nine cents, a dressy topcoat for ten dollars, and raw land for as little as thirty dollars an acre.

"Tell him he's hired," Father Andrew told the men. "I'll expect him
and the dog at Isadore in the morning."

There is no other sound quite like the baying of a bloodhound that's
caught the scent. In recent years, the fleshy tracking dogs are trained to
follow a trail silently so as not to alert a criminal on the run or frighten a
missing child, but that was not the case when Tom took up the search for
Sister Janina. Back then a loud bay was seen as a mark of skill and determination on the part of both the dog and the handler.

Scent tracking with canines is a subjective and inexact activity that
nonetheless has met with great success ever since Saint Hubert first bred
and trained a kennel of bloodhounds at his monastery in France in the
seventh century. Saint Hubert's dogs were known for their "endurance,

courage, and throatiness," and when several black-and-tan pairs were exported to England and put to work, they soon gained the nickname "Sleuth Hounds."

Sheriff Kittle's own dog, Tom, was a likely descendant of this line, as were many others in America bearing the distinctive black-and-tan coat. If that were the case, this canine could trace a longer Catholic lineage than Father Andrew himself, or for that matter, any of the other parish members of Isadore.

Though still a young dog of five or six, Tom had already put his distinguished bloodline to good use. Under Sheriff Kittle's guidance, the year before Tom had followed the trail of three prisoners who had broken out of the Big Rapids jail. Dog and man went through four neighboring towns, across a river to the bank on the other side, exited a mile downstream, and then came upon a set of railroad tracks.

Kittle could only surmise the trio had hopped a freight train, and so he wired ahead to the authorities in the next town, and the men were arrested when the train made its regular stop twenty miles down the track.

Tom also found two lost boys, one in the Mancelona woods and one in a Bellaire swamp. And he and his master were not above working livestock crimes, either. In Walton Junction, a woman reported to police that her milk cow had inexplicably been poisoned. Sheriff Kittle brought Tom to the scene and set him to work "tracking the clean boot"—following a trail without first being given a scent item to orient himself. Tom and Kittle arrived on a nearby neighbor's doorstep, and when the sheriff questioned the man who answered his knock, he was so shocked to see them that he confessed.

Most applicable to the Isadore search, however, was Tom's experience running a cold line. The dog had once helped search Michigan's vast Upper Peninsula for a missing hunter, and it was here that he proved he could do the work his master asked of him, even after significant time had passed. The ability to follow a scent trail that is days old—hunt a cold line—is what distinguishes bloodhounds from other tracking dogs like Labrador retrievers or German shepherds or foxhounds. Those breeds can track a fresh scent, but only bloodhounds can track a scent days, and sometimes even weeks, old. Tom picked up the missing hunter's trail a full five days after the man vanished and followed it for thirty forested miles. The only thing that thwarted the dog's success was the foot of new snow that fell before he and Kittle could find their man.

After Sheriff Kittle gave Tom the scent in Isadore, put him on a long lead, and allowed the dog to follow a path of his own choosing, the sound escaping his wide throat was like a large rock being dropped down a deepwater well and knocking against the hard sides on its way down. Almost instantly the dog was "giving tongue freely," and his plaintive cry echoed over the fields of the parish and into the woods beyond.

Still, it had not been easy for Sheriff Kittle to find something of Sister Janina's to get Tom started. When master and dog arrived at the convent at dawn Tuesday morning, Father Andrew, Detective Castle, a group of men from Traverse City, and two newspaper reporters were there to greet them. The new assemblage went immediately into the convent and proceeded on to Sister Janina's cell. Long gone was any thought that, as men, they did not belong there.

The room was as sparsely furnished and as bereft of personal belongings as any ascetic's quarters would be expected to be. It was strikingly similar to the cell of her order's founder, Sister Mary Angela Truszkowska, shown in a photograph of the Polish convent. No clothing on the bed, no bric-a-brac, not even so much as a handkerchief. Just a single bed with a plain wool blanket, a small desk and chair, and a cross on the wall above the headboard. So much the better to keep a nun's mind on prayer. "At some time in the day or the night think upon and call to mind all who are sick and sorrowful," instructs the *Nun's Rule*, "who suffer affliction and poverty; think especially of the Christians who are among the heathen; compassionate those who are under strong temptations; take thought of all men's sorrows."

Then, in the dark recesses of the room's tiny closet, the men found a small box and a locked trunk.

As sunrise was still several minutes away, Father Andrew lit a candle. In the flickering dawn, the men slid the trunk out into the open room and crowded around it. Someone pried open the lock, and inside they found only Sister Janina's collection of books. Father Andrew told the men that these would be of no use—Sister Janina was generous with her tiny library and all of the other Sisters had surely handled each and every volume. The box yielded nothing, either. Only Sister Janina's clothes were inside, neatly folded and recently washed.

When totaled, her possessions were few; the Felicians' vow of poverty, atonement, chastity, self-denial, and obedience had practical, as well as spiritual, consequences. Their teaching salary was rarely more than twenty dollars a month, sometimes even less. Enough money to purchase fabric to sew their habits and veils, to buy a pair of shoes, perhaps a few postage stamps and some stationery to keep in touch with relatives and with other Sisters, and the occasional train ticket for rare visits to other convents.

In the end, it was the missing nun's mysteriously abandoned rosary and prayerbook that were placed under Tom's damp nose. An account of this event written by one of those present at the scene read: "The dog was brought out, taken to the room and given the string of beads and then, giving tongue freely, he raced down the back stairs, out of the back door, and, running in a bewildered fashion, finally started for the woods back of the convent, taking [us] through a field of corn. He had evidently lost the scent and was merely hunting. For two miles Sheriff Kittle raced behind the hound, over fences and through bogs before his deep rolling bay again reached the ears of those who remained at the convent. He had evidently found a fresh trail but was unable to follow it far on account of the insufficient scent from the beads."

Sheriff Kittle would later detail the exact route his dog had taken on that first early morning search that began in Sister Janina's cell. For this initial go, it was just Kittle, the dog, and one other man, a friend of Kittle's named Pat Bowes, who went out. The other men stayed behind and planned the larger human search scheduled for that same afternoon.

From the Sister's cell, the dog ran down the back stairs and out the back door, straining at his rope lead. The door Tom used on this first run was the same door that the Sisters found ajar when they awoke from their naps days earlier and noticed Sister Janina missing.

From there the two men and the dog traveled through the cornfield and into the nearby swamp, where they made slow progress, and finally came out alongside a road. There was a fence running beside this road, and they followed it a short while, crossed and traveled down a hill and up the other side to another road, where the trail abruptly ended.

"We went through pretty fast, I know," Sheriff Kittle would later explain. "The dog was leading me and straining at the leash all the while. From the wire fence we went across that road down over the hill to another road there and quit. There was no track there. He could not find anything. I believe it was about forty rods from the road. After that, the scent was gone."

Kittle, Bowes, and Tom returned to Holy Rosary where the men ate breakfast and then joined with the lawmen, the reporters, a few curious neighbors, and the priest, to make a second run. Kittle again started the dog in the nun's cell but this time he opened all the doors of the convent so Tom could choose his own exit. The dog led his master out the front door, broke his rope lead, and then followed the exact same course he had tracked only hours earlier, which didn't surprise Kittle. Bloodhounds are known for their ability to track the same scent over and over again without ever switching scent lines, a trait known as "freedom from change" and one that was certainly strong in Tom.

"The dog, when put upon the scent, would never switch to another." Kittle said. "You could not make him. I have tried it lots of times. There might be a thousand men cross it, but he would not take any other man's track than he had the scent of. If the dog had the scent from articles owned or handled by the Sister, and she had been walking around there and went over to that church, he would have followed wherever she had been. I have seen him do that. He would go anywhere, wherever she had walked."

While these visiting men searched the countryside with the dog, Holy Rosary's women searched the convent for some article of Sister Janina's that would give Tom a stronger initial connection to the missing nun. It was Stella, the housekeeper, who found something promising. A pair of women's shoes.

"These," she said, holding the raggedy things aloft, "are Sister Janina's."

The shoes were old and worn out and had been discarded in the convent's basement, but they did belong to Sister Janina, the housekeeper said, and no one else had worn them.

Father Andrew was skeptical. Gruba, their chore boy, slept in that basement; hadn't Gruba worn the shoes, or one of the other nuns? he wondered. But Stella was adamant. Sister Janina wore out this pair of shoes months ago, she said, and had purchased a new pair. Since then, they'd been cast aside down in the basement where Stella found them; no one else had worn them.

Sheriff Kittle said it was worth a try, and so Tom was offered the shoes and put to work yet again. This time, the dog headed directly to the woods. "Over logs and through bushes, up hills and across bogs they made their way, peering into every hollow stump and searching every thick clump of bushes in hopes of finding at least the body of the nun."

It was the depths of one of these bogs that offered up the first real clue. Footprints.

A set of small muddy footprints circled the bog randomly, then led the searchers to a pool of water where, Kittle speculated, someone had knelt to drink. Kittle had brought the shoes with him on this third go-round and placed them over the set of the footprints preserved in the mud. They matched.

The men circled around the spot and looked down. These newly found impressions rested on top of the mud, they observed to each other, while their own feet sunk right down into the stuff, which quickly oozed over their boots and far up their calves. Sister Janina was a small woman, just 110 pounds or so, and the mucky ground could probably support her light frame.

The prints followed a curious and seemingly random path, and the men wondered aloud if the Sister had gone insane and was wandering aimlessly, either not knowing how to return to the convent or not wanting to.

Tom slopped through the ooze too, trotting around the footprints over and over, his nose heavy with mud. He finally let out a throaty cry, straining toward the cornfield and the road beyond.

"Circling!" Kittle yelled. "C'mon boys, he's after her!"

The men turned from the bog, crossed through a woodlot, and exited out alongside the same road Tom had taken Kittle to twice previously. Here the dog lay down, satisfied, panting happily.

"The trail must end here, because he lays down like that only when he thinks his work is done," Kittle told the rest of the group.

But the dog had found nothing at all but an empty dirt road. The spot where they stood had nothing to distinguish it—no sign of a skirmish, no flattened grass where someone might have lain down to rest, no wildflowers with snapped-off stems, nothing telling at all. Just rough grass, a barbed wire fence, and a dirt road criss-crossed with old wagon and buggy wheel ruts. Any evidence that Sister Janina had ever visited this spot was evident only to the dog.

The workings of a bloodhound's nose were not yet fully understood in the early 1900s, but the very fact that Tom's quarry was a nun could have hampered his search.

Scientists have extensively studied the dog breed and now know that bloodhounds track by following the scent of gas emitted by decaying skin cells that human beings normally shed at the rate of tens of thousands per day. The more skin the dog's quarry has exposed, the stronger the scent trail. Sister Janina was covered from head to toe in a woolen nun's habit, with even her neck and scalp unexposed, which would probably have made her scent trail weak.

The August heat didn't help the dog in his work, either. On hot days, a scent trail can hover several feet above the ground, raising it above the head of even a large dog like Tom, where he could misconstrue it, get turned around on the trail, or just miss it altogether.

Whatever the reason, even the magnificent Tom, his fine nose perfected first by more than eleven centuries of selective breeding and then by nearly one hundred searches with his master, could not find Sister Janina.

Father Andrew's financial resources were dwindling, but he seemed not to care. He had traveled to the Motherhouse on his own dime, hired Detective Castle for an unknown sum, plus paid the man's round-trip train fare to Isadore and secured him a horse. He had also paid Sheriff Kittle $45 for three days work, paid a deputy for working on his day off, and even covered the expenses of feeding the massive searching parties.

Instead of cutting his losses, though, the priest did the opposite; he pledged even more of his own money to the cause. On the morning of a fourth organized search, Father Andrew told everyone present that he would pay a reward of $500 to whoever found Sister Janina. Or found her body.

He asked the *Evening Record* and the *Manistee News Advocate* to print an announcement of the reward, which the papers did. Five hundred dollars was enough to make any man dream. It could purchase a small farm outright, stake a new business, buy a ticket to exotic lands, or convince a girlfriend to become a wife. The article did its work and brought in reward-seekers and amateur sleuths from Traverse City, but also from Detroit and Grand Rapids. One of these was Sheriff Kittle's friend Pat Bowes.

Since he had been along for the first try with the dog, Bowes decided to search the area by himself instead of going along with Kittle and Tom on the second and third times they made their runs. That decision turned out to be a good one.

Bowes found a torn piece of brown wool stuck on the barbed wire fence that ran along the road where the dog had ended his tracking. The piece of cloth was either not there when the men had scoured the area the first time or they had been too preoccupied with the dog to notice it. Bowes pulled it from the sharp point where it had become lodged and took it back to show Father Andrew.

It was an exact match to the fabric nuns used to make their habits, the priest said.

Newspaper stories about the case were beginning to take on the breathless tone of pulp novels and stage plays. Until Sister Janina disappeared, entertainment for those in the region with a taste for the macabre was provided by a surprising source: the railroad. Passenger cars regularly left the tracks, whether because of loose wheels, debris, or damage, with various degrees of human injury the result. Each of these accidents regardless of severity attracted an audience who stood or sat nearby and watched as rescue workers arrived. Sometimes this audience even arrived with blankets, picnics, and parasols in tow.

A missing and perhaps mad or murdered nun was a welcome change of pace for this ilk—and did a fine job of selling newspapers, especially with the gothic tone employed by the reporters and editors. The lead story on the front page of the September 3 *Evening Record* expressed the grave thoughts of many: "Deeper and darker grows the mystery surrounding the disappearance of Sister [Janina] from the Isadore convent."

Other oddities abounded in the local news that week. A farmer in a neighboring town found a large toadstool propped on his pasture gate, with a suicide note attached. A runaway horse pulling a hay wagon engulfed in flames ran through town at top speed, unmanned. And, by some celestial coincidence, even the night skies were acting peculiar in the last days of August 1907.

"The general disturbance among the stars and comets that has recently been puzzling astronomical students and is being witnessed all over the country has not skipped Traverse City by any means," the newspaper reported. "The large comet that is traveling at seventy miles a second can plainly be seen in the eastern sky while meteors have been falling every night for the past week."

As it turned out, the suicide was a hoax, the hay wagon had been accidentally set ablaze by a stray spark from its owner's pipe, right before he fell to the ground and startled the horses, and the sky was in the throes of a meteor shower. While these strange events could be explained away, no one had any more clues as to what had become of Sister Janina. Some of the main particulars in the case even seemed to give up hope of finding her, either alive or dead. One of these was J. R. Castle, the Detroit detective Father Andrew had hired the week previous. The one who had once been so certain that he could find out what had happened to the missing nun.

"I've been in the business twelve years," he said. "This is the most mysterious case I've ever had. The only case with as little to work on. There is absolutely no evidence."

Castle was a man impressed only by facts, and he derided the dog, the footprints in the swamp, and the ghostly singing as the superstitions of frightened Polish immigrants. He had purposely separated himself from the large searching parties and from Sheriff Kittle and his dog, and instead had scrutinized every realm of Leelanau County from his vantage point on horseback.

He put some credence in the theory that the missing Sister had been kidnapped, and so stopped every buggy, wagon, pedestrian, and rider he met on his travels. Some locals told him about strange rigs they'd seen on the road, and these Castle tracked to their destinations, finding that they were only the relatives of some area farmer, come to visit. After days of this, the detective took the train back to Detroit at Father Andrew's expense.

While the detective was disgusted with the lack of resolution in the mystery, Holy Rosary's two remaining nuns were growing increasingly frightened. They lost sleep to restless dreams and ate less and less of Stella's cooking. They could only pray, and even this had so far, to their human understanding at least, proven as futile as Detective Castle's horseback investigations.

Finally, they could stand it no more, and Sister Janina's two fellow nuns packed up their belongings and left the area as well, in fear for their own safety.

"What happened to one might happen to us," they said.

Father Andrew begged them to stay, but both demurred and, along with Castle, left on the train. Together, Sister Angelina and Sister Josephine took refuge at St. Joseph's, a Catholic parish in Manistee, some sixty miles to the south. Father Andrew would later explain away their hasty exit by saying church doctrine forbid fewer than three nuns living together under one roof. His interpretation of the Felician Order's rules was later proven false, and with the start of school only days away, the convent, usually staffed with at least three nuns who served their order by giving children a proper Catholic education, now stood empty.

This did not please the families with young children. School was seen by the Poles as a direct entry into a proper religious life. They saw school as an extension of church. One standard Polish textbook of the day, *Nauka czytania I pisanaia Wypracowana z polecenia Towarzystwa,* which translated means "Instruction in Reading and Writing," contained this definition of *Szkola,* or "School": "The place where children are sent to learn to read, write, calculate, and revere God."

In another Polish textbook, *Czytanka pierwsza* ("First Reader"), a typical day in *Szkola* is described by a young Polish student like this: "I go to school twice a day, in the morning and afternoon. When I am in school I praise God and I sit in my seat. Instruction begins with a prayer. In school I see many desks, at which sit the children. On the walls I see a crucifix and holy pictures."

The case of the missing nun had abruptly stopped the regular rhythms of life in Isadore, but until now it was the village's adults who had been affected. Now their children, too, were waiting for Sister Janina to be found.

Despite its importance, schooling of Isadore's children would just have to wait; but the souls of their parents could not.

On Sunday morning, two weeks after Sister Janina disappeared, Father Andrew said Mass as usual. After the benediction, however, another search began. This time, a Catholic understanding was not required nor even considered an advantage to join in, but a fair knowledge of the forests of northern Michigan was. A fresh crowd of searchers had been recruited, and these newcomers didn't even attend the service before venturing out into the wilds surrounding the sanctuary.

The rumor that Sister Janina had been driven insane by a combination of heredity, poor physical health, and her anxiousness over the Bishop's impending visit spread from farm to farm and church to church until it reached Traverse City and finally the lumber camps outside of town. The Sister was alive, the story went, and wandering in the swamp. The midnight melodies Holy Rosary's neighbors reported hearing were really Janina's voice, singing out her fright, madness, and last remaining shreds of religious faith.

If this were the case, it would take more than a bunch of farmers to find her. It would take a harder kind of man, a man comfortable in the darkest parts of the wilderness.

"A number of experienced woodsmen of the city have signified their willingness to go out and aid in the search for Sister Mary Janina and it is believed that many others will join in the search which will be held Sunday," the newspaper had reported. "There are a large number of young men in the city well acquainted with the woods and as such are asked to take part in this search. Despite the fact that she has been gone fifteen days it is believed that she is still alive, and in such event common humanity demands that every man who possibly can do so, whose services would be an aid, join in this search. If the missing Sister is dead, the finding of her body would bring relief as it would be known for certain then that her sufferings are at an end."

Experienced woodsmen, or "shanty boys" as they preferred to call themselves, with long blocks of unencumbered time on their calloused hands were easy to find in Traverse City in the fall of 1907. The lumber boom that had fueled the northern region's voracious logging industry for fifty years was coming to an abrupt end. Most of the white pines that had towered over the region were gone. They had all been felled, branched off, peeled, cut into sixteen-foot-lengths, floated down the Boardman River to the Grand Traverse Bay, and finally loaded onto waiting schooners bound for Chicago and the ravenous treeless prairies beyond. The foremen of the few logging camps, the so-called shanties, that were still in business had now sicced their shanty boys on hemlock, cherry, cedar, poplar, and red pine.

The men who worked with the loggers, the river hogs, the sawyers, the skidders, and the choppers, called this seemingly endless tree crop "green gold," in an effort to place this natural resource on par with California's gold rush. In one monumental logging season in the 1880s, thirteen million board feet were taken out of the northern Michigan forest. These were the kind of men now headed north from Traverse City, not to find giant trees but to find one petite nun.

Two decades after the lumbering began in earnest, if one virgin white pine remained in the region, it was left behind by accident. Virtually all of the green gold had been taken from the earth, and the shanty boys who felled them were just waking up from their clear-cutting stupor. They needed something to do, some quest that would take their mind off the fact that the backwoods goose that had laid billions of board feet of golden eggs was gone. Some of these shanty boys turned to agriculture, some followed the logs west to the prairies and became builders, some could not adjust to any life but logging and turned to liquor. Or gambling. Or crime.

Those who remained were a mixture of languages, nationalities, religions, personalities, and temperaments. They were single or married, family men or city ruffians, teenaged boys, men at their healthy peak, and old-timers. They thought themselves superior to any other laborer in any other endeavor. All were forever marked by the stain of pine tar, the feel of a crosscut saw in their hands, the bite of bedbugs large as pigeon's eggs.

Though their deep voices could be heard throughout the woods, most were not aligned with any particular religion. They did not sing hymns, they sang folksong melodies that drowned out birdsong for miles in every direction.

I am a jolly lumberman,
The pinewoods is my home;
Like many other fellows
From camp to camp I roam.
On many a raging river, boys,
I've drove throughout this land.
And now I'm on the Boardman
With a peavey in my hand.

These were the men called upon to search for Sister Janina, after the priest, the nuns, the neighbors, the dog, the private detective, the re-ward-seekers, and the law had failed to find her. For those woodsmen still in the area, searching for a missing nun provided a welcome and worthy diversion from searching for a life after logging.

On Friday, September 6, 1907 at 9 a.m. an M&N train blew its whis-tle as it left the Traverse City station bound for Isadore. One hundred woodsmen with a nun on their minds were on it.

Once they arrived at Holy Rosary, this new and manly swarm strode into the woods, undaunted by the rain and mud. They struggled most not with the conditions in the woods but with the conditions in the parish. A current of desperation had descended upon Isadore.

Throughout the morning and into the afternoon the woodsmen searched, lining up and walking in ragged formation, like some band of mismatched soldiers, each man spacing himself twenty feet from his counterpart. They fought with their fists, pulled flasks from their pock-ets and took long swallows, smoked, spit, swore, and stomped over every blade of grass, dead twig, fallen log, and stand of brush, just like those who had gone before them. They, too, found nothing. They did not intimidate the weather—it rained on them just as it had every other large searching party.

When the shanty boys returned to the church, someone in their group suggested calling upon the strange abilities of Arthur "Otto" Sorenson, the area's best-known clairvoyant. This interested the woods-men, now wet, tired, dejected, and willing to try anything, whether they thoroughly understood its methodology or not. Sorenson could be asked to come to the convent that very night, the men suggested, and could be encouraged to settle himself in Sister Janina's cell and then go into one of his trances.

This spiritually rich setting where the nun slept and prayed would eliminate the barrier between past and present that men working in the physical realm had thus far been unable to penetrate. "Yes," they said to each other, slapping backs and knees, pulling beards, and adjusting caps, "this is the best idea we've heard yet."

There was one man, however, standing directly in the path of this new idea—Father Andrew. The dark art of clairvoyance went against everything the priest believed in, and though few could claim to be as desperate as he to find the missing Sister, the priest was aghast at the idea that the powers of the occult might be summoned right here to his parish. Catholic theology looked harshly upon clairvoyance, viewing it as a function of black magic, something "beyond the power of man with the aid of powers other than the Divine." Such activity was not only forbidden but also condemned as a grievous sin. Father Andrew's own views on the matter mirrored those of his church.

"I know nothing about it," the priest remarked in a phone call to an inquirer. "It is the first I have heard of it. I would certainly forbid such foolishness."

Which he did to the woodsmen and to the clairvoyant, in short order. Otto Sorenson was not welcome on church grounds, Father Andrew announced, and if he appeared, he would be removed. Forcibly, if necessary. One look at the priest's marble-hard fists and tall shoulders set as wide and high as any war statue's and even the roughest men knew that while this might be a man of spiritual things, he could also make good on a physical threat.

But the disappearance of Sister Janina had, by now, grown into a mystery that Father Andrew could no longer contain nor control. Her fate belonged to the Isadore parish, but also to the hundreds of searchers who had looked for her in the dark and in the rain and in the mud, to the lawmen who stood guard outside the church at night, to her Sisters in Manistee and Detroit, and to her Creator. And only some on this list were members of the Catholic faith and under Father Andrew's purview.

If there ever had been a time when Sister Janina's priest was in possession of the power to forbid any mode of investigation into her disappearance, no matter how distasteful or foolish, that time was now over. The clairvoyant was contacted and his help enlisted. The woodsmen had found an obvious way around Father Andrew's imposing fists—just keep their human novelty off church property.

Not needing to use any of his special powers to know he was unwelcome in Isadore, at the men's invitation Sorensen situated himself across the street from the church the very next evening. Settled in at the edge of the oat field, he focused his mind toward "getting into the sleep." His first attempt was unsuccessful, and he blamed the publicity that dominated the case for his inability to get any psychic images that would point to the location of Sister Janina or her body. Sorenson vowed to try again, though, and on Sunday night he did.

What came into his head finally was a sense that Sister Janina was confined to the basement of a house located in a town nearby, but west. The images were vague and distant, the specifics hazy. She could have been snatched right out of the convent, or she could have gone along with her escorts willingly and then changed her mind. However her absence had occurred, she was now being held against her will—of that the clairvoyant said his visions were almost certain.

The house where the nun was being held was square, white, and built at the top of a hill. Three men had worked in concert to take Sister Janina away, for reasons unclear but without a doubt nefarious. One of those men now paced up and down the road in front of this square house, keeping a lookout. This kidnapper was stocky, coarsely dressed, and no stranger to wrongdoing, but both his expression and identity were unknowable to Sorensen, hidden as they were behind a swarthy black beard.

All of this the clairvoyant told the neighbors, searchers, shanty boys, and reward-seekers still on the scene. From them, the story made its way to Traverse City where it joined with the other rumors already circulating there.

Swirling their way through gossip circles, lumberyards, liveries, and barstool conversations were stories like these: Sister Janina's body had been found in the belfry of the school, some said. No, no, not the belfry of the school, the attic of the convent, others insisted. Sister Janina had run off with a man, and they were living together as husband and wife in Chicago. Sister Janina was insane, and not only wandering aimlessly in the swamps of Isadore, but purposely hiding out from anyone who looked for her there.

While these possibilities were shared openly, another rumor built in whispers, and sideways glances: Sister Janina was pregnant. Shame had driven her away, had gotten her killed, or both.

From among these scandalous theories, the clairvoyant's description of the place where he believed the nun was being held prisoner commanded enough merit to rally a group of his neighbors from Kingsley. They banded together and, along with Sorensen himself and a newspaper reporter, made their way to Glen Lake, the resort town west of Isadore that the clairvoyant had seen in his vision. On the way, they picked up more men in Cedar and then a deputy in Empire whose job it would be to take the bearded man into custody if they could find him.

Moblike now, with torches, guns, and a collective anger growing darker by the mile, the determined group descended upon a large white cottage on the shore of Big Glen, the lake the resort town was named for. Their arrival frightened the cottage owner's domestic staff, the residence's only current occupants. This summer cottage belonged to a Chicago businessman who hadn't visited in weeks.

The men found no sign of the Sister, no bearded kidnapper, nothing but a cook and a chore boy both now frightened half out of their wits by the searching party. Their bluster gone, the men doused their torches and relaxed their trigger fingers. Their voices all but silenced, they left as quickly as they had come.

"The case is still as mysterious as ever and no new light has been thrown upon it," reported the newsman who had accompanied the mob, in a short article he filed for the next day's edition. Sister Janina's disappearance had distressed those in the region so thoroughly that the newspaper was now running daily dispatches that reported nothing more than that there was nothing new to report.

In the early-twentieth-century newsroom, this was called a "snap," and only the most compelling ongoing stories rated daily ink even when there wasn't any news to share with readers. A vanishing nun sold papers, and so editors throughout the Midwest and the Central Plains were in agreement: Sister Janina's story was snap-worthy.

The rumor that the missing nun was pregnant could have begun as sala-cious tavern talk or front parlor chitchat, but it gained credence when Sheriff Brown leaked something scandalous. After Detective Castle re-turned to Detroit, Sheriff Brown had taken over the case and conducted a series of interviews with anyone who had interacted with the nun in the past several months. What he learned was that Sister Janina's private cell hadn't really been private at all. Not according to accepted convent protocol, anyway.

The sheriff knew that Catholic nuns were never to allow themselves to be alone with a man, not for any reason. Not illness, not grief, not a visit to a neighbor, not even death. A nun's dying breath was to be taken alone or with her Sisters. Should a priest be called to give last rites, he was to do so chaperoned by at least one other person.

"I would not that any man should see you except he have special permission from your superior; for these sins I have spoken of did not happen because the woman looked forwardly upon men, but it hap-pened through their uncovering themselves in the sight of men," states the *Rule*. "The dog enters gladly where he finds an open door."

Apparently, the male searchers who had cringed at the idea of vio-lating a nun's private space had had nothing to worry about. If the sher-iff's revelations were to be believed, two men had enjoyed regular access to the Sister's private room. Both Father Andrew and a local physician Dr. George Fralick had freely passed through the same bedroom door-way that the searchers had been so reluctant to enter.

There had been complaints that Father Andrew was too "intimate" with the Sister Superior, visiting her regularly in her cell. Not only that, but for the past six months Dr. Fralick had been attending to the nun, making frequent house calls to the convent and being allowed, un-escorted, into her room. Whatever business these men had with Sister Janina, it was conducted behind a closed door.

The sheriff's revelations stopped short of saying outright that any-thing untoward had taken place between the nun and her male visitors, but the rumormongers were more than happy to take it from there. What else but animal urges, they whispered to each other, could have expressed themselves there?

Dr. Fralick, who operated a medical practice and a drug store in nearby Maple City and was also his city's postmaster and a county coroner, traveled throughout Leelanau County in his black iron-wheeled contraption, a doctor's bag perched on the seat next to him. He was enamored of man-made inventions and owned the county's first automobile. He was favorably thought of for his friendliness and medical skill. "Everything which tends to bring to man the key to that complex mystery which we call life is of interest to him," stated a local historian, "and his reading and research have been broad and long continued, bringing to him accurate and comprehensive knowledge of the best methods of eradicating disease and restoring to man his most priceless possession."

Still, despite such flattery, word that the doctor had been allowed into Sister Janina's cell weekly and sometimes even more often for half of the past year fueled the scandalous rumor. The protocol for the physician's visits was later described in detail by none other than her other visitor, Father Andrew.

"Sometimes he was accompanied to her room and sometimes he was not. When he first came here I would ring the bell and the Sisters would come and accompany him to the place where he was to go, and usually Sister Janina would come out because it was her task to come. She was Superior. I would introduce the Sister to the doctor, and she would take him to the proper place. I did not always accompany the doctor to the door. Sometimes, when he was called upon to make a visit, he would ring the bell I understand, but he would go to see the Sister without my knowing it. Without the other Sisters knowing it."

Public accounts describe Dr. Fralick as an honorable man, sincerely vested in the health of the residents of Leelanau County. A native of Michigan and an only child, he studied at the Michigan College of Medicine and Surgery in Detroit, graduating in 1893 and setting up his practice in northern Michigan that same year. Like most country doctors of the day, Dr. Fralick, by necessity, was a generalist. He tended farmers who had been injured in agricultural accidents, relieved the discomfort of the old and infirm, responded to train accidents, and set broken bones.

He also did what he could for children beset by disease for which immunizations were yet unavailable, and he was one of two county coroners. Dr. Fralick also provided prenatal care, such that it was, and he delivered babies. In all this, publicly he was considered quite competent, and his practice was successful.

"Concentration of purpose and persistently applied energy rarely fail in the accomplishment of any task, however great, and in tracing the career of Dr. George W. Fralick, a well-known physician, it is plainly seen that these things have been the secrets of his rise to a position of prominence and respectability," reported an early 1900s guide to the area's leading citizens. "His knowledge of the science of medicine is broad and comprehensive, and in his professional labors he has shown that he is well qualified to cope with the intricate problems which continually confront the physician in his efforts to prolong life and restore health."

Privately, Dr. Fralick was known by some as a flirt and a womanizer. In piecing together the events leading up to her disappearance, Father Andrew told Sheriff Brown that the doctor last examined Sister Janina a week before she disappeared. A few days later, she requested another visit with him, but because of his busy practice, or for some other reason now unknown, as far as Father Andrew knew this visit never took place.

"During the week before her disappearance she wanted to see him and asked for him," said Father Andrew. "The housekeeper was going to town and I told her to leave word for him and she said she did. He didn't come, and I was reminded by the Sister to notify him. I stopped his rig and asked him to be kind enough to call on the Sister, and he said he would. He did not call to my knowledge."

All of this Sheriff Brown shared with the people he interviewed as part of his ongoing investigation, and they passed the titillating news on further. Of course, there were logical reasons for the Sister to meet with each of the men. She would have needed to talk to Father Andrew about church matters and to the doctor about her health and the health of the convent's two other Sisters. But behind a closed door?

Sister Janina's struggle with tuberculosis would surely have brought the doctor to her bedside. If that were her only condition that required medical treatment, would she have needed him weekly and sometimes even twice a week or more? The talk had begun, and people said they knew of friends and relatives who suffered the same affliction as the Sister and they certainly didn't need to see the doctor every week. Why, people wondered, should the Sister be any different?

The rumor of her relationships with these men and her possible pregnancy was widespread enough to make its way to at least some of the reporters covering her disappearance. The local newspaper, for one, attempted to quell the scandal, stating, "When she was 18 years of age, she took the holy vows of the church and became a nun. She is about 33 years old now and as she has never come in contact with the world, the idea of any love affair is preposterous."

Talk, once it is loosed, cannot be stopped by one journalist's opinion, and in northern Michigan in the early 1900s opportunities for titillating entertainment were few; plain newsprint was no match for the stories of forbidden love and broken spiritual vows now traded from ear to ear. The same determination to find the Sister that had once recommended Father Andrew now turned against him. Could his tireless acts be not the kindness of a dedicated priest but the guilt of a lovesick and grieving full-blooded man?

Rumors of Sister Janina's pregnancy also affected Dr. Fralick's reputation unfavorably. Some said he had performed an illegal abortion on the nun, which had ended badly. The procedure had killed her, this rumor went, and her body was buried somewhere secret, where no one would ever find it.

"And it is written of Eve, the mother of us all, that she looked upon the forbidden apple and saw it fair," the *Rule* warned. "Thus did sight go before and prepare the way for guilty desire; and death followed, to which all mankind is subject. This apple, dear Sisters, betokeneth every thing that excited guilty desire, and delight in sin. When thou lookest upon a man, thou art lookest upon the apple."

At 9 p.m. on September 17, 1907, an anonymous letter addressed to "Mother Superior, Isadore Convent, Traverse City, Michigan" was postmarked in Chicago. It arrived at the Holy Rosary rectory three days later, where it was opened and read by Father Andrew. If anything could distract attention away from the scandal of a wayward nun, it was the contents of this letter. "Sister Mary [Janina] who disappeared from the convent was not abducted or murdered. She simply was tired of her job so slipped quietly away, knowing that was the only method which would be successful. You are foolish to have raised all this hew and cry. It was a mistake which I presume you now realize, and so for appearance sake, gave it to the public that she was abducted. Nonsense! Let her alone! Give her a chance. You probably won't find her and she won't want that you should—Protestant Pup."

Father Andrew was certain he had obtained an important clue to the Sister's whereabouts, and he examined the letter carefully. It was handwritten, and upon several rereadings he thought he recognized the penmanship. It looked remarkably similar to the writing he'd seen on notes and prescriptions scrawled by none other than Dr. George Fralick.

Unless the doctor had something to do with Sister Janina's disappearance, Father Andrew could think of no reason why he would write such a note and then not sign his name. He immediately turned the letter over to Sheriff Brown. Despite the sheriff's initial reluctance to get involved, he was now in full control of the case. Detective Castle had gone back to Detroit, and each of the miscellaneous bounty hunters lured by the priest's $500 reward had lost interest.

The sheriff read the letter with interest, but his theory on the author was quite different than Father Andrew's. The letter had been postmarked in Chicago, the city of the Sister's birth and the home of two of her brothers. Perhaps she had fled the convent and was living with them, and they had sent the letter to stop the search for her, so that she could enjoy her newfound freedom without having to account for her decision.

Sheriff Brown located Frank and Emil Mezek, and posted a letter to each of them, asking if they'd seen their sister, and if either of them were the mysterious Protestant Pup. The brothers wrote back straightaway, denying any knowledge of the strange letter. Other correspondence from them followed. Neither had seen their younger sister, they said, since she entered the convent. It was the church that had lost her, and they expected the church to find her and to keep them informed of any progress in the matter.

One of these letters read:

Dear Sir,

In relation to my being in Detroit Michigan, and meeting my Sister a year ago, there is no truth in it. The last time, and the only time I was in Detroit, was when my sister and me went to the Convent when my father died, twenty-five years ago, and none of my relation was in Detroit the last sixteen years, and we don't know anything about her.

Please write when you get any clue of her,

Very respectfully,
Emil Mezek, 8855 Aberdeen St. Chicago Ill.

The priest and the sheriff decided not to take these brothers at their word, however, and instead convinced another lawman, Traverse City police chief William Ashton, to go to Chicago on the sly. Ashton complied and did not announce his visit to the Mezek men but instead spent his first day in Chicago observing the comings and goings at their house on Stewart Avenue. The next day, the police chief knocked on the doors of Frank and Emil's neighbors and asked whether anyone had seen a woman about the Mezek place in the past few weeks.

She would be just over five feet tall, he told them. With a slight frame, reddish brown hair, and olive skin. Pleasant looking, if not exactly pretty. They might have heard her singing, he added, and if so, they would have remarked to each other upon the loveliness of her voice.

No, the neighbors told Chief Ashton. No one had seen any women around the Mezek place; certainly not one like the woman he described. After canvassing the street and receiving this same answer at each doorway he visited, Ashton returned to Traverse City empty-handed. Upon his arrival, Father Andrew and Sheriff Brown sent him to question Dr. Fralick. The doctor also denied sending the letter, and acted put out by the suggestion. Either because they were afraid of the doctor's reaction, or because it didn't occur to them, neither policeman compared the handwriting on the letter to the doctor's, and it became yet another mystery associated with the nun's disappearance.

Still, Father Andrew continued to puzzle over it privately, long after the letter had left his possession. Someone had mailed it to Isadore from Chicago, in order to confuse the searchers, vouch for Sister Janina, or exorcise their own dark secrets. Though Father Andrew couldn't know with certainty who that person was, or say which of these possible motives had inspired the correspondent to put pen to paper, never again would he share a polite word with the doctor. He regretted that he had relinquished the letter, and that control of this piece of important evidence now rested with the law, and not with him.

The onset of cold weather was another thing Father Andrew could not control, and by the beginning of October, Sister Janina was no longer on the front page of the newspapers. Occasionally, a single paragraph buried in a back section would inform readers that there was nothing new to report about the missing nun. By November, these "snaps" had ceased and she wasn't anywhere on these inside pages, either. She had been missing for nine weeks, and had become a non-story. Readers had other things to be titillated by, and to worry about. So did the Catholic Church.

Advent and all that season's accompanying holy days required preparation, there were still several weekly Masses, and the school was open again. Sister Josephine and Sister Angelina had returned to the convent to teach and were joined by Sisters Regina, Raphael, and Leonissa, from Detroit. In late September, a group of orphaned boys had arrived from the St. Joseph Home in Jackson, Michigan, 230 miles to the south. Another branch of the Felician Order operated this orphanage for boys, it was overcrowded, and so a group was sent to board at Isadore for a Catholic, and country, education.

The convent's newly appointed Sister Superior was Sister Regina. In the absence of Sister Janina, it was her appointed job to see that the classrooms of children were following their lessons, that the nuns were attending to their duties, that prayers were being recited, and that holy days were properly observed.

In early November, Holy Rosary parish was planning a Forty Hours' Devotional, and so Sister Regina was given her first important assignment. She was in charge of decorating the church's altar so that it looked special for the priests who would be visiting Isadore from around the state to add their prayers to Father Andrew's. This was the same task Sister Janina had been given three months earlier in preparation for a visit from the Bishop, who had been coming to bless the new brick school. Sister Regina could not have helped but face it with some trepidation.

One afternoon, a few days before the gathering of priests was to take place, Sister Regina went to the church basement where the paper flowers and other decorations were stored. This ordinary task was what many thought to be Sister Janina's last act on the day she disappeared. Sister Regina woke from her afternoon nap, rose from her bed, and knelt down and prayed. She walked downstairs, left the convent, and walked across the churchyard to the church basement. She opened the small door, stooped down, and pushed inside to the earth-smelling dark. And here Sister Regina's path diverted sharply from Sister Janina's. Sunlight reflected on something down on the ground at her feet, and the glint caught her eye. She bent down to see what it was and found a pair of small wire-rimmed eyeglasses.

Sister Regina picked them up and turned the glasses over in her hand. She wondered if they had belonged to her predecessor. They were the type that the nuns who needed glasses wore, and she remembered that when she met Sister Janina in Detroit, the missing nun had been wearing eyeglasses.

The box of paper flowers forgotten, Sister Regina ran back to the church, where she found Father Andrew preparing the altar. She showed him the glasses, and before she could even speak, he reached out and snatched them from her hand.

"Where did you get these?" the priest demanded.

"Under the church, down in the basement," Sister Regina answered. "Right inside the door."

Father Andrew said they did indeed look exactly like the pair Sister Janina wore. Two months had gone by since she went missing, and in that time every speck of that dark area beneath the church had been gone over, and then gone over again. Lawmen, woodsmen, townsmen, and hired men had searched there. Why weren't the glasses found then?

Father Andrew left the church then and took the glasses with him. Sister Regina hurried to the convent and assembled the four other nuns. She described her find and asked them what they made of such a strange occurrence, so long after their Sister had gone missing. She wondered aloud to Holy Rosary's other nuns if the eyeglasses had belonged to Sister Janina, and if they were a clue to her disappearance.

Two of those present, Sister Josephine and Sister Angelina, had been under Sister Janina's rule here in Isadore for a year before she disappeared. They taught with her, prayed with her, ate with her, and worshipped with her. Describe the glasses to us, they said. Sister Regina did her best, but the area where she had found them was shadowed by the basement, and the glasses were clutched inside her hand in the few minutes between finding them and showing them to Father Andrew. Then, Father Andrew had taken them away.

They were of a common enough style, she said, with nothing to distinguish them. Perhaps they'd been the Sister's, but perhaps not.

Father Andrew was receiving no satisfaction from the local lawmen, nor from the Mezek boys, and he continued his one-way correspondence with the Felician Motherhouse, hoping for some clue. His letters went unanswered, and he began to think the Sisters in Detroit might know something that they weren't sharing with him.

Months passed, and near the Thanksgiving holiday Father Andrew finally received a letter from one of the Detroit nuns. Sister Mary Paul had been a teacher in Isadore when Father Andrew was first posted there, almost eight years ago, in 1900. Sister Paul had served at the parish school for three years, and she and Father Andrew remained on friendly terms after she returned to Detroit.

Sister Paul would turn out to be one of the few people, besides Stella, to ever speak ill of the missing Sister.

November 25, 1907

Reverend Father,

It would be my most welcome opportunity if I could help you in any way in your noble efforts.

It is too bad that I was so distant from Sister Janina. I didn't like her conduct and on that account I didn't try to have any closer relations with her.

You say, Reverend Father, that the Sisters are unwilling to furnish you with information. Well, it is hard to swim against the current.

They know very well in how great estimation Sister Janina was with Mother Kiatana, who strongly intimated in advance that nobody should even dare to suppose that she would leave the Convent willfully. Of course, I could not follow this direction, and neither do I support this opinion.

So far as I know Sister Janina, I know she was petted too much—
to the limit, and she was not a nun, only by her garb. I never saw
her at community prayers and meditations. She slept as long and as
often as she wanted and never came to community table. She never
touched any harder work and was difficult. She always relied on
others and I don't know by what law.

The Superiors were delighted with her and allowed her
everything.

Now Reverend Father, don't worry. Don't waste any money. Your
health and time are too valuable. We will pray to Jesus and Saint
Anthony for that intention . . . and we will commend this matter to
Jesus.

Sister Mary Paul

This letter may have provided some friendly and spiritual support to
Father Andrew, but it didn't contain what he was primarily seeking:
hard evidence as to the whereabouts of the missing nun. Around the
grounds of Holy Rosary parish, and in the woods and fields beyond, the
only visible signs that the Sister was still missing were the footprints the
priest himself left in the snow when he went out looking for her. These
daily and eventually weekly sojourns he now made alone.

The swamp that had once seemed such an impediment was frozen
hard enough for even a man of his robust size to walk on. The brambles
and mud that had vexed the searchers in August and September no
longer kept his search at bay. Cold day after cold day he traveled every
square foot of it, to no avail.

The corn stalks were brown and flattened in the field, no longer
taller than the shoulders of a small woman, but instead frozen hard to
the ground. Snow clung to the tree branches, muffling all sound in the
woods. No one heard the voice of a woman singing again; no one saw a
flickering candle weaving in and out of the trees at night.

If any part of the Sister remained in these wild places surrounding
the church, by now Father Andrew believed it could only be her bones.
If he found any comfort at all, it was in the obvious thoroughness of his
own actions. "I have done all I could to find her," he reassured himself.
"All in my power, officially and otherwise."

The priest may have been driven by curiosity, or guilt at being unable to learn her fate, or an inner sense of justice, but his actions could also have been those of a grieving man in love.

For all activity but these searches, Father Andrew had to work hard to keep himself going, and he threw himself fully into the yoke of his spiritual responsibilities at Holy Rosary. The missing nun mystery had done nothing to improve his standing with his flock. If anything, most of the parishioners mistrusted him more than they ever had. He wasn't liked or even admired by them, but he could claim one small edge of acceptance. Alongside mistrust was a grudging respect for his work ethic. That was something all of the immigrant families of Isadore could understand.

By December, the roads from the farms to the school became impassable many days, and so the orphan boys from Jackson were joined by some of the local schoolchildren who now had to winter in. Some of these students stayed during the week, returning home on weekends, and some boarded at the school all winter long.

The children who stayed during the week arrived on Monday morning in a sleigh pulled by a team of horses owned by one or another of the area's farmers. Packed into the open-air sleigh, along with their schoolbooks and Bibles, were their bedding, their clothes, and whatever vegetables and meat their families could spare. Between eight and twelve families sent their children to board at Holy Rosary in the winter of 1907, plus the orphan boys from Jackson, making the school building and convent home to five nuns and approximately thirty children. Another seventy youngsters came to school in the morning and returned home in the afternoon. Educating this group was a given; feeding them was quite a laborious undertaking.

"Every family brought their own meat and platter on which the meat was served," according to Michaeline Brzezinski Pleva, who began her schooling at Holy Rosary School as a first grader in 1912. "Parents had to supply potatoes, and any vegetables that were available, to cook up into soups and such so the Sister in charge of cooking could prepare the necessary meals," according to Dorothy Galla Popa, who was a student at the school several years later, in the 1920s. Little had changed. The menu was still dominated by potatoes. Potato pancakes, potato stews, mashed potato, fried potato, and potato dumplings.

"The meats were mostly home-canned beef, pork, etc. Breakfast was nearly always oatmeal and coffee. Lunch was just a pick up. Something quick from the supplies brought from home; a slice of bread, an apple, etc. The meals for students and the Sisters were all prepared on one wood stove."

Girls slept on the first floor on the south side of the school building, which was also used as the auditorium. The boys slept in the northwest corner of the basement. Family washbowls were kept on a bench in a basement hallway where the children lined up, brushed their teeth, and washed their hands and faces before school every morning and before bed every night. Older girls peeled potatoes and carrots for the next day's meals and then helped with the cooking. All the children took turns doing the dishes, their own of course but also the Sisters'.

First and second grades were taught catechism and Bible history in Polish; and arithmetic, spelling, and reading in English. Third, fourth, and fifth grades were taught religion, Polish and English reading, spelling, arithmetic, and grammar. A "Spelling Down," or friendly competition, was held every Friday. Sixth, seventh, and eighth grades were taught catechism and Bible history in Polish; arithmetic, spelling, geography, physiology, U.S. history, and civil government in English.

Besides school lessons and meal preparations, classrooms had to be swept, stove wood cut and stacked, water carried in from the well, and chamber pots emptied and scrubbed. Between the boarders and the children who commuted back and forth to school every day, Holy Rosary had one priest and three to five Sisters to see to the spiritual, intellectual, and practical requirements of more than one hundred children. "I pray you, that you be never idle, but work, or read, or be at beads, and in prayer, and thus be always doing something from which good may come," instructed the *Rule*. In Isadore, this was not difficult. There was more than enough work to keep one from idleness.

The nuns were to accomplish all of these tasks, every day, without giving the impression of hurrying, which was considered unseemly. Walking was to be done calmly, hands tucked out of sight behind their scapular; eyes were to be focused down; talk was to be limited to necessary communication: "Let a Sister, whatsoever she be, keep silence as much as ever she can and may. Let her not have the hen's nature. She grinds grit who prates idly. The two cheeks are the two grindstones; the tongue is the clapper."

These labors kept the remaining nuns at Holy Rosary busy and Father Andrew's mind occupied. He thought of Sister Janina less often through the Christmas season and into the New Year. He took weekly instead of daily walks now, weather permitting. She could not be in the woods or fields, he believed, or he would have found her body by now. His walks had become less of a search and more of a chance for solitary meditation and prayer.

He likely prayed: *O Divine Eternal Father, in union with your Divine Son and the Holy Spirit, and through the immaculate Heart of Mary, I beg You to destroy the power of your greatest enemy, the evil spirits. Cast them into the deepest recesses of hell and chain them there forever. Take possession of your Kingdom which You have created and which is rightfully yours.*

At the end of these walks, as the white church came back into view, Father Andrew always arrived at the same conclusion. It was time to inform Sister Janina's next of kin that the search had been all but abandoned. It was time to ask her brothers one last time if they had received any word of her. His own health was suffering mightily from these walks and the ongoing worry they sustained. There was no diagnosis, just a general malaise.

As a last chance effort, the priest considered the wisdom of asking the newspapers for help. They had certainly covered the mystery, whether he liked it or not, but so far his relationship with the local paper had been standoffish. Like many Polish priests of the day, he was reticent to open up the goings-on of his parish to the larger outside, and secular, world. In normal times, it was none of the public's business what he did or how he did it, but perhaps he should make an exception now. Her brothers might have an opinion on this idea, and he would ask them.

Considering that Father Andrew was rumored to have been in love with the Sister, it was curious, but probably only a coincidence, that he began his next correspondence with the Mezek brothers on St. Valentine's Day. A feast day on the Catholic calendar until 1968, it commemorates a decision by a fifteenth-century pope to purify what had been a pagan holiday. Until the pope's intercession, Romans would hold a lottery on this day, and young men would draw the name of a young woman to be their intimate companion for the coming year. The lottery remained, but saints' names replaced the women's, and men were encouraged to draw one at random and spend the year emulating their selection's more pious characteristics.

With this tradition in the background, on the feast day of St. Valentine, Father Andrew sought some final assistance from the Mezeks.

February 14, 1908
Mr. Frank Mezek, Chicago, Ill.

Dear Sir,

In searching and making inquiries for your sister Josephine, we satisfied ourselves that she is not in the woods as we suspected. She has been here only one year, but everybody in the neighborhood was so attached to her and liked her so much, that we decided to continue our work until we find out something sure.

For this reason I write you this letter to give us your helping hand and give us all the information you can. If you learn that she is alive, write us and we will be satisfied to stop our work, which costs a good deal, as soon as we hear from you.

If you do not know whether she is alive, write us anyway and we will have her picture printed in all the big daily papers of Chicago, New York, Detroit, Grand Rapids, and so forth, and ask the public to send their information to us. We have money on hand for that purpose. I believe it will not cost us very much because the papers are anxious to help us in this case.

We found her picture in her prayerbook and will have it enlarged for that purpose. Don't you think this would be a good idea? Of course we would not like to do that for her sake, but if she is dead, it will not hurt her, and will interest the public, which maybe able to give us some information.

Kindly answer at once and oblige.
Yours truly,
Andrew Bieniawski

When six weeks passed with no word from Frank Mezek, Father Andrew had not published her photograph in the newspaper, and sent a letter to Sister Janina's other brother, Emil.

March 26, 1908
Mr. Emil Mezek, Chicago, Ill.

Dear Sir,

We have been looking for a letter from you ever since we informed you about your sister's disappearance. Not hearing from you by this time we are coming to the conclusion she must have gotten tired of her hard work in the Convent and left the place, in order to join her relatives. If this would be the case, we would be glad to hear from you at least these words: "Yes, she is here." Or "Yes, she is alive." And we will be greatly obliged for your kindness.

She has been highly respected by everybody here and liked by all, therefore it is natural that we all are anxious to find whether she is alive and safe. We spent much money about this matter and are ready to spend more, provided this will bring her necessary help if she needs it.

Will you be kind enough to write me whether she is alive? Your kind information will be indeed a great favor to us and a great relief to the Convent authorities where she spent many years in hard and noble work.

I would come and see you personally, but my health is poor now, and my physician has warned me that my heart is in bad condition and I should take rest for some time. If I get better, I would come to see you, if it will make no inconvenience to you.

Please write me at once.
Andrew Bieniawski

This time, Father Andrew received a response in short order. Just four days later, a letter from Emil arrived in Isadore.

March 30, 1908
Rev. Bieniawski, Isadore, Mi

I have wrote two letters since I have known that my sister
Josephine has departed from the convent and the last time I wrote
you. I have not seen Josephine in at least fifteen or twenty years.
Don't get it in your head that if we know anything about my sister
while we would be asking to let you know. No don't let anyone tell
you that she is with us, and I haven't written to anyone at Isadore
that she is with us; and if you don't hear from her soon, you had
better look in deeper, and if/when you want to come and see us in
regard to that matter, let me know as we would be glad to meet you
at any time. Don't let anyone tell you that she is with us. I would be
too glad to let you know.

> Yours very truly,
> Emil Mezek,
> 8855 Aberdeen St.
> Chicago.

In the tiny Polish-Catholic outpost in northern Michigan, the needs
of the living precluded the needs of one nun now presumed dead, and
the fate of Sister Janina receded for almost ten years from the consciousness of Isadore.

Officially, the Diocese of Detroit and the lawmen of northern Michigan had ceased looking for her. The only evidence that she had lived at
all came once a day inside the chapel at the Motherhouse in Detroit. The
sound of Sister Mary Janina's name was just one beat in a long rhythmic
list of other names read aloud during her Felician Order's ritual prayers
for the dead.

Revelations

Spring, 1917

> Confession of secret sins ought also
> to be always prudent, and made to a
> prudent man, and not to young priests,
> nor yet foolish old men.
>
> —*The Nun's Rule*

AN UNGODLY AND BURDENSOME PREDICTION ushered in Isadore's new priest. On May 15, 1917, in a simple ceremony, Father Edward Podlaszewski was installed as the new parish priest at Holy Rosary Church. He was 31. Though short in height and slight in stature, Father Edward's plans for the parish were mighty. He was the church's third resident priest, the second man to lead the parish after Father Andrew's abrupt transfer in 1913, and his route to Isadore had been circuitous.

In the decade after the disappearance of Sister Janina, Father Andrew had been transferred out, replaced first by Father Leopold "Leo" Oprychalski, from St. Joseph's in Manistee, from 1913 to 1917 and then by Father Edward. The shift in authority between Father Andrew, Father Leo, and Father Edward had been ordered by the diocese in Detroit.

After Father Andrew failed to find Sister Janina or determine what had happened to her, the Isadore farmers could no longer sustain any faith in his leadership, and the senior clergy in Detroit found a creative way to replace him. In 1913 he and St. Joseph's Father Leo had been asked to change places. Father Leo took over for the unpopular and indelibly tainted Father Andrew, and Father Andrew moved to the more prosperous St. Joseph's, where the parish was not so familiar with the gossip surrounding the missing nun.

Rumors that Father Andrew was somehow involved in the nun's disappearance had never entirely faded away, despite his steadfast efforts to find her, and his forceful protestations of innocence. Still, these whisperings were confined to Isadore and to correspondence within the upper echelons of the Catholic Church; people in his new town of Manistee knew little about them. St. Joseph's was, strangely, a promotion for the very priest Isadore had discarded.

"When Father [Andrew] removed himself . . . it could be said he was forced," one of the area's first settlers later said. "He was a different type of priest who behaved rudely toward the parishioners."

Father Leo, a baby-faced man with an enveloping kindness, a history of accomplishments, and an approachable manner arrived in Isadore in 1913 with the assignment to right the wrongs of his predecessor and restore Holy Rosary to its rightful place of leadership and spiritual example among the local farm families. It was a challenging task, but Father Leo was undaunted. His work at church-building was well documented and admired by church leaders and parishioners alike. He, too, brought with him his own ambitions.

In 1889 he had taken over St. Mary's in Alpena after a devastating fire had leveled the church, the rectory, and two hundred neighboring homes. It took only a few years for him to dedicate a new church, rebuild the rectory, found the Rosary Society, and staff the convent school with Felicians from Detroit. At St. Joseph's in Manistee, he had been further credited with building a new school after the first one burned down, and frescoing the inside of the church, giving it a dramatic and European sensibility.

Father Leo saw the opportunity of replacing the simple white church building in Isadore with something much more grand, and planned to raise the funds for a new building to bring Holy Rosary out of its spiritual isolation and insular mindset. All Father Leo needed was time and money. He had secured both in Alpena and Manistee, and when he arrived at Isadore there was nothing to convince him that he couldn't do the same in this new outpost, despite its remote location.

In the previous century, rural parishes were known to hold on to their priests for decades, some holy men even spending their entire working lives at a single church. This had not been the case at Isadore. The church had been built in 1882, and Father Leo was its fifth resident priest in thirty-one years. Two of these had been traveling priests who ministered to several rural churches, and then the next three men were dedicated to Holy Rosary only. Father Leo was of Polish descent, just like most of the Isadore community; the parishioners liked and even loved him, and by all accounts his tenure at Holy Rosary should have been a long and fruitful one.

But within a few years of his arrival, something happened to turn his head and heart against this parish, and in 1917 Father Leo walked away from the dreams and ambitions he'd once had for the place. He requested a transfer to another church, and was posted again in Alpena, all the way across the state on Michigan's opposite coast. He knew the parish well—he had served there for a decade before his tenure in Manistee. The warning he gave to Father Edward about what was buried under the old wooden church was his only good-bye to the place he had once had such great plans for. Church records list his last official act as a baptism on May 11, 1917.

"Why he didn't want to stay with us was made clear during the investigation," said the same local settler who had earlier criticized Father Andrew. "He was too honest and did not want his good name to be involved in criminal proceedings. [Father Leo] was a great loss and everybody was sorry to see him go when he left Isadore."

Into this sorrowful vacuum came the ambitions of the introspective, mannerly, young and handsome Father Edward. Holy Rosary would be his first church. In his other posting at St. Joseph's in Manistee, he served as assistant to first Father Leo and then to Father Andrew, with little authority or visibility. All of the important sacraments and ceremonies and parish decisions had been made by the head priest, sometimes even without so much as a word of Father Edward's input or opinion.

In 1913 he sat in the pew and watched while Father Leo was honored for his twenty-five years in the priesthood with a silver jubilee high mass and given a silver chalice and a matching silver ciborium. The celebration lasted for an entire day. An orchestra played, the children's choir sang, priests from around the state gave sermons extolling the virtue and faith of Father Leo, and the boys of St. Joseph's school even gave a gymnastics performance in his honor. Much was made of the fact that Father Leo had been ordained by Bishop Richter himself.

Father Edward had also been ordained by Bishop Richter, and now that he had his very own church to lead, things were finally going to be different, he must have assured himself. It was God's blessing that he had been posted here in the remote north, at this plain church so very ripe for improvement. The anonymity that he so despised would soon be a thing of the past.

Through his own spiritual will, Father Edward vowed that he would rally the town into action, calling for a commitment of both the people's muscles and their money. Under his tenure, Isadore's faithful would replace the unremarkable and outdated wooden church with a modern and proud brick-built one to match the school. Its spire would stretch toward heaven and the windows would have real stained glass to reflect the divine light from above into the hearts of these common people. The stature of his new church would be more in keeping with Father Edward's view of the Catholic Church itself, and his own rightful place within it.

Before he could build a new church though, the old one would, of course, have to be torn down. A task that anywhere else could have been accomplished with a team of horses, a throng of men swinging axes, and a bonfire. Here in Isadore however, that task would not turn out to be quite so straightforward. Father Edward was soon to learn that before he could point his flock toward the future, they would have no choice but to face Holy Rosary's past. He was right about one thing, however. These were indeed the waning months of his anonymity.

Just two days after his position in Isadore was made official, Father Edward received this mysterious warning: "I'm afraid there will be a scandal in this parish. I heard a Sister who disappeared here some time ago was buried under the church."

This disturbing omen came from none other than Father Leo. It seemed that even now, when Father Edward was finally given his own church to lead, he was still expected to take direction from his former superior. Just the idea was insulting and while Father Edward may have listened politely to Father Leo's parting words, he put little stock in the admonition. Isadore had potential and so did he. Together, the young priest and the old village would attain their full spiritual reward.

Inscriptions in the Roman catacombs dating from the first century bear witness to the ancient Catholic ritual of reciting prayers for the dead. According to church law, these prayers were to be voiced aloud not for the blessed, nor for the damned, but only for those souls trapped in between. Prayers for the dead were to be offered not to ease the grief of the living, but to hasten the time a soul spent in purgatorial purification.

Lord Jesus Christ, these prayers read, *deliver the souls of all the faithful departed from the pains of hell, and the deep abyss.*

The Felician Sisters who lived at the Detroit Motherhouse in the early 1900s were responsible for praying for so many such souls that they needed a special book to keep track of them all. In a separate section inside this book, the religious lives of all of the Sisters of their order were documented. The date they entered the convent, the date they were made a novice, the date they took their final vows, and the day they died were all duly noted inside its pages.

Sister Mary Albina held the office of Recorder Secretary, and it was the black inked script in her hand that added Sister Janina's name to the list of souls receiving these sacred prayers for the dead. The missing nun's entry read:

"Sister Mary Janina—Josephine Mesick. Father's name is John, mother's name is Josephine; is from Chicago, Illinois; born January 24th, 1874; was made a postulant, September 20th, 1888. Received small black veil, October 4th, 1888; received the habit September 12th, 1892. Final or perpetual vows August 25th, 1901. Lost the 23rd of August, 1907, from the Mission House at Isadore."

"Lost" was a spiritual state of being as well as a physical one. Though as far as they knew there had been no direct evidence that Sister Janina departed the earth having committed a mortal sin, there had been rumors. Rumors that she was tired of religious life and snuck away from the convent, only to perish in the swamp. Rumors that she had rendezvoused with a forbidden lover. Rumors that she had been having a love affair with Father Andrew and was pregnant when she disappeared. Even rumors that Janina had died from a botched abortion.

These stories, still without any evidence to support them, came with enough credence, and were repeated so boldly, that the local newspaper reported them to its readers. "[A] story circulated was that Sister Mary [Janina], in trouble because of intimacy with the priest in charge of the diocese, had been spirited away from the vicinity to cover her alleged shame."

The Detroit Sisters did not actively believe any of these terrible things, but they could not say unequivocally that they were false, either. A fellow nun's mortal soul was not to be trifled with. The Sisters' Catholic teachings told them that a person could live the entirety of their life in obedience to God and adherence to His commandments, but sin just before death and be forever trapped in purgatory. These unfortunates would be "seized upon by the flames of the purgatorial fire, to be severely chastised, and cleansed until the Day of Judgment, from the filth of their vices."

Unless, of course, their souls were set free by virtue of God's mercy, which perhaps could be inspired by their own prayers for the dead. And, they knew, the prayers of the righteous were many times more powerful than the prayers of unrepentant sinners. If Sister Janina's soul was trapped in the searing furnace of her sins, the women of the Felician Order of Detroit were duty-bound to do what they could to release it to heaven. And so they took the only action they could. They prayed.

The final one-word entry in Sister Janina's record, "Lost," was made in their book of records sometime during Father Leo's brief tenure in Isadore. By the time Father Edward arrived to replace him, the possibility that Sister Janina's soul was burning in the flames of purgatory had already been dealt with by her fellow nuns.

Through some mysterious circumstance, the women who walked the halls of the Detroit convent, the cloistered women who spent their lives in prayer, hundreds of miles to the south and shuttered away from the outside world, perhaps knew more of Holy Rosary's secrets than the farmers, and housewives, and the holy men of Isadore did.

Father Edward went about his new duties at Holy Rosary as if he had not heard a single word of Father Leo's warning. The reasons for this were probably twofold: one, he was secretly thrilled to be in a leadership position for the very first time, and two, his own nature was to passively observe situations that made him uncomfortable, instead of confronting them—a trait that was to surface again and again in the coming months.

Father Edward had obediently listened to Father Leo for years, and to any number of seminary priests before that, and would do so no longer, despite the dire substance of his predecessor's warning. Isadore was his now, he would make his own decisions here, and a scandal simply did not figure anywhere in his ambitious plans. Father Edward began this new role as head priest by the most practical of actions: setting up housekeeping.

Even an inconsequential Catholic mission like his had substantial domestic needs. The buildings required regular maintenance, the garden and the farm animals needed daily attention, and laundry was an endless task, as the northern Michigan geography did not treat holy garb at all kindly. Between the teaching Sisters, the laborers, any visitors, and Father Edward himself, there were also at least six appetites to satisfy during the summer and on weekends. When school opened in the fall, all of these tasks would multiply overnight like mushrooms in a damp forest. Father Edward and the new Sisters could not possibly accomplish all this on their own; the parish needed laborers.

A few stragglers from Father Andrew's household had stayed behind in 1913 when he left for Manistee and had continued to work at the church when Father Leo was installed, but by the time Father Edward arrived by train in late May 1917, none of the original Sisters, and not one member of the lay staff, remained.

The grim but capable Stella had moved across the big lake with her daughter, Mary. Mary had come of age and married a local farmer's son named Joseph Flees. Father Andrew had pronounced them man and wife on October 18, 1910, the newlyweds had taken a steamer ship across Lake Michigan, and, with Stella, they joined the large Polish community in Milwaukee, Wisconsin. Later, they moved away from the city to the rural town of Friendship.

Father Andrew was now fully installed in Father Leo's old church, St. Joseph's in Manistee. He had taken his sister, Susan, with him, but her health had deteriorated. His household did not have the same orderly competence that it boasted in Isadore under Stella's tenure, and he missed it. In 1916 he had written to Stella and asked her to leave Milwaukee and return to his service, to help him run the parish in Manistee and care for his ailing sister. Stella obliged him, and the pair now functioned at this posting much the same way they had in Isadore.

The two nuns who had been the teachers at Holy Rosary School under the leadership of Sister Janina had also taken their leave. Sister Angelina and Sister Josephine had each moved on to serve in other convents far across the Atlantic, in eastern Europe. The Detroit Motherhouse had replaced them with newcomers.

And Theodore Gruba, the teenage chore boy who had lived in the school basement and accompanied Father Andrew and his sister on the fateful day of the fishing trip years ago, was rumored to have moved to the Upper Peninsula of Michigan or to Canada. Gruba left Isadore a few years after Sister Janina disappeared, and despite subsequent efforts by Father Andrew and others to find him, he had not been heard from since.

Each of these vacant positions at Holy Rosary Father Edward filled with his own choices, but none of them took on more significance than the role of his housekeeper. The new priest's style of running the parish and managing his own domestic affairs could not have been more different than Father Andrew's.

While Father Andrew was stern and chose favorites among his parishioners, Father Edward was a unifier, kind and welcoming, if also a little shy or perhaps just socially awkward. While Father Andrew was harsh and sometimes even violent with the schoolchildren, especially the boys, Father Edward was encouraging and helpful. Discipline had been meted out by Father Andrew regularly throughout the day, every day, with coarse language and even rougher fists; Father Edward was too busy with his own thoughts to notice a wayward schoolboy or a raised eyebrow from one of his parishioners.

Even the two men's physiques were opposites. Father Andrew was tall and muscular, his rafter-beam shoulders and imposing form being once described by a newspaper reporter as "magnificent." Father Edward was short and slight, fine-boned and almost pretty, an intellectual and an amateur philosopher, cut through with a streak of the romantic dreamer. Except in size, the cassock they both wore was identical on the outside, but on the inside signified absolute authority to one man, and devotion, sacrifice, and even love to the other.

Despite their obvious differences, it's possible, perhaps even probable, that both Father Andrew and Father Edward were inspired to join the priesthood by the same saint. The words of St. Bonaventure spurred

many young men of the day toward their ultimate path to the monastery. According to the Franciscan archives and the *Catholic Encyclopedia,*
no religious writer from the Middle Ages was more widely read or
copied. More specifically, it was St. Bonaventure's "Man of Prayer" sermon that inspired generations of boys and young men all over Europe to
become Franciscan priests.

Where Father Andrew and Father Edward were concerned, however, it was as if each man had focused their vocation on a separate line
of the Saint's stirring call to service. His stern and ridged nature assures
that Father Andrew would have responded to these words from the famous sermon: "If you would gain power and strength to overcome the
temptations of the enemy, be a man of prayer." And Father Edward to
these: "If you would sustain your soul with the richness of devotion,
and keep it ever full of good thoughts and desires, be a man of prayer."

These differences between the two men showed themselves quickly
in Father Edward's new household. While Father Andrew favored the
rigorous and middle-aged Stella to manage the parish's domestic affairs,
Father Edward was willing to sacrifice experience and culinary skill to
add someone friendly, young, and pleasant to look upon to his household. That person turned out to be Martha Miller.

Martha's father Joseph was a farmer and one of the area's early settlers. Joseph Miller was also one of the few in the parish to come from a
line that sought acculturation partly by changing their surname. The
lengthy and consonant-rich Polish names most of Isadore's residents
bore with pride were foreign to American eyes and tongues, and some
immigrants grew so tired of mispronunciations, misspellings, and prejudice that they changed their last names to make them more palatable to
the tongues of their new countrymen. Some Milczewskis, Przy-
siewkowskis, and Mikowskis in Michigan Polish communities became
simply "Miller."

While the name sounded more American, and was certainly easier
for many to spell and pronounce, the families behind it retained their
Polish traditions. Where their daughters were concerned, these Old
World traditions, very much alive in Isadore, dictated that upon reach-
ing maturity, the girls had only two real choices: marriage or the convent.

Martha Miller was seventeen years old and a few weeks shy of her high school graduation in May 1917 when the new priest was installed. Still living with her parents, Joseph and Franciska, Martha faced the end of her childhood with neither a waiting marriage proposal in plain view nor an inclination toward the convent.

Without a serious suitor, a job, or a calling, Martha's prospects in Isadore after high school would have been narrow. The unmarried daughters of Polish immigrants who lived in the urban areas in the south found employment in cigar factories, bakeries, laundries, and hotels. They worked as domestics for wealthy families or trained as governesses. Those options were not available to rural families like Martha's. She could continue to live with her parents and work on the farm, she could have her relatives actively seek a husband on her behalf from within their small community or perhaps back in Poland, or she could reconsider the convent.

With Martha's three sisters and one younger brother to raise, Joseph Miller and his wife, Franciska, must have felt something close to relief when their daughter was offered the paid position of housekeeper by Father Edward. Their firstborn was certainly blessed by God to have been presented with such a timely and chaste opportunity. With several women of the congregation to choose from—widows, mothers whose children were grown, maiden aunts—their daughter had been selected from among all of them. Though the *Rule* did not govern her life, she could have benefited from one of its admonitions: "Believe secular men little, religious still less. Desire not too much their acquaintance."

As for his motives in hiring the attractive and naive local girl, Father Edward would have been wise to heed yet another line from St. Bonaventure's memorable sermon: "If you would mortify your will with all its affections and lusts, be a man of prayer."

Autumn arrived and with it the acrid scent of burning leaves, the security of farmers' corncribs stuffed to overflowing, and their root cellars packed with potatoes. There was ripe squash in the garden, their stems as hard as shovel handles, and a riot of color in the forest. Father Edward passed his first autumn in Isadore unscathed by local gossip, even though the scarlet of the sugar maples matched the color of his own heart.

Almost from the first week he moved to Isadore, the priest had been unable to keep his vow of celibacy; he was falling in love with his young housekeeper and she with him. Something would have to be done, and yet the passive kink in his nature dominated all of his other inclinations, no matter how well-advised, and he did nothing.

Father Edward couldn't bear to leave the priesthood, especially now when his career was just gaining a foothold, and he couldn't keep his vows, either. As far as Father Edward knew, his sins with his house-keeper weren't known by anyone but the two of them. It could end now, and perhaps no one would be the wiser. He could have ended it anytime and escaped what was to come, but he didn't.

Locals called October the "month of the mad moon," and as proof of its inherent strangeness reported seeing animals engaged in bizarre and self-destructive acts. Songbirds beat themselves to death with their own wings. Usually shy game birds purposely flew into windows, breaking their own necks. Small mammals threw themselves under slow moving wagon wheels. Children were restless and ill behaved, the taverns were full, and even usually friendly people were sometimes bad tempered.

"Students of bird life and nature know this as the month of the mad moon," the newspaper reported on the front page, after a local woman found a dead partridge in her bedroom. The bird had gone berserk, she said, beating itself against her window, breaking the pane with such force that pieces of glass landed in the center of the bedroom. The bird's feathers had all been ripped from its body in the struggle.

If they knew of his habits, the people of Isadore could have said Fa-ther Edward, too, was in the grip of the mad moon. Even if he had been accused of such a charge, priests did not believe in this kind of folklore or superstition. Such ideas were just holdovers from the past, when people were uncivilized heathens and had not had the benefit of a Catholic education. The thought that the moon could cause strange be-havior in living creatures went against the idea of an all-powerful God and was, instead, evidence of dark arts afoot.

Church matters turned the priest's attention away from his own troubles with Martha, and as the frost buckled the farmers' fields and the wagon tracks in the roads froze into solid and unending ruts, Father Edward felt the chill of his church's bloody secret for the second time.

～

"There is a rumor in the convent, Father."

The voice belonged to one of Holy Rosary School's new teachers, Sister Leoncia. She had sought Father Edward out and had asked to speak with him about a private and pressing matter.

It was unusual for a nun to speak with a priest about innuendo or impropriety in the convent; they usually kept their conversations to mundane church matters and upcoming school schedules. The Sisters prayed for their priest, and he, in turn, prayed for them. He took their confessions and oversaw their lesson plans, but gossip was not normally part of their exchanges. Even with Father Edward's submissive nature, it would have taken a lot for a Sister to approach her priest about a rumor circulating among the women of the convent.

Priests of the day, on the whole, already thought nuns had a proclivity to spend too much time chatting and not enough time praying. In comparison to many secular women of the day, nuns had a career in the church and could even aspire to high office and accomplishment if it was within the confines of belief and a life of prayer. Still, they occupied a lower rung than men and were careful about what they revealed about their convent life to their priest.

As far as many nuns were concerned, there was no sense in giving the priests anything that could be construed as proof that they were less serious about their work than men. Even their *Rule* addressed this issue: "People say of Sisters that almost every one hath an old woman to feed her ears; a prating gossip who tells her all the tales of the land; a magpie that chatters to her of every thing that she sees or hears; so that it is a common saying, 'From miln and from market, from smithy and from nunnery, men bring tidings.' This is a sad tale, that a nunnery, which should be the most solitary place of all, should be evened to those very three places in which there is the most idle discourse."

Personal stories were rarely shared with the priest; it would only prove them right about the talk between the Sisters. Unless it was absolutely necessary, detailing a rumor would certainly fall into that category. But in the autumn of 1917, Sister Leoncia had determined that it was indeed absolutely necessary.

"A rumor?" he inquired.

"Yes, Father. The Sisters have been talking about Sister Mary Janina. The one who disappeared. We heard she was buried under the church."

This was the second time Father Edward heard this same implausible revelation, and the topic irritated him. He asked Sister Leoncia to name the rumor's source. She did, and it was surprisingly reliable: Mother Mary Antonia, the Mother Superior of the Felician Order in Detroit. The Order where the missing nun had taken her vows and the Order that was still responsible for staffing the Holy Rosary School with teachers.

"What are the details of this?" Father Edward inquired further.

"They are saying that Mother Superior came to Isadore last year for a visit. This was before you came here, and she came with another Sister. They are saying that Mother Superior and this other Sister searched in the basement of the church."

"Well then," Father Edward asked, "what did they find?"

"Nothing," Sister Leoncia said. "The search was unsuccessful. They didn't find anything except an old pile of boards. But the rumor still won't go away."

Using the church's telephone, it would have been possible for Father Edward to trace this rumor right then. It would also have been possible, even with what little authority a young and inexperienced country priest such as he possessed, to ascertain whether the rumor was true or false. Surely that is what Sister Leoncia was hoping he would do; otherwise she wouldn't have risked any further ridicule of her gender by bringing the matter to him.

If he had pursued the Sister's story further, Father Edward would have found that the reliability of its source only grew in stature the closer he came to its conception. Mother Mary Antonia had heard it from Mother Mary Veronica, the aging and powerful Mother Superior at the Felician convent in Milwaukee. And Mother Veronica had heard it from none other than the new Wisconsin Bishop himself, Father Edward Kozlowski. Investigating even further back, he would have found that the rumor's genesis added yet another layer of scandal to an already disgraceful circumstance. The Bishop had heard the story from one of the priests in his diocese, who had heard it in the confessional, directly from the killer's own lips.

But while Father Edward was a man of intense thought, he was not a man of decisive action, and again he fell into his characteristic inertia. He told Sister Leoncia that he did not believe such a fantastical tale; that he thought it was, as she had feared, only convent gossip.

The dominant trait that had steered Father Edward's actions since he'd arrived in Isadore continued to prevail, even though it had not served him well. He could have ignored the charms of Martha Miller, but he didn't. He could have ended his forbidden relationship with her before it was too late, but he didn't. And he could have used his holy station to finally find out what had happened to Isadore's missing nun, but he didn't do that, either. "It has been sufficiently shown how the good man is never safe from all temptations," states the *Rule*. "As soon as he hath overcome one, he immediately meets with another." Father Edward was a good man and a good priest, but he had his weaknesses.

Autumn turned into winter. The "mad moon days" of October were long forgotten, and without their red leaves the maple trees changed into tall skeletons, their long limbs glazed with ice. Snow blanketed the corncribs, and the squash from the garden had been picked and stored alongside the potatoes in the rectory's root cellar. With the shortened hours of daylight, the chickens stopped giving eggs, and visits from neighbors were fewer. For reasons unspoken, Sister Leoncia left Isadore and went to teach at another Catholic school, miles away in Parisville, another Polish community in Michigan's Thumb Area.

The pressing cold and the spiritually reflective season of Advent turned Holy Rosary's focus inward, and the fate of Sister Mary Janina hibernated until spring.

In May, Isadore's black secret awoke in an unexpected location. At the same time the rumor of bones buried under the church was spreading throughout the state from convent to monastery, the Detroit Diocese was preparing an unrelated ritual to appease what it saw as the general anger of God. A Forty Hours' Devotion, a sacred tradition begun in the fourteenth century to pay homage to the forty hours that Jesus' body lay in the tomb, would be held that very spring in churches around the state.

Altars would be prepared, the cloaked men would gather, and their litanies would be recited aloud and unceasingly for each minute of the nearly two day devotion. Night and day, from the Mass of Exposition until the Mass of Deposition, the holy men would pray in unison for forty unbroken hours. Bound together like a climbing rope to heaven, each man's voice would be like a knot giving their prayers solid footing, their words moving closer and closer to God. The atonement of parishioners from every corner of Michigan would certainly be heard.

Father Edward was determined that his voice would join the others, and he made plans to travel to the magnificent St. Adalbert's Church in Grand Rapids where one of these rituals would be held. He would add his prayers to those of his brethren, and when the Devotional was completed, perhaps he would even have the opportunity to fill the other priests in on his plans for a new church.

Amid his secret personal battles, Father Edward had not abandoned this ambition, and he was looking forward to the auspicious opportunity to pray for its success this coming weekend with his brother priests. He had already paid an architect to draw up plans for the new building and had even placed an order for the bricks. The new church was going to be magnificent compared to the little white wooden building that was there now, and he was looking forward to sharing the design with the other priests. Cerebral and quiet, Father Edward was determined to accomplish what his predecessors, the physically powerful Father Andrew and the gregarious Father Leo, had been unable to. He would be the holy man to further God's plan in Isadore and finally put the forgotten little outpost on the Catholic map.

Despite his feelings of anticipation, bragging rights were not bestowed upon Father Edward when he arrived in Grand Rapids. At St. Adalbert's, the only priest who paid him any heed at all was more interested in what was buried in the basement of his current church than his ornate plans for a new one. Father Edward had traveled more than one hundred and fifty miles to the site of the devotional, but the rumor that had retired over the winter, the rumor that he had thought was only convent gossip had kept pace with him, mile for mile. He had been naive to think that bricks and mortar would be more interesting, even to his fellow holy men, than bones and scandal.

At his destination Father Edward had been a guest of the famed Father Casimir Skory, who presided over St. Adalbert's. Father Skory invited several of the visiting priests to enjoy their stay in Grand Rapids in his own rectory. There was plenty of space; everything about St. Adalbert's, dedicated only a few years earlier in 1913, gave the impression of grandeur. Built at a reported cost of a staggering $130,000, one thousand electric lights glowed in the sanctuary, gleaming off the red oak pews. The rectory was red brick trimmed in white brick and occupied an entire city block. Father Edward was one of Father Skory's guests, and so was a priest from Detroit that Father Edward struck up a conversation with. His name was Father Joseph Lempke, and he ministered to the Felician Motherhouse.

The men had been praying in shifts, and when they were not in the sanctuary, they were relaxing by the fire in the fireplace, enjoying each other's company, and catching up on news from the other churches around the state. It was in this intimate setting that Father Lempke made a point of introducing himself to Father Edward and told the younger man that he knew all about Isadore's history as he was the priest of the Felician Motherhouse, where Holy Rosary's teaching nuns had been trained.

For the first time Father Edward understood that neither years nor distance would put the missing nun to rest. It was as if he had to leave Isadore entirely in order to finally see the situation there clearly. Such a conclusion would have been his only option after one particularly memorable conversation.

"I intend to build a new church at Isadore," Father Edward proudly told a priest from Detroit.

"Have you selected a building site?" Father Lempke asked, innocently enough.

"Oh yes," Father Edward told the other priest eagerly. "It will be built on the same site as the present church. As soon as that one's torn down, my new church will be built in its place."

If Father Edward had been expecting to impress Father Lempke with this news, he was now gravely disappointed. The reaction of this city priest to his news from the north country was far from what he must have hoped.

Father Lempke leaned in close. "Well then," he whispered to the younger man, "what are you going to do with the bones?"

And so, there it was again. This rumor that had been only sleeping and would not die.

"What bones?" Father Edward asked.

"I heard from Bishop Kozlowski that Sister Mary Janina, who disappeared at Isadore some years ago, was buried under the church. I believe you'll find her body down there, under a pile of boards."

Father Edward was aghast. His vanity and passivity were now in direct conflict with each other. If he wanted a new church, he would have to take some action on this rumor detailing a gruesome answer to the mystery of the missing nun. Though he had played no part in her disappearance, nor in spreading the rumor of her demise, he was now being forced into ascertaining its truthfulness. His submissive nature won out, and instead of bragging to the older man about his ambitious plans, he asked Father Lempke for his counsel.

"You must remove the remains secretly," the senior priest advised, "*before* you tear down the church, or they will be discovered. It would be best to avoid all the trouble that would certainly cause. Do it yourself, so that no one else will know. Do it at night and rebury the bones in your cemetery there."

In the past months Father Edward had been so determined to believe that the rumor was false, just a fanciful story germinated in the fertile atmosphere of the convent, that he had not considered any other possibilities. A frightening thought must have occurred to him now. If the rumor was true, and Sister Janina had been buried in the dirt-floored basement of the church, someone had done the digging.

"Do you know who is responsible for this?" he finally asked.

"The rumor that Father Bieniawski was implicated is untrue," Father Lempke said. "I am not positive of this, but the information I received stated that she was buried there by his housekeeper. By Mrs. Lipczynska."

Sister Janina had been murdered, the older priest said, killed by a blow to the head from Stella's garden spade.

Father Edward returned to Isadore the next day and, against all reason, heeded none of Father Lempke's advice. He ignored the man's words as completely as he had ignored those of Father Leo on the same topic many months prior, and then Sister Leoncia's. Spring turned into summer and the priest still did nothing. The local farmers' children enrolled at the parish school, a fresh crop of Felician Sisters moved into the convent to prepare to begin teaching them in a few weeks, and building plans were moving ahead for the new church.

Productive activity dominated the church grounds, just as Father Edward had envisioned all those months ago when he had looked upon his parish for the very first time. Despite the increasingly reliable sources of information, he refused to entertain the idea that something sinister lay literally underneath all this good work.

Masses were full. His congregation was happy. He had more volunteers for church projects; most of them, he had to admit, were admiring women from his flock, but they devoted time to the church just the same. And his heart, though edged with guilt, was brimming with an unexpected love for Martha.

When Sister Janina first went missing more than a decade before, some four hundred people had turned out to look for her. When the local newspaper dispatched reporters to cover the searches, thousands of readers followed the mystery of the missing nun, hoping for an answer to the question of what had become of her. When the search proved fruitless, newspapers around the state, and even throughout the Midwest and as far east as New York City, told of her unusual absence to hundreds of thousands more. Her brothers and her fellow Felician sisters continued to wonder at her fate, as did the law. Now, one man had it within his reach to finally give them all an answer, and he did nothing.

Despite his deepening feelings for Martha, Father Edward was increasingly preoccupied with his own troubles. Troubles that had occurred in the here and now, and not a distant decade ago. Troubles that affected the living, and not just the dead. Troubles so severe, they could determine the fate of his soul and its eternal salvation. Or damnation.

Martha Miller, his teenage housekeeper, was pregnant, and he was the father of her unborn baby. She was only a few months along, so he could have taken some comfort in the fact that no one knew their secret. The girl was as determined as he to keep their relationship private. He still had a little time.

What he didn't have was the fortitude to deal with the certain repercussions both a murdered nun and a new baby would bring down upon him. Being an intellectual man all of his life had given Father Edward a weakness. He operated as if all problems could be solved by simply thinking about them. Action was for those without his intellect.

Years ago when the lawmen searched Isadore with a bloodhound, no one noticed how poor the beast's eyesight was. It was his nose everyone focused on. In that same way, Father Edward's inability to respond to conflict with action was, until now, easily hidden and perhaps even unimportant in a vocation where his thoughts and meditations were highly prized.

Where the problems of the two women now in his life were concerned, one missing and presumed dead and one very much alive, his characteristic passivity won out, and, for the last time, Father Edward dealt with neither. He would later confess that he felt strangled by these dilemmas. If each of these feminine creatures would only take their strangling hands from around his neck, all would be well. The idea that he could pry open the fingers of fate by doing something about his predicaments apparently never occurred to him.

By the end of the summer, Joseph and Franciska Miller knew they had a serious problem. Not only was their unmarried daughter pregnant, she refused to name the man who was the father of her unborn baby.

If she would only tell them who he was, her parents would convince him to marry Martha, or even demand it if that were required, and the whole lurid episode could be made right before it was too late. Joseph Miller might not have been a learned man, but he didn't have the same fatal personality flaw that Father Edward did. Joseph had no trouble taking action where action was required, and as soon as he found out who had stolen his daughter's innocence, he would have the couple married, one way or another.

The alternative was unthinkable. Joseph Miller shared a faith, a cultural heritage, lifetime friendships, and his farming vocation with his neighbors, but that would not matter one whit if they found out that his unmarried daughter was pregnant. Once the people of Isadore learned that Martha had allowed a man to have relations with her without the legitimacy of marriage, she would be ruined. The event would reflect poorly on his other children as well. Joseph and his wife tried pleading, they tried kindness, and they tried threats, but nothing would loosen their daughter's tongue.

She was still only a teenager, but Martha had been brought up in the Catholic Church, had been educated in both facts and faith by the nuns, and she knew full well that she had sinned. But it was even worse than that. She had committed a mortal sin; her faith told her that in frightening detail.

As a priest Father Edward was considered to be married to the church, and so by lying with him she had committed adultery. She committed it with full knowledge of its moral gravity, and she did so in a deliberate way, with complete consent. That meant, as far as the Roman Catholic Church was concerned, that she had committed a mortal sin, and unless she confessed fully, her soul was condemned to hell. Confessing fully meant admitting details about the context of each sin, why it was committed, and against or with whom, as well as the number of occurrences and any related factors that might affect her responsibility. Martha's link with God had been ruptured, and until she confessed these details to a priest, his saving grace was no longer available to her, the Church believed. She could, if the priest so deemed, even be excommunicated.

All of this Joseph related in a paternal way to his daughter, but she remained adamant. Martha told her parents that she had thrown herself at the feet of God and was regularly praying for His mercy. Whatever plans He had for her, she was prepared to endure alone.

Faced with their daughter's stubbornness and the certain harsh judgment of their neighbors, the Millers turned to the only refuge they had: their church.

As personal counselors, priests did not and could not make distinctions between giving members of their flock direction about spiritual matters and giving them direction about daily life. Despite his own flawed behavior, to men like Father Edward, there simply was no distinction. Life was to be lived in accordance with Catholic teachings regardless of a person's earthly circumstances. So powerful were priests in their immigrant Polish communities that many even became known as "priest-titans."

"Immediately upon his arrival in a Polish community, the burden of leadership fell upon him," wrote Henryk Sienkiewicz, one of the first ordained priests to visit Michigan from Poland. "They must be energetic and heroic men because the people consider their priest their advisor, teacher, and leader."

When it came to personal matters, these Polish priests did not give advice so much as make decrees.

While Father Edward was far from being considered a titan and was not known to be either energetic or heroic, he was the moral authority of Isadore, and so it was his advice that the Millers sought shortly after finding out that their daughter was pregnant. They met with him privately and asked him to decide what their next course of action should be. This was difficult for the Millers not only because their daughter was unmarried and they were ashamed, but also because of the long-held Polish traditional belief that it was bad luck to talk about a pregnancy, even when the child was wanted and expected.

"It was universally believed by Poles . . . that a pregnancy was concealed for as long as possible, and when the condition became obvious it was not remarked upon or discussed in any detail," writes folklorist Sophie Hodorowicz Knab. "Anyone who made too many inquiries was immediately suspect. The secrecy was necessary to protect both mother and infant against jealously, witchcraft, and the evil eye."

As Catholics and parents the Millers thought they were sharing their distress with their priest—they had no idea they were also sharing it with the unborn baby's father. For his part, Father Edward said nothing during the meeting to enlighten them further. Instead, he offered to broker an adoption of their daughter's baby. Perhaps when this whole sordid episode was over, Martha would be the wiser for it, would change her ways, pray for God's mercy, and live a good life here in Isadore. Perhaps when they saw how repentant she was, how well the family had handled such a delicate situation, their neighbors would forgive or even forget her sin, or at least not hold it against the rest of her family.

Father Edward had to be cringing inside as he gave them his counsel. Perhaps he had believed that sin could not find him in such a remote location, but he had been quite mistaken. Even the *Nun's Rule* warned of the spiritual dangers to the Church's holy pioneers. "Go, however, very cautiously: for in this wilderness there are many evil beasts. Let not anyone of remarkably pious life think that she may not be tempted."

The Millers accepted Father Edward's offer and thanked him for what they believed was his obvious wisdom and his divine kindness in not judging their family too harshly. A plan was made. In December, Father Edward would drive Martha to a charity hospital in Ann Arbor where she would stay until the baby was born. The child would be anonymously placed for adoption with a Catholic family, and when

Martha was well enough to travel, he would go back to Ann Arbor, re-
trieve her, and bring her back home to Isadore. If she liked, and her
parents approved, she could even continue working as his housekeeper. It would be, he assured the Millers, almost as if none of this had
ever happened.

The plans for the new church were proceeding nicely, and Father Edward had, through the growing respect of his station, been given what
could only be considered a divine respite from his difficulty with his
housekeeper. The solution freed him up to direct his energy into his
longtime dream.

Teams of volunteers had been organized for the demolition of the
old church and the construction of the new one. The brick manufacturer
had assured Father Edward that the company would be able to fill his
large order. The architect's plans for the church had been tinkered with
by Father Edward until, in his eyes, they were perfect. Ordering Zettler-
crafted stained glass windows from the famed Royal Bavarian Art Institute, the Vatican's very own glassmaker, was even being considered.

After the old church was demolished, construction would begin immediately. Each farmer of the parish would bring the largest and most
uniform stones from his fields to be mortared together and used as the
new church's foundation. The three stories of brick and the towering
steeple that would be seen from miles around would be built upon these
stones, making the weight of the new church, and that of the worshippers within, rest literally upon the toil and sweat of its parishioners.

It was almost fall now; the work was scheduled to begin in six
months or so, after the spring thaw. As the days became shorter and
cooler, it was in the evenings that Father Edward's thoughts turned finally to Sister Janina.

Once it was dark outside and his household quieted, he could not
seem to keep his mind within the walls of the rectory. It wanted only to
travel out the door and across the churchyard, visit the church basement, then think its way under the pile of boards Father Lempke had described, and scratch with imaginary fingers at what might be buried
there.

Backward, he calculated. The new church would be built in the
spring. First, the old church would be demolished. In the process, the

bones of the buried nun, if they were even there at all, would be discovered. Then, the scandal that he had been warned of would become a reality, with his good name forever attached to it like one of the greasy wood ticks that latched onto the barnyard's unsuspecting peacocks.

Father Edward's nightly figuring of this eventuality included different variables but always ended with the same final answer; if something wasn't done, and done soon, his new church would not be the magnificent example of faith and accomplishment he'd dreamed of, but rather an ugly house of shame, plucked clean of all virtue.

His natural tendency for deep thought and shallow action had to be overcome if he was to avoid disaster, and for once, he knew it.

On a November 1918 afternoon, Father Edward walked from the rectory across his churchyard to the three-quarter door that secured the church basement from the elements, stooped down, and entered the earthy dark. When his eyes had adjusted to the dimly lit space, he looked over the slanting ground for the pile of boards Father Lempke had told him about all those months ago. He saw nothing.

The priest then took a few hesitant steps away from the door, deeper into the dark, and scraped at the dirt with his foot. It was as impenetrable as dried peat moss, and looked undisturbed. He could see no evidence of a grave, or, for that matter, of any activity at all.

The wood foundational walls, though bleached thin with dry rot and age, muffled the birdsong and shut out any sense of a breeze blowing through the sunlit trees just outside. The door he'd come in seemed to recede past all understanding, like a reflection in some fun house mirror. He knew the door was almost a yard wide, he'd walked through it dozens of times but it looked much narrower. The longer he stared at it, the more it seemed to shrink even further under his gaze. Though it was overcoat weather outside, Father Edward could feel himself sweating under his cassock. "This task is too gruesome for me," he said out loud. The words were left hanging in the cloistered air, and the priest bolted outside and sucked in a deep breath.

Though Father Lempke had advised him months ago to take care of Isadore's dark secret alone, he found he simply could not heed this advice. He would have to share his burden with someone less squeamish than he, and then in God's name swear that person forever to secrecy. There was only one man he could think of who might be a match for this grisly errand.

This man was already in service to Holy Rosary. He was an Isadore native and a farmer, raised a Catholic from one of the four corners' founding families. He would not want to sully the ground his own forefathers had settled, of that Father Edward was fairly certain.

This man also had one mental advantage that the priest himself did not, sheltered as he had been first by the seminary and then by the priesthood. This man was a farmer and raised livestock for food. He did the slaughtering and the dressing himself. If Jacob Flees, the man Father Edward had just hired as the church's new sexton, could slit a hog's throat and slaughter chickens by the armload, perhaps he had the stomach to exhume the bones of a nun.

Straining against his proclivity to wait things out, Father Edward approached his sexton the very next morning. Jacob Flees was standing by the door to the basement, the same door Father Edward had made his hasty exit from just the day before. Jacob was looking for scrap wood to repair the rectory's ice shed. He had no warning of the chill his next chore for the church was about to send down his spine. Though he had done odd jobs for the priests of Holy Rosary many times before, he had been the church's official sexton for only three days when the priest slid up alongside him and unburdened himself.

"I received information from a certain party that a Sister disappeared here some years ago," Father Edward said to Jacob, speaking in a low voice. "This same party said that she had been buried under the church. Under a pile of boards."

A longtime member of Holy Rosary Church, Jacob was past sixty now, but he had been a young man of just twenty-six years when the first church building was erected by Isadore's founding settlers during the summer of 1882. He had worshipped faithfully inside Holy Rosary's plain sanctuary and sent his children to the Holy Rosary School to be instructed by the nuns.

Jacob had known Sister Janina, had liked her as well as he liked any nun, and had helped search for her in the woods when she first went missing more than ten years ago. His whole life was forever tied to this church, and he had certainly been privy to the chain of rumors about her whereabouts. His nature was stoical, and little excited the man, but he could hardly contain his surprise.

"That can't be!" he said. "Who would do it?"

"The priest who told me about it said a well-known woman did it. Mrs. Lipczynska."

"No!"

The men discussed the possibility further, and Father Edward said that if the bones were there, they had to be removed. Otherwise they might be discovered during the upcoming excavation for the new church and their scandalous location made public. Slowly, Jacob's response turned from shock to practicality.

"I know the exact pile of boards you're talking about, but they ain't in there no more," he told the priest. This Father Edward already knew from his own failed attempt to locate the grave.

"But the grave still may be in there somewhere," he told the sexton. "I'd like you to help me look for it. And whatever we find is to be kept secret, and nobody else is to ever know anything about it. It's a secret of the confessional, Jacob, a secret of the Church. Get your tools."

By late afternoon, Father Edward and Jacob were together just outside the basement door of the church. Jacob had brought with him two shovels, a potato fork, a wheelbarrow, a lantern, and a rectangular wooden grocery box he'd found discarded in the common room of the school. Father Edward had brought along only what tiny amount of inner resolve he had been able to summon.

The two men went into the darkness one after the other and began a course of halfhearted scratching with the shovels in random places in the hard-packed dirt. The basement was one long open space forty-five feet wide, ninety feet long, and just high enough at its tallest end for someone quite short to stand up. The low ceiling did nothing to make the space feel manageable. To Father Edward, it still seemed endless. An eerie, earthly purgatory.

There was so much area to cover, hundreds of shovelfuls, perhaps even thousands, that it was hard to know where to begin. After only a few minutes of this, Father Edward again made his exit without learning anything more about the truthfulness of the hideous rumor. Could it be false, as he'd suspected all along?

"Keep looking," he told Jacob. "Come and fetch me in the rectory if you find anything."

Jacob did exactly as he was instructed. With the priest out of earshot, he jabbed deeply at the ground with his shovel. When he struck nothing but dirt, he stepped a few feet away and jabbed down again. Nothing. He continued this for several tries and then focused on a more specific spot.

Straight back from the three-quarter door, five or six healthy strides of a man toward the north wall, was the place where the scrap lumber pile had been haphazardly stacked. Jacob stooped down—his eyes had adjusted to the dark—and in the light from the lantern he could see a slight incline and what could have been an area of disturbed soil. After several more tries in this spot with the shovel, he struck something hard eighteen inches down.

When the metal of his shovel struck the hard object he would recall later that it sounded like he'd hit a large stone. Jacob dug out some dirt, and then kneeled on the ground and reached down with his hands, expecting to unearth a chunk of granite or even a rare pudding stone. The soil was looser here, once he'd broken through the crust, and his fingers touched the thing. He felt immediately that it was long and thin and the same shape as his shovel handle, except with knobs on either end. No stone was shaped like this. He gripped the object tightly in his fist, pulled it out of the dirt, and held it up to the lantern. Bone.

"Father. I found a bone."

Jacob's voice, calling to him from his doorway so soon after he'd left the man in the basement, was the very last sound Father Edward wanted to hear. The sexton was not known to be much of a conversationalist but he had plenty to say now. He described his brief search, the feeling of the bone in his hands, and his certainty that more of its kin would be unearthed with even the slightest effort. The sexton's find was almost certainly proof that the rumor had been true. There would be no going back to the safety of ignorance from this point on. Not for either of them.

"I believe it's the Sister," Jacob told him.

The priest grabbed his own lantern and together the pair made the short, solemn walk from the rectory back into the church basement and stood over what they now thought to be Sister Janina's grave. Jacob had already placed the wooden grocery box next to the spot, and each man put their lanterns down and picked up a shovel. Father Edward made no attempt to escape from his duty now and, with the sexton, began digging. Under two feet of loose soil they found her.

Sticking up at a sharp angle was one of her thigh bones. And then the other. Below them, her ribs. Next to her ribs, hands and arms. Further below, the spine, and around the lower spine some miniature bones they hardly dared speak of.

"A whole torso," Father Edward whispered, when they'd uncovered it.

"She's all doubled up, like she was throwed in here on her back and just drew up her knees," Jacob said.

Jakie zycie taka smierc, the Polish proverb went: As you live, so shall you die. Death from illness or old age was mourned, but also accepted and understood. Sudden death could be the work of a powerful curse or punishment for secret sins. Murder was surely the result of the strongest dark forces, and without an open window or door, or any other opening here, ancient Polish belief stated that the Sister's spirit might be present. Perhaps the angels and Satan were still even fighting over it.

"Be very careful with her, please Jacob," the priest told him. Neither man mentioned the tiniest bones they found in a tight bunch next to her spine. The little skull no bigger than a new potato, the twigs of arms and legs. The whole of it would fit in the palm of a big man's hand, with room leftover.

Deeper, three feet below ground or more, Jacob unearthed Janina's much larger dirt-covered skull, cradled it in his hands, then held it up out of the hole and handed it to the priest. Father Edward took the skull and put it in the wooden box with the rest of what they'd recovered. Looking down at its resting place, even in the weak glow from the lantern, he could see that the dirt around where it had lain was several shades darker and had a different texture than anywhere else.

For two hours they dug, filling the small box. Jacob used the potato fork to lift out some of the bones, trying to make sure he didn't leave any behind. A few feet away from where they'd exhumed her skull, the men found both of her tiny leather shoes, with foot bones still rattling around inside. Rotting pieces of dark-colored wool disintegrated in their hands. Intact was a five-foot length of the braided black waistcord with a knot in it that the Sisters wore as a belt. This, too, they put in the box.

When their probing yielded nothing more, the men climbed out of the grave, stood up as straight as they could under the low ceiling, and looked down at what they'd unearthed.

"She needs a proper box," Father Edward said.

"Yes, she does, Father," the sexton agreed.

"Leave her here for now then, but build her one. Soon as you can."

"Should she be buried in the cemetery then?" Jacob asked the priest.

"Yes. Under the big cross. Come and tell me when it's done. And then I don't want to ever hear another word about it. Not ever."

Jacob put the cover on the box and tamped it down. The men extinguished their lanterns and went back out into the daylight, leaving the nun behind for what was not yet to be the last time.

That evening, the Felician Order at the Motherhouse in Detroit prayed, just as they did every evening, for Sister Janina's eternal soul to be released from the flames of the purgatorial fire. But she was not in heaven and she was not in hell, she was in a too-small wooden box, dusted with the dry dirt of Isadore, waiting.

The next afternoon, the common room downstairs inside Holy Rosary School was filled with the smell of freshly cut pine boards. Jacob had just finished making the new wooden box Father Edward had requested. It was two feet long, a foot wide, and at least that deep, with a tightly fitting cover to keep the neighborhood's stray dogs and barn cats from molesting its intended contents.

It was traditional for a Polish village's carpenter to make coffins only when they were needed, and never ahead of time, for fear of tempting death. If there were a bunch of coffins waiting, the thought went, surely evil spirits would soon make sure they were filled. Tradition also deemed that pay was not to be levied or accepted for this task; it was considered the *ostatnia przysluga*, or the last favor bequeathed to the deceased. Though he was a farmer first, Jacob had good carpentry skills and would be the one to do this last favor for Sister Janina.

The sexton carried the box to the church basement, set it down beside the smaller grocery box, knelt, and set to his foreboding task bare-handed. When he was finished, and the grocery box was empty and the new box was filled, he stood up and put on the cover. Before he left, he filled in the large hole that he and Father Edward had dug the night before, gathered his tools and the now-empty grocery box, and went back out into the daylight.

Whether because there were other people about the churchyard that day, or because his soul needed a rest from what he and the priest had discovered buried in sacred ground beneath the church, or for some other unfathomable reason, Jacob left the box he'd made and its contents in the church basement for two more days. Enough time for Father Edward to share their secret with two more people, Sister Superior Hillaria and Sister Gastone, Felician teachers at the school.

The mystery that had hung over Isadore for ten years like a gauzy shroud was beginning to lose its transparency and take on a distinct shape of its own. From the confessor, to the Bishop and his confidants, to Holy Rosary's household, fully ten people scattered in two states now had some knowledge of Sister Janina's terrible end. These were Bishop Kozlowski, Father Novak, who was the Wisconsin priest who had reportedly taken the housekeeper's confession, Mother Mary Antonia, Sister Veronica, Father Lempke, Sisters Hillaria and Gastone, the sexton, Father Edward and, of course, the killer. A group large enough for small utterances to break through their promised silence.

Holy Rosary's Sister Gastone said that she found Father Edward's tale unbelievable and wanted to see the evidence for herself. He gave her permission to do so, told her the basement door was unlocked, but said he would not accompany her. He had been back to the basement once that day already, satisfying himself that the grave was filled and the new box Jacob made was sufficient, and so he told the nun with some certainty that he would not be going inside the place again.

Sister Superior Hillaria had no desire to see such a hideous thing, and so on her own Sister Gastone went into the basement, lifted the lid on Sister Janina's makeshift coffin, and looked inside. After a moment she took a piece of the rotted cloth surrounding the bones in her hands and carried it with her out into the daylight. She compared the fragile piece of cloth in her hand with the skirt of her own wool habit. Time and unknown other insults had ravaged it, but still, they matched.

"I was particular in comparing them, that it was the same material," she would say later. "I found that it was."

On the fourth day after first unearthing Sister Janina's remains, Jacob waited until dark and then dug a new grave in front of the large crucifix in the center of *Cmentarz Kalwawyi*, Holy Rosary's Cemetery.

He lowered the box he'd made down into the grave, then removed the cover at the last minute and filled the hole with dirt from a nearby flowerbed. The cover, he worried, would eventually rot, cave in with age, and cause a suspicious dent in the ground if he'd left it on, and so the nun was again exposed to the raw earth. This time, though, a marble Jesus preserved in His holy agony on the cross was looking down upon her from the ten-foot crucifix that decorated the cemetery and now marked her new and anonymous resting place.

That night, Jacob went to bed anxious over what he and Father Edward had done, but full of resolve. He would keep the church's business private, even from his wife, Mary, who was sleeping soundly right next to him.

It was autumn now, the season of remembering the dead. Only three days ago he'd sat in church with the rest of Isadore while candles were lit to observe *Zaduszki*, All Souls' Day. Some in the parish believed that the dead came back to visit the earth on this holiday, and they even set extra places at the table in their ancestors' memory, heaped the plates with food, and recited special prayers. *Holy sainted ancestors, we beg you, come fly to us. Eat and drink what we offer. Sainted ancestors, come fly to us.*

While soul bread was baked to a golden brown in the church kitchens, Jacob did not say whether he believed that the ghosts of his own ancestors were active, but he couldn't deny that Sister Janina had chosen a spiritually appropriate time to communicate from beyond the grave. Despite the reverence of All Souls' Day, Jacob did not share her presence or her reburial with anyone.

Before spring broke, Mrs. Mary Flees and the whole country would know what he'd done, but not because he let the secret out.

"I did this all in the dark of night, so nobody could see me, and I never on my part told anybody."

Martha Miller had been showing her condition for some months and was nearing her time of confinement. The snow and ice of winter arrived, along with the season of Advent and its admonitions against the expressions of levity in all the good Polish households of Isadore.

Serving meat at dinner, hosting parties, or planning celebrations was forbidden. Catholic priests were not allowed to perform weddings now, and if a baptism was required it was accomplished quickly and without the usual fanfare. Not even the sound of people singing Christmas carols would be heard until Christmas Eve. Evergreen trees could not be decorated until that day, either. Fish, preferably carp or pike in gray sauce, was the proper entrée to be served for Christmas Eve.

"Advent is a time of fasting, prayer, reflection, mourning, and reconciliation," Catholic Church documents of the period state. The merriment that Protestants and unbelievers observed was an insult to God.

It was during this introspective season in 1918 that Father Edward drove a pregnant and teenage Martha Miller to St. Joseph's Sisters of Mercy Hospital in Ann Arbor and left her there. She had with her only a single small piece of luggage, her parents' good-byes, and Father Edward's promise to return for her, after their unfortunate situation was satisfactorily resolved.

For the next month and a half she would stay at the hospital among strangers, during what had to be the most frightening and confusing time in her young life. She would miss the Christmas Eve celebration, as well as the *turon,* or caroling, in observance of the Feast of the Three Kings.

She would miss the fortune-telling of New Year's Eve, when all her unmarried girlfriends would knock on the doors of neighboring chicken coops, hoping to hear the crowing of a rooster in response. If they did, it meant they'd be married within the year. She would miss the simple act of wishing her neighbors "*Bog cie stykaj,*" or "God's good graces touch you."

Before she returned to Isadore she would give birth and see her baby adopted away, ponder her own family's conflicted feelings about both her pregnancy and her continued silence over the circumstances that led to it, accept that she and Father Edward had no future together, and finally consider what meager prospects might await her back at home. She would contemplate her own soul, and its place in eternity. Quite a lot for a sheltered teenage girl to ponder and pray over.

"Dread greatly this doom;" says the *Rule.* "If he is tempted so that he sin mortally through thee in any way, with desire toward thee, or if he seek to satiate on some other the temptation of thee, which is awakened through thy conduct, be fully certain of thy doom."

Father Edward kept his promise, though, and returned for her on January 24, 1919, but when he did it's no wonder that it was a very different Martha Miller he encountered than the one he'd left behind six weeks earlier.

Together, the two of them made the journey back to Isadore, and something prophetic happened on that trip. Whether it was because he could sense how mature she'd become, or because he needed to confess the sin to someone, or because he felt guilty about her circumstances and wanted to share his own suffering as a form of comfort, or even because he loved her, Father Edward told Martha Miller about the bones he'd found buried under the church.

When he finished telling her the story, eleven people now knew the whereabouts of Sister Janina, but Martha was the first and only person not employed by or bound to the Church to be taken into Father Edward's confidence. The bonds of secrecy, stretched thinner and thinner, were about to break.

On February 2, Candlemas Day, the Feast of the Purification of the Blessed Mother, ended. The Polish called it *Oczyszczenie Matki Boskiej*. Holy Rosary's parishioners observed the holiday by carrying their own candles with them to Mass where they were lit with glowing shims kept burning by the acolytes. Father Edward blessed each one.

At the end of the service, a flickering procession exited the church in unison, then the individual flames were carried home by their owners, who were careful to protect them from the winter wind. Tradition held that if they stayed lit the priest's blessings would carry from the church into their households. If death, sickness, or grief visited their homes that winter, the candles would be lit again and prayed over.

Though he could not know it, this protective ritual was to be one of Father Edward's last acts as Holy Rosary's priest. A week later, on February 9, 1919, he would make his final entry in the church's archival book. A baptism. By February 25, his parishioners would be begging the diocese for "a Father who would take charge of this parish . . . to give a mission here as soon as possible." Never again would Father Edward say a public Mass.

For their part, the Miller household could also have no knowledge of how soon they would need to relight the candle their priest had just blessed. Before the month was out, Martha found that she could hold onto the secrets that pressed inside her no longer. One evening, she told her father all.

She named her lover and the father of her baby, now forever lost to her. She told of her feelings for Father Edward and those that he expressed to her. "He was good to me," she said, "and he loved me."

Martha told her father of the lonely days she spent in regret at the hospital in Ann Arbor. Of suffering through childbirth with only strangers for comfort. And finally, word for word, she told her father the scandalous confession Father Edward had made to her on the couple's trip back home to Isadore.

"He asked me if I knew where Sister Janina is," Martha said. "I replied that I heard that she is supposed to be dead. He told me that he exhumed her and Flees assisted him in this work."

Anyone who still wondered what happened to the missing nun, she said, had only to look at the base of the large cross in the church's own cemetery.

Within hours, her story went beyond the confines of Isadore and was reported by the area's daily newspaper. In February 1919 the *Traverse City Record-Eagle* ran this news of the startling developments in the case.

"It was along in December, 1918, when this girl was taken to Ann Arbor," the paper reported. "Upon her return her father, suspicioning something, compelled her to tell of her alleged intimacies with Father [Edward] Podlaszewski, and in the course of the recitation of these revolting details, she gave away the story of Sister Mary [Janina]. The people of the vicinity are aghast at the revelations."

The secret of the nun's murder had been stretched thin over two forbidden love affairs and two unholy burials, one Catholic confession, the ambition of a young priest, and a dozen years of cloistered church gossip traded among the most powerful clergy in the state. Finally, it took a disgraced and homesick teenage girl to snap it in two, and it was her father who made it official. Joseph Miller left his daughter's side to pay a visit to Leelanau County sheriff John Kinnucan.

Holy Rosary Church, Isadore, Michigan, after Sunday services in 1883.
(Courtesy Traverse Area Historical Society.)

Holy Rosary Church today.

Father Andrew studying for the priesthood in Warsaw, Poland, in 1891. He was seventeen years old. (Courtesy University of Notre Dame Archives.)

Stella Lipczynska, Father Andrew's housekeeper, who was arrested, tried, and convicted for the murder of Sister Janina. (Courtesy University of Notre Dame Archives.)

Cross monument in the center of Holy Rosary Cemetery. (Courtesy Traverse Area Historical Society.)

Stella Lipczynska's daughter, Mary Lipczynska, in an Isadore orchard with a book. Circa 1910. (Collection of Jack Sweeney.)

Left: Wedding day of Stella Lipczynska's daughter, Mary Lipczynska, to native of Isadore, Joseph Flees, October 18, 1910. The ceremony was performed by Father Andrew. (Collection of Jack Sweeney.)

Below: Father Andrew's sister Susan shows off a northern pike caught in Lake Leelanau. Her brother was often heard saying, "God does not subtract the time I spend fishing from my allotted time on earth." Circa 1907. (Collection of Jack Sweeney.)

Facing page, top: Holy Rosary parishioners and staff in front of the church rectory. Father Andrew is on the far right with his pet crow on his shoulder. His sister, Susan, is on his immediate right, and next to her is Mary Lipczynska. The other people are unidentified. Circa 1905. (Collection of Jack Sweeney.)

Facing page, bottom: Sexton Jacob Flees, Father Andrew (second from left), and two unidentified local men show off the spoils of a winter hunt. Circa 1910. (Collection of Jack Sweeney.)

Father Andrew's menagerie of bee hives, fowl, badgers, a fox, and an alligator was housed here, behind the rectory. In the coldest months, the alligator lived inside the rectory. Circa 1910. (Collection of Jack Sweeney.)

Typical convent cell of a Felician nun in the early 1900s. The cell pictured here belonged to Sophia Truszkowska, founder of the Felicians. (Courtesy University of Notre Dame Archives.)

Father Leo Oprychalski, who replaced Father Andrew and served as priest of Holy Rosary from 1913 to 1917. It was he who warned Father Edward, "I'm afraid there will be a scandal in this parish." (Courtesy University of Notre Dame Archives.)

Father Edward Podlaszewski in 1912, five years before he was assigned to Holy Rosary. It was Father Edward's ambitious plans to tear down the old wooden church and build a lavish brick one that precipitated the discovery of Sister Janina's remains. (Courtesy University of Notre Dame Archives.)

St. Bonaventure
Monastery in Detroit
where Father Edward
was sent to appear before
Catholic leaders in a
Church trial. (Courtesy
University of Notre Dame
Archives.)

Photo of Bishop Edward
Kozlowski reprinted from
his biography, published
to honor his twenty-five
years of service. It was
the Bishop who allegedly
gave permission for a
Milwaukee priest to give
Stella Lipczynska absolu-
tion after she confessed to
murdering Sister Janina.
(Courtesy University of
Notre Dame Archives.)

Mother Mary Antonia, Mother Superior of the Detroit Felician convent, who heard the rumor of the confession from Mother Mary Veronica and passed it on to Father Lempke, who passed it on to Father Edward. (Courtesy University of Notre Dame Archives.)

The only known photograph of Sister Mary Janina. (Courtesy University of Notre Dame Archives.)

Dr. George Fralick, Sister Janina's physician and Leelanau County coroner. (Courtesy Traverse Area Historical Society.)

St. Joseph's rectory in Manistee, Michigan, where Stella was arrested and Father Andrew was questioned. (Courtesy University of Notre Dame Archives.)

St. Joseph's Church in Manistee, Michigan. Father Andrew, Father Edward, and Father Leo all served here. This was where Father Andrew was posted when his housekeeper, Stella, was arrested for the murder of Sister Janina. (Courtesy University of Notre Dame Archives.)

Postcard featuring Stella Lipczynska, inside the Leelanau County Jail, Leland, MI, circa 1919. (Collection of Dave Tinder.)

Aerial view of Isadore, circa 1975. (Courtesy Traverse Area Historical Society.)

Still from a performance of the Broadway play *The Runner Stumbles,* by Milan Stitt. (Courtesy Traverse Area Historical Society.)

Scenes and Figures in Nun Mystery Case at Leland

Top, left—Leelanau county courthouse where Mrs. Stanislawa Lypczynski is being tried on a charge of murdering Sister Mary Janina, a nun, at St. Isadore's convent. Bottom, left—The jury in the case (left to right): John Westcott, Glen Arbor; Joseph Bussey, Leland; Benjamin Wilsey, Cleveland township; George Shalda, Cleveland township; John Young, Empire; William Challender, Sutton's Bay; C. H. Treat, Empire; Welby Ray, Glen Arbor; John Bright, Kasson; Herbert Lindley, Bingham; John Shorter, Kasson; George Eckardt, Cleveland township. At right—Mrs. Lypczynski and Fr. Andrew Bienowski, pastor of the Isadore church at the time of Sister Mary Janina's disappearance, and for whom Mrs. Lypczynski was housekeeper.

Grand Rapids Press coverage. (Courtesy Traverse Area Historical Society.)

The Sinners

Winter, 1919

> The heart is a full wild animal, and
> makes many wild leaps, as St. Gregory
> saith, nothing escapes from a man's
> control so soon as his heart. When
> a man so holy, so wise, and so wary
> suffered his heart to break loose,
> others may well be sorely anxious
> lest it should take flight.
>
> —*The Nun's Rule*

ON AN ICY MORNING IN LATE FEBRUARY 1919, Father Edward stood outside the train station and wept. Tears dripped down his cold cheeks, and he made no attempt to disguise his grief. He was ruined.

"Don't blame the girl," Father Edward told the small group of still-loyal parishioners, all women, who had assembled to see him off. "It's not her fault. I truly loved her. All the fault rests with me, on my shoulders."

Gone were his dreams of saying Mass inside his own majestic brick church. Gone was his first opportunity to lead a parish to salvation all on his own. Gone were the blueprints he'd labored over, the imported stained glass windows, the trust people here had bestowed upon him, and the naive idea that he could hide his carnal sins. Before the law could get to him, Father Edward was summoned to Detroit by his superiors.

While he said his good-byes, two very different factions of authority were preparing to sit in judgment of him: the lawmen of Leelanau

93

County would judge his deeds, and Michigan's leading priests would judge his soul. Neither group portended good things for Father Edward.

Leelanau County sheriff John Kinnucan, the former sheriff, Martin Brown, who was now a probate court judge, and Holy Rosary sexton Jacob Flees were in the church cemetery, exhuming the body of Sister Janina. Bishop's administrator Peter Paul LeFevbre was awaiting Father Edward in Detroit at St. Bonaventure Monastery, where the administrator and his advisers had already scheduled a hearing to decide the young priest's future. Or to decide, rather, if he was to have any religious future at all. If the Church had to offer up Father Edward as a public sacrifice to spare its reputation, it would do so. Cooperation with law enforcement, publicly at least, would be immediate.

"Every power of the Church will be brought to work on this case," said LeFevbre. "I deeply deplore the fact that the name of the Church has been brought in simply because of the alleged machinations of unworthy dignitaries."

This came as a relief to Sheriff Kinnucan.

"Without the help of the Church," he said, "our chances of figuring all of this out are hopeless."

Early that morning while Father Edward had been packing, the sheriff, the probate judge, and two Holy Rosary Church board members stood outside the door of the Flees farm. Sheriff Kinnucan knocked impatiently and called out Jacob's name. There were no niceties exchanged.

"Where did you bury the Sister?" the lawman demanded, when the sexton opened his door.

Jacob couldn't be sure when it would come, but he had expected this day. After a brief exchange, the sexton agreed first to give an affidavit detailing his activities, and then to accompany the four men to the cemetery and point out Sister Janina's grave. He put on his coat and glanced back at his wife, Mary, who was still groggy from sleep.

"The stone is off my head now," he told her, then turned to leave with the men.

"Better bring a shovel," the sheriff told him.

The men went first to the church basement and then to the cemetery. As requested, Jacob had come prepared with a shovel but also a hand sled. Someone else had brought along a shovel too, and two pickaxes. Jacob pointed to the spot in front of the large cross, and the men set to work. It was February 20, the ground was snow covered and frozen into a brittle crust, the frost line twenty inches down or more. They hacked at the earth with their tools, and two feet down they struck the edge of her small coffin.

Sheriff Kinnucan would later describe what they unearthed. "The box was not covered with a lid, metal or otherwise. We moved the earth from the box until we got down so we could feel the bones. We took that dirt off there as much as we could take off. The box was filled with dirt near up to the top, and we removed the dirt from the top of the box. We took it up with our hands. When we got down there we could feel the bones, and we discontinued taking off any more dirt."

They pried the box out of its cold rectangle and with a groan lifted it up out of the ground. When they'd set it down next to the open hole, each man looked first inside the small coffin, then at Jacob's face.

"That's the box I buried," he told them. "It's the same box. It's her."

Sister Janina's lidless coffin was light enough for just one man to fasten it onto the hand sled, and Jacob took this task upon himself. The group walked across the street to the neighboring Rosinski farm, Jacob pulling the sled through the snow and over the crusty drifts at the edge of the road, the sexton finally hefting his burden up onto the farmhouse's front porch. The sheriff went inside and made a phone call to one of Leelanau County's two coroners.

"We left the box on the porch and awaited his arrival," the sheriff would later say, under oath, in an open courtroom. A true statement, verified by witnesses, but nonetheless one that left much to the imagination. What did the men talk about, there in the dry cold, guarding the bones?

Waiting together outside on that porch were church board member Jake Rosinski Jr. who was a descendant of original Isadore settlers and owner of the farm; Sheriff John Kinnucan and sexton Jacob Flees; Judge Martin Brown; and another church board member, Mike Gatzke. Neighbors John Panek and Toni Odi had wandered over, too. Their seemingly coincidental arrival was conspicuous; the wind was cold enough to split stones, and no one was just out walking for their health. Even in the below-zero air, the party telephone lines throughout Leelanau County must have been ready to catch fire from the exchange of news.

It took more than two hours for the coroner, Dr. J. F. Slepica, to arrive.

Two hours for the assembled huddle to think back to the Sister's disappearance, to share their theories of her murder and burial, to consider judgment of her killer. Two hours to ponder the crime's brutal blow against their little immigrant mission church.

Each man present had a personal stake in what this exhumation had wrought. Jacob Flees must have worried over his own culpability and the security of his new job; he had been loyal to Father Edward, kept the man's secrets for him, and now the priest had been run out of town in disgrace. Would he face the same treatment? With the involvement of the sheriff and the judge now, it must have occurred to Jacob finally that what he and Father Edward had done was not only immoral but illegal, too. He was in his mid-sixties, and jail time would have been tantamount to a death sentence.

Sheriff Kinnucan's post was an elected one, he was serving his second term, and now he had the unenviable task of investigating what looked to be a murder. Before becoming sheriff, he'd been a farmer himself, and even though he was not part of this tight-knit group of Poles, he understood them as well as any outsider could be expected to. If a murder had been committed, it had happened long before he was in office. If Kinnucan could bring the perpetrator to justice, his future would be secure. If not, this incident would be a dubious legacy, and someone else would surely be elected to replace him.

Judge Brown had been unable to find the missing Sister when she first disappeared. He was sheriff in 1907 and had been unable to determine if there even had been a crime connected with her disappearance. He was a probate judge now, and he just might have been given another opportunity to help solve this mystery. Second chances like this one were rare, and he planned to take advantage of it.

Mike Gatzke and John Panek each had children who attended Holy Rosary School, as did Jake Rosinski. They had gone to the school themselves when they were youngsters, and their families had always been the leaders of this village. If there was a murderer on the loose, they wanted him, or her, caught and jailed, for the safety of their wives and children.

Mike, especially, had a proud family history to live up to. Mike's father, Michael Gatzke Sr., had been one of the first white settlers in the area in the early 1880s, years before the church had been built. Visiting missionaries had said Mass in his house, and he had helped prepare his son and the other Isadore children for their first Holy Communion. Once the church was built, the senior Gatzke would often be the lay reader of the Gospel and the Epistle during services. He was also the church's first sexton, he provided living quarters in his house for the priests before the rectory was built, and he and his wife even sheltered the nuns when the first school and convent had burned down. Mike was now a leader of the church himself, but as Michael Gatzke's son, he had enormous shoes to fill.

And finally, waiting there on his own porch along with the other men, was Jake Rosinski. Though his father, too, had been an original settler of Isadore, had helped Michael Gatzke, Sr., organize the construction of the first church, even helping to select the building site, it was a more current event that would probably have occupied the younger Rosinski's thoughts.

A few years after Sister Janina disappeared, Jake remembered sitting under a tree in his front yard, relaxing after a hard day's work. He was a farmer, ran a general store and the post office out of his house, and was the town's postmaster, too. His workplace was always busy, especially when the children got out of school and stopped by the store for a piece of pink wintergreen-flavored candy, and he enjoyed sitting outside just before sundown and taking in the stillness at the end of the day.

During one of these early evening respites, he remembered hearing women's voices and recognized them as his wife's and Stella Lipczynska's. The two women were standing on his porch, in exactly the same spot he and the other men were standing now.

Stella was there to tell his wife good-bye. After years of tension with his parishioners, exacerbated by the missing nun, Father Andrew had just been transferred to Manistee. Stella would be leaving too, she said. And then Jake heard Stella say Sister Janina's name.

"That Sister is not worthy of being called a Sister!" the housekeeper hissed.

Then Jake's wife said something that he couldn't hear, and then the housekeeper spoke again.

"Father was always over there. He was over there too much. He went to the Sister's and it made more work for me. I warmed up his meals and the food got burned, and then it's not so good. It makes more work, cleaning up the dishes. So much work! He always had something to do with that Sister Janina."

Jake sat silent in his place under the tree that evening all those years ago. The women, he knew, had not seen him there. He remembered that they went into the house, closed the door, and kept up their gossiping even though he could no longer make out their exact words.

He had to be wondering about this overheard conversation now, though. Wondering if Sister Janina had already been dead and buried, her body hidden in the basement of the church when Stella came to his house and said her guilty good-byes right here on this very spot.

A human circle of dread surrounded the wooden table. Standing in the middle of the workroom in the basement of the church school, the gathering point was a long rectangular piece of furniture, designed for utility and not style. It was more commonly used for small arts and crafts or construction projects, and not assembling evidence.

Now, though, each set of eyes present watched as Dr. Slepica reached into the soiled box with his bare hands. His audience knew what was inside, and they were here to see if medical science could bring some logic to what thus far they had no way to understand. The doctor went about inspecting the nun's bones. He pulled out the larger ones, dusting off the dirt and holding them up to the light, then placed them, one by one, on the table. Finally, he removed the skull, turned it over in his hands, and examined the brown strands of hair still attached.

Interspersed around the table among the lawmen, the doctor, the sexton, and the curious, were four nuns, the sameness of their brown habits and black headpieces contrasting with the mismatched suits, weathered overcoats, and patched knees of the men. There was one other time that this same table had been brought into use for Sister Janina: It was here that Jacob Flees fashioned the pine box that now held her remains.

That was not even four months ago. To Jacob, that autumn day, when he built the tiny coffin, and he and Father Edward still believed they had sequestered the secret of her end forever, must have seemed like it belonged to some other era entirely.

Dr. Slepica, one of two Leelanau County coroners, was a physician with a general practice in Suttons Bay, a coastal town eight miles northeast. Along with his contemporary, Dr. Fralick, it was his job to record every birth and death in the county, and to document a condition of the former and a cause for the latter. Birth and death certificates were issued and filed at the Secretary of State in Lansing.

But despite her being missing for eleven years, five months, and twenty-eight days, neither coroner had issued a death certificate for Sister Janina and would not as long as the rumors persisted that she had left the Felician Order of her own volition. It's difficult to imagine anything putting the rumors to rest more abruptly than what those present now witnessed lying upon the table in front of them.

As for Sheriff Kinnucan and Judge Brown, they each promised to the small assemblage that they would right the wrongs committed against the Sister, in whatever way they could, using all the investigative tools at their disposal. Our good faith efforts, they told the group, will begin this very evening.

"Officers took no chances with the remains of Sister Mary Janina," the newspaper later reported. "These they dug up, examined, and now have hidden and guarded, that they may not be lost as evidence in the final clearing up of the case."

What happened after Sister Janina's informal and private autopsy was this: The coroner dusted off her bones and returned them to the box; the sheriff and the doctor loaded the box into the sheriff's rig, snapped the reins of the team of horses hitched to it, and made haste to the county seat of Leland. They came to a stop at the jailhouse just after dark. The sheriff pulled out his key ring, unlocked an empty cell, put the box inside, and locked the door.

The lawmen would be leaving soon to conduct an inquiry in Manistee, and neither one of them was going to risk having the nun disappear again while they were gone.

"Never in the world would I raise a hand against a Sister!" sobbed Stella. "Please, I don't know anything about a murder."

With arrest warrants in hand, Sheriff Kinnucan and Judge Brown traveled to Manistee and pounded on the front doors of the gothic-styled rectory at St. Joseph's. Inside they found a bewildered but angry Father Andrew and his frightened housekeeper.

"I am innocent," Father Andrew told the men. "I remain firm in my denial of any knowledge of this tragedy."

The lawmen had brought with them two arrest warrants, duly signed and notarized. The case of the missing nun might have sat suspended for nearly twelve years, but now things were moving quickly. It was Tuesday, February 24; three days after the coroner had declared Sister Janina dead, four days after Father Edward had left his post at Holy Rosary, and five days after Martha Miller had confessed her intimacies with the priest and told the story of the nun's burial.

In less than a week the bones had been exhumed and examined, affidavits had been taken, and arrest warrants issued. Despite their protestations of innocence, the names written on those arrest warrants in looping black script were "Stanislawa Lipczynska" and "Andrew Bieniawski." The charge—murder in the first degree of Sister Mary Janina.

Sheriff Kinnucan and Judge Brown did not exercise these official papers immediately, however. Their plan was to first question the pair, withholding judgment on whether both, one, or neither of the suspected killers would be arrested, until they could gather more facts via a thorough interrogation.

While Stella seemed genuinely shocked by their arrival, the presence of the sheriff and the judge was not entirely unexpected by Father Andrew. The surprise for him had come the day before. A Chicago newspaper reporter had called the rectory's telephone and asked the priest if he would care to comment on the news that Sister Janina's body had been found.

"Are you sure the bones are found?" Father Andrew asked the caller.

"Oh yes," the reporter replied.

"Are you sure they are the bones of the Sister?"

"Oh yes."

"Where did you get this news?"

"The Associated Press."

"Well, I don't know whether or not this is fact."

"How can we find out?"

"By calling up Cedar."

Father Andrew could not believe that, if such a story were true, he would not have heard of it from someone within the Church or at least from one of his former parishioners. How could a reporter all the way in Chicago know about such secret and shocking doings in his former parish before he himself did? It must be a lie.

"I believe it is some trick, some frame-up," he told the reporter, and then hung up, only to quickly lift the earpiece again and make a telephone call himself.

Even though Father Andrew had been gone from Isadore for six years, and had not been at all liked while he was there, he did still have friends he could call on. He telephoned one of those men now, a Polish farmer, and the man's daughter answered the phone.

"How is everything at home?" Father Andrew asked the girl.

"All right," she said.

"Anything new?" the priest asked.

"No."

"Well, is it true . . . is it true that the body of . . . that the bones of the Sister were found under the church?"

"Yes."

"Tell your father to call me up."

From the girl's father the priest learned that the story the newspaper reporter had told him was, incredibly, true. Not only that, the farmer said, but the authorities believed the nun had been murdered and that he and Stella could have had some part in the heinous crime.

Father Andrew was livid. How could anyone believe that he of all people had played a part in something so horrible? Had no one taken notice of how diligently he had searched for the missing Sister? Long after everyone else, even her own family, had given up he'd walked in the frozen woods alone looking for her. He still had the frostbitten toes and weak heart to prove it. The idea that Stella could have perpetrated something like that right under his nose was ludicrous as well.

Sister Janina had been sweet natured, almost childlike, and inspired only feelings of lighthearted happiness and a certain spiritual calmness inside those in her midst. Especially when she was singing or playing the piano. Who could possibly want to *murder* her?

The telephone call got Father Andrew thinking about who could have done the deed, if the body was even that of Sister Janina, which he doubted. So, while he may not have expected the sheriff and Judge Brown to bang on his door, slipping arrest warrants from their coat pockets, their arrival couldn't have come as a complete surprise.

Stella, however, was obviously caught completely off guard. The law men immediately decided to separate the two suspects before either was questioned, and Sheriff Kinnucan took Stella to the Manistee jail. He told the local sheriff his business and asked if the man could find him a Polish interpreter. Someone without pending obligations would be best, as many hours of work might lie ahead.

The lawman's strategy was to get harsh with Stella and cozy with Father Andrew. Of the pair, Kinnucan was the tough guy, Brown the negotiator, making their assignments obvious. And so while the sheriff dragged a protesting and tearful Stella off to jail, Judge Brown remained at the rectory with Father Andrew.

The judge and the priest knew each other well, Brown having interviewed Father Andrew several times during the days when the nun first went missing. As sheriff back in 1907, Martin Brown had helped Father Andrew organize citizen searches of the woods and swamps, and even took the occasional walk in the woods with the priest long after the rest of the community had stopped looking for her. The judge and the sheriff agreed that Brown had the best chance of finding out whether Father Andrew knew more details about the crime than he had so far revealed.

News that suspects had been publicly named in the case titillated the readership of northern Michigan, who were eagerly following each new development: "The first thing they did was to separate the couple, and then they proceeded to 'sweat' them," the Traverse City newspaper reported. "Neither warrant will be served until every possible means has been exhausted to wring a confession out of one or both. It is understood that the sweating was continued throughout the night and into today, in the possibility of getting a confession. Separating Father Bieniawski and Mrs. Lipczynska is believed to have been the strategic move that will get this confession if either of them are guilty."

If there was a limit to how far Sheriff Kinnucan was willing to go in order to build a case against Stella Lipczynska, he had yet to reach it. When he told Sister Janina's fellow Felician Sisters, the county coroner, and the church leaders that he would use all legal means to solve the case, he meant it. Thus far Kinnucan had urged a church sexton from his bed, detained a priest inside his own rectory, summoned nuns to view human remains, and then stored those remains in the most secular location imaginable, a locked jail cell. If anyone dared call the sheriff to task for these aggressive tactics, he may very well have replied that he was just getting started.

That the sheriff would interrogate his chief suspect off and on for twenty-four hours hardly seems out of character. Even if she was a diminutive Polish immigrant who had to raise her eyes to see even a height of five feet. To one confidant, the sheriff revealed that Stella's small stature was not an indication of her innocence but rather quite the opposite. He was suspicious of it beyond measure. How else, he posited, could she have raised a shovel above her head to strike the victim, in a basement with such a low ceiling? If the nun was indeed murdered by this type of blow to the head, and the crime had taken place under the church, the killer would have been someone without much height to them. He'd swear on his badge that she was guilty.

The housekeeper had yet to be formally arrested, but a day and night had passed and she was not allowed to leave the Manistee Jail. Present during the questioning, besides Sheriff Kinnucan and the housekeeper, were Manistee County sheriff E. M. Hallock and the clerk of the Probate Court, Blanche Srsinska, who was fluent in both English and Polish.

When Kinnucan asked for an interpreter, it was Srsinska who was called into service. She acted as interpreter for Stella as needed, though many of the housekeeper's answers were given in heavily accented English.

SHERIFF KINNUCAN: From the evidence we have gathered in this matter, it seems to us that you must know something about this crime.

STELLA: No, I don't know. I know nothing.

SHERIFF: Where were you on the afternoon that Sister Janina disappeared?

STELLA: Working about the house and in the garden. I had lots of work to do. Geese and chickens to look after and all these many things to do.

SHERIFF: What time did the other Sisters report to you that Sister Janina was missing?

STELLA: Along in the evening sometime, between four and five o'clock. I couldn't tell you the exact time. I didn't look at a clock.

SHERIFF: Did Sister Janina have any enemies, anyone who would want to hurt her?

STELLA: No. She was a good Sister. There was never any trouble between Sister Janina and me.

SHERIFF: Then how is it that her body was recovered from underneath the church?

STELLA: I know nothing of this! I know nothing of this until the present time, until I know that I am accused of this crime of murder.

(re-created from trial transcript)

On February 25, 1919, Stanislawa "Stella" Lipczynska was placed under arrest by Sheriff John Kinnucan, charged with murder in the first degree of Josephine Mezek, a.k.a. Sister Mary Janina, and locked in a cell inside the Manistee County jail.

∽

The arrest of Stella was "insanity," Father Andrew declared—a characterization that turned out to make the priest a more accurate prognosticator than even he could have anticipated.

Not only was the priest convinced that his housekeeper was innocent of all charges, he also protested that the box of bones recovered from underneath Holy Rosary Church had been improperly identified. That it was a foregone conclusion to everyone else that the remains were indeed the nun's mattered to the priest not one whit. Father Andrew had never been swayed by public opinion, and he had no intention of beginning that simpering practice now.

"I do not believe that the body that has been found is that of Sister Mary Janina," Father Andrew said. "She wore a heavy brown wool dress. The goods would not have decayed in eleven years, to any extent. I have no idea whatever as to the identity of the body that was found. I did not know of the existence under the church of this body, or of its reburial. Sister Mary had no enemies to my knowledge. She and my housekeeper were on good terms, so far as I know."

In the minds of the public, however, the case had progressed far past the suggestion that the bones might not be those of the missing Sister Janina. Who else could they possibly belong to? The identity of the skeleton had been firmly established; if not by the evidence, then by the banner headlines. Newspapers around the state, the region, and even the country, stated: "Arrest in Nun Murder," *New York Times;* "Woman Confesses to Murder of Nun," *Nebraska Evening State Journal,* "New Evidence in Nun Murder," *Grand Rapids News;* "Chain of Evidence of Slaying of Nun Leads to Manistee," *Manistee News-Advocate;* "Seek Solution to Murder of Nun," *Traverse City Record-Eagle.*

That there had been a lack of train accidents that winter was hardly noticed by those who once flocked to the railways, picnic baskets and wool blankets in tow, to view the carnage. Northern Michigan's aficionados of calamity had a much more thrilling mishap to observe, and this one couldn't be cleaned up in a day or two. Plus, no travel was required to be among its audience; the newspapers brought it straight into their parlor, where they could read all about the case of Sister Mary Janina and her deranged female killer at their leisure.

"Despite a grilling covering nearly 24 hours of both Fr. Bieniawski and Mrs. Lipczynska, the northern officers have still failed to solve the mystery surrounding the nun's disappearance," the *Manistee News-Advocate* announced to its readers. "Under questioning all yesterday afternoon, at Fr. Bieniawski's home and also at the courthouse, Mrs. Lipczynska threw no light as to the murder of Sister Mary Janina."

Even though a confession was thus far out of their reach, from these accounts the law still seemed to observers to be competent enough. But besides giving the community assurances that the fate of the nun had been discovered and that the guilty party had been found, officers accomplished something else when they placed Stella under arrest. Something they did not anticipate. They had secured for her an indefatigable patron—Father Andrew, who had convinced the arresting officers so thoroughly of his own innocence that they decided not to exercise the warrant they had for him, now began laboring on his housekeeper's behalf.

He sent his sister, Susan, to visit Stella in the Manistee jail before officers took her to Traverse City. He hired Manistee attorneys Howard L. Campbell, Thomas Smurthwaite, and Peter T. Glassmire not only to defend her innocence, he said, but also to identify other suspects. The reward he had offered all those years ago for the whereabouts of Sister Janina he now pledged toward Stella's bail. And he demanded that the lawmen immediately cease behaving as if the case were solved and instead continue to gather evidence.

"I will not be satisfied with the dismissal of charges or casting aside of suspicion toward my housekeeper, Mrs. Lipczynska, or to myself. I will insist that a thorough investigation be made to clear up the mystery beyond the shadows of a doubt. For this purpose I have engaged [attorneys] who have been directed to conduct inquiries which will lead to the persons responsible for the bones being in the basement of my former church at Isadore. I want everything sifted as to whom the remains belonged and who were the perpetrators of the crime. The case has taken a different trend and we will follow up every clue to bring to justice the persons involved."

Father Andrew was used to giving orders, and he did so as a matter of course. In Isadore and in Manistee his word was its own law, and he was accustomed to making decisions and having the actions he decreed by those decisions carried out in short order. It must have come as a shock to realize that he held no authority over the sheriff or the judge. They didn't argue with him, they did something considered far more insulting by an authoritarian man like Father Andrew. They ignored him.

As far as the law was concerned, a crime had been committed, the guilty party had been located, and she would be taken back to their county to face the consequences of her deed. If the priest wanted to do something for her, they guessed that he could pray if he liked.

Before Sheriff Kinnucan and Judge Brown hauled Stella away to the train station, bound first for Traverse City, then for Leelanau County, and finally to a hearing, a furious Father Andrew gave them one parting absolute. This well-known miser pledged Liberty Bonds from his own vault to her cause, as well as the $500 in gold he had locked inside a little black money chest.

"Take it if you need it," he demanded of the men. "She must not be put in jail."

If anyone who'd followed the case still believed that Sister Janina had left the convent and moved to Chicago in order to live with her brothers, the following letter, addressed to Traverse City's top lawman, John Blacken, and received the day after Stella arrived in his town from Manistee, put that theory immediately to rest.

Chicago, Feb. 24
Chief of Police, Traverse City, Mich.

Dear Sir: We, Frank and Emil Mezek, brothers of Sister Mary Johns, who was Josephine Mezek before she entered the convent, are ready to assist you and any of the authorities in any way possible to bring light on the story.

Josephine has never been in Chicago, to our knowledge, and she never even visited in our homes after she entered the convent.

We have letters from A. Bieniawski which were received during the search for her, after her disappearance, and some a year or so later from Sister M. Nepomucene, which may be of great assistance to you.

Signed: Frank Mezek, 7527 Stewart Avenue,
and Emil Mezek, 911 West 86th Place, Chicago

When the letter from her brothers was made public, any chance Father Andrew had to convince a single living soul that the bones found under his former church belonged to someone other than Sister Janina quickly evaporated. The priest was, however, able to secure the freedom of his housekeeper. At least temporarily.

After her arraignment, Stella was freed on $4,500 bail. This figure was far too large a sum for the priest to raise from his personal savings, and so the services of a bail bondsman, James W. Markham of Traverse City, were required. Particulars at a local bank had initially offered their support but soon thought better of that idea and withdrew it at the final hour.

The *Traverse City Record-Eagle* made much of this development. "The original plan had been to provide bail through the Traverse City State Bank, this having been talked over some time ago. But the State Bank decided it did not care to have anything to do with the matter."

Whether because of shock, anger, shame, guilt, the advice of her attorneys, or simply her language barrier, Stella stood mute as the charges of murder in the first degree were read against her in front of Justice

Charles Borrough, in his Greilickville courtroom. A silent response to the accusation of a crime was not uncommon, even for a crime of premeditated murder. Still, the audience, especially the newspaper reporters, undoubtedly had been hoping for more.

Stella's attorneys entered a plea of not guilty on her behalf. Their client would be vindicated, one of the attorneys said, and as proof of this eventuality assured the public that Stella's defense team had inside information that the investigation into the nun's murder was already moving in a new direction.

"There have been developments in the case at Leelanau," said Howard Campbell, one of Stella's attorneys and the former prosecuting attorney for Manistee County. "In view of the fact that both Father Bieniawski and his housekeeper, Mrs. Lipczynska, are firm in their denials of knowledge of the tragedy, officers have changed their attitude toward the pair and have become convinced that the chain of evidence continues further."

A hearing to decide whether there was enough evidence to proceed with trial was scheduled to begin March 11, 1919, in the Circuit Court of Leelanau County, in Leland. Because of the complex nature of the case, the difficulty finding witnesses within the cloistered environment of the Catholic Church, and the continued search for evidence, delays were a foregone conclusion.

Until the hearing would begin, the priest and the housekeeper were free to return to St. Joseph's parish in Manistee, he to preach and she to cook, and they did so, almost as if nothing unusual at all had transpired over the previous days. On March 3, Father Andrew conducted Sunday services exactly as usual; Low Mass and communion at 7:00 a.m.; High Mass and sermon at 9:00 a.m., and then again at 10:30 a.m.

Bail was not an unusual privilege accorded someone arrested for murder, even at the turn of the century; the Constitution guaranteed it, in most cases. Still, the fact that it had been bestowed upon Stella seemed to irk the public, and the newsmen. Any tone of objective curiosity in newspaper articles about the case had turned quickly from impartiality to the surety of Stella's guilt.

"Opportunity to obtain a confession from Mrs. Stanislawa Lipczynska . . . was apparently lost when the housekeeper was allowed to go on bail, a most unusual thing in a first degree murder case. The woman has returned to Manistee away from the Leelanau County officers, where she is again with Father Andrew Bieniawski. While officers can go to her and question her they cannot subject her to the ordinary methods usual in such crime cases of sweating the accused until their nerve breaks. Mrs. Lipczynska will miss the third degrees and other grilling methods that would tend to make her admit her guilt or complicity in the crime and she will go to the hearing March 11 confident in the knowledge that she has won the first bout with the prosecution."

As for the investigation, defense attorney Howard Campbell was correct about one thing: Sheriff Kinnucan *was* headed off in new directions, but these were geographic in nature and not, as he suggested, evidentiary. The sheriff was en route to Milwaukee, Chicago, and then Detroit, not to clear the name of Stella Lipczynska but rather to gather more evidence against her. He was not shy about contradicting Mr. Campbell, or for that matter, the theatrics of the newspapers on this point, either.

"We are on the right track," Sheriff Kinnucan said. "We believe we will be able to reveal the gruesome details within a few days. The rumor stories now extant are true basically, although as yet the public is not aware of one-half the awfulness of the crime."

In Milwaukee, Sheriff Kinnucan called on Stella's daughter, Mary Flees. He found her at home with her two young children, in a state he would later describe as "acute distress." She met him at her door, her face swollen from crying.

A planned trip across the blue plain of Lake Michigan to Leelanau County to support her mother had been delayed when the steamer ship she had booked passage on stayed in port due to a coming storm. Mary knew of her mother's arrest but had heard only scant details of the investigation. The personal visit would have informed her of the rest, and the wait was agonizing.

Just days earlier, before the sheriff's visit, Mary had sent her mother the following letter, written in English, obviously not her native language:

Milwaukee Wisconsin March 1, 1919

Dear Mother?

Though I am feeling well; wanted to start Saturday on our trip, but because the boat did not start, and also because it is with children during this time, it is impossible.

I thank you for the news and consolation. Truly I almost was losing my head, and I thought the same of you, not knowing anything, and not having a presentment in my life, and from also calumny, suspicion, and condemnation; feeling a little better and having my confidence in Jesus and His Mother, God is the best judge, but nobody will ever pay for our sufferings and tears. I thank the Reverend Pastor and Susie for their heart feelings. I will never forget this kindness.

Did you receive my letter? Truly when I was writing it, I was half in my grave about what happened of it.

Little Eugene is praying constantly to Jesus for the Grand Mother and little Stella is kissing the cross. The conscience and heart are telling me that Jesus has sent this to us for our good and greater reward in Heaven.

If the weather clears up next week and will be favorable, we expect to console you.

> Your sincerely loving children and grand children, Joseph, Mary Flees, and the children.

Ps. What about my present. What is it? I am longing for it. Good souvenir for the 11th of March, my birthday.

Sheriff Kinnucan was not altogether an unfeeling man, but the tears of a distressed woman, caught between caring for her two young children and worrying about her incarcerated mother, had little effect on him when it came to investigating the biggest murder case ever to land in his county. In between her erratic outbursts and earsplitting sobs, he grilled her.

Despite her obvious distress, Mary Flees had submitted to the sheriff's questioning willingly, saying, "I want to tell all so that my conscience will be clear." Though her first language was Polish, Mary provided her answers to the sheriff in accented English. She did not appear to need an interpreter and did not ask for one. Before Sheriff Kinnucan left, he secured Mary's solemn promise that she would return to Michigan for her mother's hearing. Once there, she told him she would testify to the fact that she could not account for her mother's whereabouts in the first few hours after Sister Janina disappeared. Though she told the sheriff she wanted desperately to believe in her mother's innocence, she also vowed to use what influence she had to convince her mother to confess all she knew of the crime.

"I know Father Bieniawski is innocent," Mary said. "That is why I sent him a letter to give to my mother to tell her to tell the truth. If my mother is guilty, she must take her punishment, and suffer in this world and save her soul in the next."

The sheriff stayed in the Flees home at 338 Arthur Avenue for only a few hours, but after he left even the Great Lake was not barrier enough to keep a lid on the case. Word traveled through weather that passenger ships could not, and the news soon spread across Lake Michigan that the sheriff had accomplished much on this first leg of his investigative journey. Even the suspect's own daughter had cast suspicions upon her.

In Traverse City, an anonymous telegram was received in the offices of the *Traverse City Record-Eagle*. It was printed in the newspaper without attribution, and with the further caveat that the missive was "impossible to verify."

Milwaukee—Michigan sheriff has secured deposition from Mrs. Lipczynska daughter, Mrs. Joseph Flees. Says she begs the priest to have her mother confess to the murder.

On Wednesday night, Sheriff Kinnucan left Milwaukee, bound first for Chicago and the doorsteps of the Mezek brothers, and then to Detroit and the innermost circle of St. Bonaventure Monastery. Though news of his interview with Stella's daughter was soon spread throughout the region, the sheriff still kept at least one secret of the investigation to himself. For now.

While in Milwaukee, he had paid a secret visit to the Wilson Detective Agency and there met with the organization's chief investigator. The sheriff told the unnamed man that he required the services of an experienced woman operative for a most delicate matter in his jurisdiction of northern Michigan.

This assignment could take several weeks, the sheriff explained, and the woman for the job would have to be both a Catholic and a native speaker of Polish. She would also need to possess a robust attitude, and a certain coarseness to her nature.

"This is not an assignment for a proper lady," the sheriff said.

The agency chief responded that he knew of a woman whose quali-
fications and personality made her well suited for such a job.

"When do you need her to be in Isadore?" he asked.

"Soon," the sheriff replied. "Very soon."

While the sheriff was covering mile after midwestern mile collecting the
evidentiary nails for what he promised would be Stella's courtroom coffin, his cohort, Judge Martin Brown, was busy collecting other important
items back in Isadore at the scene of the crime. The sheriff had left the
judge in charge while he was away, and he wasted no time in continuing
the search for clues.

At the judge's direction, the other Leelanau County coroner, Dr.
George Fralick, had also examined the bones. As Sister Janina's personal
physician, Dr. Fralick was in the very best position to say whether the recovered skeleton was indeed his former patient. On this point, he was
curiously silent, though he did offer a medically inspired opinion on another crucial issue. What had been buried in the cemetery was not a
complete skeleton. Bones were missing, and this would have to be reme-
died or it could cause a problem for the prosecution if they went to trial.
Dr. Slepica, the first coroner to examine the skeleton, agreed.

Dr. Fralick informed the judge that the human body had approximately two hundred bones; only 146 bones of an adult female had been
recovered from the unmarked grave in the cemetery. Missing were fifty-
four bones, the doctor said, including two ribs, a piece of the breastbone,
and many small bones of the hands, wrists, and feet. Some, he posed,
could have disintegrated over the years. Where, though, were the rest?

If the lawmen let this fact stand, the defense, they knew, would use
it at trial to dispute the chain of evidence. Perhaps, Stella's attorneys
could argue, there were truths of the crime as yet untold, and perpetrators as yet unnamed, if not even the alleged victim's full skeleton could
be accounted for. These unanswered questions alone could be enough to
provide reasonable doubt in the minds of a jury.

With the sheriff away, Judge Brown took over the task of locating the
rest of the nun's remains. He aimed to find each and every one of the Sister's missing bones, and find them before the hearing, which was now
scheduled to begin in just one week.

Judge Brown rallied Jacob Flees and a posse of men from Isadore—Jake Rosinski and Deputy William Dalton and at least four others—and led them back to the church basement and the site of the still open grave; the sexton was again equipped with shovels but this time also brought along a metal hand sieve and a large wood-framed wire screen.

Jacob and the deputy dug while the other men sifted. The screen was mounted between two wooden planks and while the diggers filled it with shovelfuls of dirt, the other men shook it back and forth as if panning for nuggets of gold. What eventually appeared in the dark when the sandy dirt was shaken away was, to them anyway, of almost equal value.

"We found a wooden cross with an image on it, a piece of newspaper, a little metal cross, a piece of cord, a spool, a scapular, a thimble, a ring, and some buttons," Judge Brown said. "And bones, too. We found many more small bones and a rib. And smaller particles of clothing; it was so decayed though that it would work right through the screen and mix with the sand."

Most of the material recovered in these siftings was taken to the Leland jail and added to the contents of the box of skeletal evidence already sequestered there. But a small portion the doctors and the judge deemed so indecent that not even the iron bars of a locked jail cell could protect polite society from the crisis that would surely erupt upon any public announcement of its discovery. Some of the smallest bones snagged in the sieve were those of a human fetus.

A gentleman's promise was made. Neither the doctors, nor the judge, nor any other man present would reveal what they had found. All anyone else save Sheriff Kinnucan needed to know was that additional remains had been discovered and added to existing evidence. That the deceased had been pregnant would not be revealed for any reason. Their community's faith had already been shaken quite enough. None of them was ever to tell of it. Not at trial, not to their wives, and certainly not to the newspaper reporters.

This latter group accepted the men at their word when they exited the church basement and made a public announcement about the success of their efforts. Certainly whatever their sheriff was uncovering in Milwaukee and Detroit was of much more consequence than one more trip into the church basement.

"Methodically," the newspaper reported, "the investigation is proceeding hourly. Anticipating that the arrival, from Milwaukee, of Sheriff John Kinnucan will result in shedding additional light on the alleged mysterious murder . . . authorities are 'standing pat' on the matter in hand, unshaken in the belief that the ever increasing threads of evidence can eventually be woven into a satisfactory solution of the grim tragedy that is thought to have been enacted at the Leelanau village of Isadore in 1907."

If the citizens of Leelanau County and the neighboring town of Traverse City were expecting a big announcement from the sheriff when he returned to northern Michigan, they were sorely disappointed.

"There is absolutely nothing to tell you," Sheriff Kinnucan told the large group of onlookers waiting for him at the train station when he arrived on Saturday. "When the time is ripe, we will tell you everything. It will be material for a bigger story than you have yet had on the Sister Mary case."

In truth, the sheriff had discovered few new clues from his interviews with either the Mezek brothers or Father Edward. Certainly nothing to rival what had been found in his absence. Sister Janina's brothers had already told all they knew, which was very little, and Father Edward was in such a state of despair over his personal transgressions as to render him, for the time being anyway, quite useless.

Privately, the sheriff called a meeting of his team. Assembled with him in the front hall at the Leland jail were Judge Martin Brown, Deputy Dayton, doctors George Fralick and J. F. Slepica, another physician from Northport by the name of Robert Flood, and Leelanau prosecuting attorney Ralph Hughes. Also present was Martin Martinson, director of the Martinson Funeral Home.

In preparation for what was about to take place, the sheriff had unlocked the cell, removed the box of bones, and placed them on two square tables he pushed together for just that purpose. The missing bones only recently found were placed where they belonged, and for the first time since she had been exhumed, the remains of what most believed to be Sister Mary Janina were assembled into a nearly complete skeleton.

The doctors began their first official examination, making notes of their observations.

They measured the skeleton, taking into account the space that would have been occupied in life by cartilage, and estimated the person to have been between sixty-two and sixty-five inches tall. They examined the pelvic bones and labeled the victim female. They looked inside the rotting leather shoes and saw at least some of the missing foot bones.

"Is that a crack?" Hughes, the prosecutor, asked the doctors, indicating a place on the skull.

When Dr. Fralick examined the skull more closely, he saw what looked exactly like a crack about an inch and a half long on the left side, about two and a quarter inches from the eye socket. The crack appeared to originate from inside the skull. Dr. Slepica agreed with this observation, and all present watched as Dr. Fralick retrieved a small handsaw from his medical bag and, without preamble, cut the skull in two.

When they looked inside, the crack looked larger and deeper. It was also quite dark in color, and the men thought they saw a discoloration of the area around it. Though the others may not have recognized this, the doctors thought immediately that they had just discovered the cause of death. The crack bisected the location of the meningeal artery.

"A fracture there in a living person would cause a hemorrhage of the artery, a breaking of the artery, unconsciousness, and pressure on the brain which, if not relieved, would cause death," Dr. Slepica explained. "Such a fracture as this might be produced by a blow from a dull instrument applied to the outside of the head."

A dull instrument such as Stella's common garden spade.

The next afternoon, Sheriff Kinnucan made his first public announcement in more than a week: When the hearing of Mrs. Stella Lipczynska was called to order on Tuesday, in the Greilickville courtroom of Justice Charles Burroughs, the prosecution would be ready.

Father Andrew had something bothering his conscience. A memory was eating at him, and no matter how urgently he tried, he couldn't satisfy himself that it was without substance. The priest wondered if an ongoing feud between himself and another Michigan priest might well be the impetus behind his housekeeper's arrest. The idea that Stella could be guilty was unacceptable; there must be some other explanation for the suspicions that had been cast upon her. Though he still didn't fully believe that the remains belonged to Sister Janina, there was little he could do to combat the general belief among the public and the law that they were, indeed, the nun's. The presumed guilt of his loyal housekeeper was an entirely separate matter, and one that he might be able to influence.

A longtime hatred had existed between Father Andrew and a powerful priest from Bay City. Could the man he was thinking of hate him so thoroughly that he would exact his revenge by framing him and Stella with the Sister's murder? The possibility was almost too awful to entertain.

Though casual and even acute observers of the case believed that the first inkling of the crime had come to light only weeks ago, when Father Edward's love affair was made public, Father Andrew knew differently. There had been an important clue to the murder delivered to him much earlier, but he had ignored it.

Father Andrew remembered the incident with a vividness that was unnerving, especially for a man of his usually sensible constitution. It had happened in the autumn of 1914, when Sister Janina had already been gone for years. Father Andrew had been removed from Isadore by then and was serving as priest of St. Joseph's in Manistee, and the church had just bought him an automobile—"my machine," he called it. He liked the contraption so much that he used it to run errands and visit parishioners more often than he used the horse and buggy he had once been so proud of.

When he returned to the rectory one afternoon, Stella announced that someone had come to call while he was out.

"Guess who was here to pay you a visit?" she asked coyly. The tone was uncharacteristic of his usually stern and no-nonsense housekeeper, and it didn't suit her. Which was exactly what made it stand out in his memory.

"I don't know; I can't even guess at it," Father Andrew replied. He was rarely in the mood to play games, guessing or otherwise, and he felt no special need to do so then. If he'd had a guest, he told his housekeeper, he'd appreciate it if she'd just tell him who it had been.

"Father Krakowski," she told him.

Father Andrew remembered being surprised upon hearing this. Isadore was not the only place that he'd made enemies. There were those in the Catholic Church who wished him ill as well, and Father Krakowski was one. He and the other priest were barely on speaking terms ever since he'd opposed the man's nomination for bishop. Krakowski served at a parish in Bay City, way on the other side of the state. Whatever his business was in Manistee, it could not be anything helpful, of that Father Andrew was certain.

"I wonder what he wants," he said to Stella.

"He didn't say. But he's at the depot, waiting for the train to Isadore, and you still have plenty of time to catch him if you'd like."

Father Andrew jumped in his "machine" and drove the few blocks to Manistee and Northeastern. Once there, the two men spied each other immediately, and Father Krakowski angrily motioned Father Andrew over.

"What are you going to do about the bones under your old church?" he hissed.

"What bones?" Father Andrew asked.

"Sister Janina's," the other priest said.

Father Andrew blanched at the memory of the names he'd called Father Krakowski then. How dare he make such a revolting suggestion. It was just a way to discredit him, he'd believed at the time; revenge for their differing politics, and proof in Father Andrew's mind that'd he'd been right all along: the man would have been a poor choice for bishop.

"Who are you to judge *me?*" Father Andrew shouted back. "If you think this thing is true, then you should notify the officers."

That had been Father Andrew's parting remark, and he spun around and left the depot, insulting the other priest under his breath as he went. At the time, he remembered being furious that Father Krakowski would go to such lengths to discredit him. Now, he wondered if the wicked plot his enemy had planted more than four years ago actually had roots, in fact, and was about to bear its poisonous fruit by the bushel.

Father Andrew made up his mind then and there that regardless of whether or not he was subpoenaed, he planned to be in attendance for the opening of Stella's hearing.

As it turned out, Father Andrew and everyone else interested in the case had to wait a bit longer to learn what questions, if any, would be answered in the courtroom. For all of Sheriff Kinnucan's public bravado,

the preliminary examination of Stanislawa "Stella" Lipczynska was officially delayed for two weeks. The delay was by mutual consent between
the prosecution, the defense, and the judge. It was the last time the three
would agree on much of anything.

When the hearing finally did begin on the morning of March 27,
1919, the expected revelations were in short supply, much to the consternation of the vocal crowd of spectators. Farmers from miles around
had arrived at the upstairs courtroom in Greilickville, a little dust-wipe
of a town a mile north of Traverse City, just inside the Leelanau County
border.

All the town could claim for its own, besides a hotel, one tiny store,
and the courtroom, was a public beach. The most common crime committed here to date had been local boys taking pot shots at seagulls. The
arrival of Stella Lipczynska caused a sensation.

Even in late March, spring was still at least month away, but spectators packed together in the chill of the unheated room, waiting for whatever the prosecution could extract from the tough and silent Polish
housekeeper. They walked, came on horseback, arrived by automobile,
wagon, and buggy. They came in from the fields, away from their
chores, out of their shops, and closed up their offices, but they came.
How disappointing, they complained bitterly to each other, that there
was so little to see. Where were the outbursts and the gore? Where was
the tearful confession? The spectators had expended some effort to secure a place inside the courtroom, getting up early, skipping important
chores, shirking farmwork and missing lunch, and they acted entitled to
some satisfying dramatics for their efforts. It was almost as if they were
ticket-holders for an expensive but lackluster theater performance.

They were at least able to see all of the people they'd been reading
about in the newspapers. Stella and her attorneys were present and so
was Stella's daughter Mary Flees, her son-in-law Joseph Flees, Sheriff
Kinnucan, the prosecuting attorneys, and Judge Brown. Father Andrew
was there, along with two nuns from Manistee and two from Detroit. So
far, the Felicians had released no public statement and given no interviews, and people were curious as to what they thought of Stella. None
in the gallery learned their opinions that day, however, or much else either. The proceeding lasted only a few minutes and the only people talking were the attorneys.

A technicality had made Stella's original arrest warrant invalid, so she was released by the prosecution then immediately rearrested on a new warrant. That, and a change of venue to Leland, where the courtroom had a boiler and was heated, was the extent of the drama for the day.

"It was a disappointed crowd that witnessed the brief transaction in court this morning," the newspaper reported. "The little courtroom over the only store building in Greilickville was crowded to capacity. Fully a hundred persons were present, many of them having driven several miles to hear the examination; several dozen having walked a far as three or four miles to be present."

For their considerable efforts, all they saw was a bundled-up Stella being escorted out of the courtroom between Sheriff Kinnucan and Judge Brown. Accompanied by her daughter and son-in-law, the accused was then hurried off in the sheriff's automobile.

It was not only the spectators who were disappointed; the newspaper reporters, too, had been expecting revelations from the prosecution and now would have to wait for them, along with everyone else.

"The general impression among those who have followed the case is that the prosecution has something up its sleeve, of which the public is not yet aware," wrote one.

Polish religious custom once marked Friday as the single unluckiest day of the week. No good outcome would result from beginning something on the same day as the Lord's death. Even the *Nun's Rule* respected the day. "Pain is always to be understood by the cross. Every Friday of the year, keep silence."

But those in charge of exacting justice in the death of Sister Janina were not of Polish descent, and few were Catholic. The judge was the Honorable William C. Nelson, the prosecutors and special prosecutors were Ralph E. Hughes, Clinton L. Dayton, and Parmius C. Gilbert. The stenographer was Claude M. Curtis. Englishmen and Protestants all, and so on a Friday, March 28, 1919, the examination of Stella Lipczynska began.

The first witness was Father Andrew.

"I remember the 23rd of August, 1907. On the morning of that day I was at home, 'round the school, the premises, 'round my bees, my barn, my pheasants, alligator, foxes, and rabbits. I must have seen Sister Jan-ina twice or three times. The boy Gruba and my sister were with me when we went fishing that day. We drove straight for Carp Lake [Lake Leelanau]. East. As I was leaving I saw the Sisters at the back of the school, out on the porch. Sister Janina was with them. They waved their hands for good-bye."

The priest said that Stella and her daughter were outside at the time, too, standing in the churchyard apart from the nuns, and his fishing trip lasted well into the evening. The entire time he was away from the church, Father Andrew said he was fishing, was never alone, and made no side trips anywhere else.

"The boy Gruba and my sister were with me all the time," he testi-fied. "I never saw Sister Janina after that."

"What is your intention in the future?" Prosecutor Dayton asked his first witness, before excusing him. Father Andrew raised his chin and clenched his fist, resting it on his lap. "I want to sift this down to the bot-tom, no matter how long it will be dragged."

With this testimony the priest established his alibi on the first day of the hearing, naming not just one but two parties who could corroborate his story. It didn't take a well-trained legal mind to deduce that the priest was not implicated in the crime, as he couldn't possibly have struck the killing blow from the middle of Lake Leelanau. This may have impressed Judge Nelson and the attorneys, but to the people of Isadore it made little difference.

Their former priest might not have cracked the Sister's skull, or even known that she had been murdered, but many believed that he'd unconsciously put the nun in harm's way. The ripples of sin spread wide but always lapped on their intended shore. His love affair with the nun had inspired murderous ire, some whispered. Though it was his housekeeper sitting in the defendant's chair, gossip that Father An-drew bore some responsibility for the nun's gruesome end continued unabated.

Stella did not testify at her hearing. Leelanau County's team of prosecu-tors called thirteen witnesses to testify, each one providing a piece of their case's detail. When combined, Prosecutor Dayton told the court, the only logical action that could arise from the combination of their stories was to try Stella for murder.

"If it will throw any light on the case, we will procure it," he said. "The prosecution feels satisfied it has sufficient evidence to carry the case to Circuit Court."

After Father Andrew, the prosecution's lineup of witnesses included Stella's daughter Mary, church sexton Jacob Flees (Mary and Jacob were cousins by marriage), three Felician nuns, the two county coroners, and assorted Isadore neighbors. Their time in the witness chair was brief. Dayton and his staff had the task of pulling out just enough of their stories to convince Judge Nelson that there was sufficient evidence a crime had been committed and that Stella was the guilty party, but not so much that they gave their entire case away to the defense.

In this, they were masterful. Stella's daughter Mary was made to look like a flighty girl and could not give her mother an alibi. Jacob Flees told of how his shocking discovery had weighed heavily on his conscience, the Felician Sisters detailed the path of the rumor of the crime within their order, and the coroners briefly discussed cause of death and identification of the remains.

The prosecution managed to have all these elements entered into the court record without objection, and without producing the skeleton or allowing the defense to examine any of the bones—an oversight Stella's defense attorneys pointed out with first disbelief and then rancor. Attorney Peter Glassmire had remained uncharacteristically silent up to this point but could stifle himself no longer.

"This person is entitled to know what she is to be confronted with, and they have refused it to us this morning," he barked to the judge. "We are going into this examination blindly. We are entitled to know; and we should be permitted to see that skeleton, now being held in their possession. We don't want to take anybody's say-so for it and what it shows. We would be derelict in our duty if we did not object to it. We desire to have that skeleton produced and these bones, and make a demand for them now."

Judge Nelson made no ruling on the demand from the defense, but Prosecutor Dayton and Special Prosecutor Gilbert both offered to allow Stella's attorneys to examine the bones in a private setting outside the courtroom. What had been kept from the defense was now being offered freely, but Glassmire was skeptical.

"We attempted that once before . . . and it was denied at that time," he said.

"I am not saying anything about that," Special Prosecutor Gilbert replied, "but I am saying we are ready and willing to do that if you care to enter into the arrangement. We do not desire to produce them now. We object to their being hauled about, and moved about, as they would necessarily be, to produce them here in open court and in this room."

Glassmire held firm. "We want to see them now," he said.

Judge Nelson took this opportunity to make a ruling: "The court will allow the evidence to stand." Everything the prosecution had presented, and even what it had not, would remain in the court record. The impact of this was immediately clear to both sides.

"We ask the respondent be bound over to the Circuit Court for trial on the charge of murder," said Prosecutor Dayton.

"We ask that she be discharged," said Glassmire. "There is no evidence in the case to warrant her being bound over, or to warrant the court in finding that an offense has been committed, or probability to believe the respondent is guilty of the offense. They have introduced no testimony to establish either one of these propositions, and have failed to establish the corpus delecti. They have failed to establish the fact that this woman ever was killed, and there is no testimony whatsoever that this skeleton, which they refuse to permit us to see, is that of the missing Sister. There is no testimony to show that she is dead at all. There is no justification in the court binding her over on the testimony so far before it, and I ask for her discharge."

"I don't think, your honor, it is necessary to take much time," said Special Prosecutor Gilbert. "You ought to entertain the request made by Mr. Dayton, and in fact, we simply insist upon that as being our position. I think we are fully justified in doing so, without discussing it more in detail at this time."

Justice Nelson took almost no time at all in formulating his response. "The court finds, by the evidence, there has been a murder committed, and in his opinion he has just cause to hold the respondent to appear at the Circuit Court, which convenes at this Village on the second Tuesday in May."

"What do you fix her bail at?" asked Glassmire.

Prosecutor Dayton objected. "On that," he said, "this is a charge that is not bailable."

"The Court can fix the bail, if there is a bail established here," argued Glassmire.

"This Court cannot fix it, can it?" asked Dayton.

"She will have to remain in the County Jail until the next term of court," said the judge, "which begins May 13, 1919."

So much for the defendant's constitutional right to bail.

Perhaps Judge Nelson thought Stella was a flight risk and might return to Poland. Perhaps he believed she was a danger to herself or unnamed others. Whatever his reasons for denying bail, they did not make it into the court record, and he told no one, publicly at least, what they were. With those parting words, Stella Lipczynska was escorted by Sheriff Kinnucan and Judge Brown on the short walk next door, to the jail cell that would be her home, her prison, and eventually her confessional, for most of the next six months.

Purgatory

Spring, 1919

> An angry woman is a she-wolf. As long
> as anger is in a woman's heart, though
> she say her verses, and her hours, and
> her paternosters, and her aves, yet she
> do nothing but howl. Anger is a kind
> of madness.
>
> —*The Nun's Rule*

HOWARD CAMPBELL KNEW he had a long day ahead of him, but he could have had no way of knowing just how little he'd accomplish by nightfall. The middle-aged attorney got into his car early on the morning of May 8 and started out on his trip from Manistee to Leland. His law practice was here in Manistee, where he maintained an office, with all of his important papers and files, his compact but efficient library of law books, his circle of influence, and his small staff. Before he left town, he stopped to pick up one of these staff people, his loyal co-council and chief rabble-rouser, Peter Glassmire.

As the county's former elected prosecutor, serving two terms from 1914 to 1918, Howard Campbell had important connections in Manistee, and it was here that his word was honored. By the end of his second term, he had won convictions on his reputation alone. For the case that necessitated today's travel, Campbell was a bit out of his element, both philosophically and geographically. Not only was he the attorney for the defendant, but he was also headed north, far outside the boundaries where his word held any sway. He did not have fond memories of his last appearance in court there, at Stella's hearing where little had gone his way.

Leland was seventy miles to the north, beyond the spread of either Campbell's or Glassmire's strongest influence, a fact made obvious by their previous inability to get even their most obvious points across in court. No matter. Justice, the two men agreed on the trip up, could be garnered with facts, honest testimony, and knowledge of the rule of law, and that was exactly what they planned to provide to the court in Leland.

Though they had spent almost no time with her, Campbell at least was convinced of his client's innocence. Many years later, when he was an old man, this would be the case he would discuss with his grandchildren. Along with Glassmire's capable assistance, he planned to prove Stella's innocence, just as soon as the defense was allowed to finally examine the evidence, question the coroners, and meet with their client.

The attorneys' day was already planned. It was a three- or four-hour drive to Leland, depending on how the roads had fared during the spring thaw. The men had an afternoon appointment with Sheriff Kinnucan and Judge Brown to make the examination of the dominant piece of physical evidence, the skeleton. This had been unfairly denied them at the hearing, and both were hell-bent to see it now.

That the particulars of this evidence were certainly far from secret made their lack of access all the more insulting. The parish priest, many of the nuns, the church sexton, the county's two coroners, random visitors to the Leland jail, and even many of Holy Rosary's neighboring farmers had already seen the skeleton; finally, the defense was going to be allowed to examine the bones found under the church for themselves. The two men would then have the opportunity to confer with their client and begin piecing together their trial strategy. The fact that both the bones and their client were being held inside the Leland jail struck them as an odd convenience. After announcing themselves at the courthouse, they'd have to make only one stop.

When the men arrived just after the lunch hour, they headed directly to Sheriff Kinnucan's office inside the Leland courthouse. It was there that they met with their first obstacle. The county clerk told them that both the sheriff and his crony, probate judge Martin Brown, were out of town.

"The sheriff has been gone since Tuesday last," the clerk told the men. "I don't know where he is, when he'll return, nor how to reach him. He left me no telephone number and no telegraph office."

This was not welcome, or expected, news to the out-of-towners.

"We are the attorneys for Mrs. Lipczynska," said Campbell. "If we can't meet with the sheriff and Judge Brown, we'd at least like to see our client. We need to prepare affidavits and draft papers to present in court for her defense."

"Well, you're not going to be able to see her now, sir," the clerk replied. "She is being guarded against all visitors."

Glassmire silently witnessed this exchange between his fellow attorney and the clerk and, along with Campbell, grew more frustrated by the second. Did men this far north have no regard for the law, or were they simply unschooled in it? At the hearing he and everyone present had seen how firmly local sentiment was turned against Stella, but never had they known criminal attorneys to be kept from speaking with their clients, no matter how convinced the community might be of the prisoner's guilt. The men decided it was futile to plead their cause any further with someone obviously so woefully ignorant, and they hurried next door to the jailhouse.

Campbell rapped hard on the front door. A woman opened it and asked the men their business.

"Mr. Glassmire and I are two of the attorneys for Mrs. Lipczynska," Campbell told the woman. "We would like to see her for a few minutes."

By now it was two in the afternoon and despite their sincerest efforts, the men had gotten nowhere. Without the sheriff they would not be able to examine the skeleton or any other possible evidence, and now they were being thwarted even further. The hearing was scheduled to resume in a week, and they were far from prepared.

"I'm sorry, but you cannot see the prisoner," the woman replied.

"What do you mean we can't see her?" Campbell asked. "Don't you know that I am her attorney?"

"Yes," the woman replied, "I know that you are one of her attorneys."

"Well," Campbell gestured to the man next to him, "do you recognize Mr. Glassmire here?"

"Yes," the woman answered, "he is also one of her attorneys. But you still cannot see her. The sheriff is away, and he left me orders not to allow her attorneys to see her for any purpose."

The men could not believe what they were hearing. They had not come up against ignorance of the law, as was their initial impression, but something far worse: defiance of it. And, by orders of the county's chief lawman, no less.

"This is outrageous!" Campbell exclaimed. "Is there a deputy present we can speak with?"

"William Dalton is a deputy, and he lives just down the road here," the woman answered, crossing her arms over her chest. "You can go and see him, but it will do you no good because I am not going to let you see Mrs. Lipczynska."

Just then a man ran up to the jailhouse door to see what the disturbance was about. He stopped to catch his breath before he finally spoke.

"What do you want?" the man asked Campbell and Glassmire between quick breaths. Campbell turned to face him and took a step forward.

"What do *I* want? What is your name?" he demanded of the newcomer.

"My name is Jim Anderson. This is my wife. We have charge of this jail."

"Are you a deputy sheriff of this county?" Campbell demanded.

"We have been deputized, yes sir."

"Mr. Anderson, do you know who I am?

"Yes. You are Mrs. Lipczynska's attorney."

"And do you know who that gentleman is?" Campbell pointed a finger at Glassmire.

"Yes. He is also an attorney for Mrs. Lipczynska."

"Do you have Mrs. Lipczynska in your jail here?" Campbell asked.

"Yes," the jailer said. "She's in there."

"Well, then we *demand* to see her. We have come all the way from Manistee to talk with our client about her case. To prepare her defense. Court opens in just days and we need to have her sign some of these affidavits. We have petitions to draft and motions to make. We need to see our client immediately and you cannot keep us from her."

"Oh, but I can and I will, sir," Anderson said, standing his ground. "I don't care if you get a judge to order it, I am not going to allow you, or anyone else, to see Mrs. Lipczynska. I have my orders from the sheriff. He gave them to me before he left, and I expect to carry them out regardless of what you say or do."

With that the Andersons retreated inside the jailhouse and shut the door on their unwelcome visitors. Campbell, who had spent more time inside a courtroom than most other attorneys in the area, more even than some of its judges, could think of no argument that would sway this stubborn couple. And Glassmire, known for both his smooth oration and his seemingly limitless vocabulary, was struck speechless.

The momentary silence allowed a pitiable sound to escape from inside the brick walls of the jailhouse. It was a woman, and she was crying. Campbell put up his finger for quiet, and the two listened carefully. The sobs changed first to a strange barking, then to hysterical laughter that made gooseflesh rise on their skin, and finally to a bereft-sounding wail. After a pause, the men could make out just a few words of the Catholic rosary recited in a foreign tongue. What they heard almost did not sound human, but the men still recognized the voice. It was Stella's.

Though the windows of the jailhouse were fitted with wrought iron bars, the window frames had been opened to let in the spring air. Campbell and Glassmire circled the building quickly, ducking down as they passed the front windows to stay out of sight of the Andersons. They soon found the origin of the perplexing sounds. Campbell grabbed hold of the metal bars and hoisted himself up so that his chin was level with the bottom edge of the open window. This particular one looked out from Stella's cell, and he peeked inside.

There, huddled in the furthest corner of the little room and crouched down on her knees, was his client. Stella pressed her face against the concrete wall and Campbell could see that her skirt had been drawn up around her slight form, almost covering her head. He watched as she pulled at her hair and tugged at her clothes. The strange sounds continued: first crying, then laughing, then praying. The tone was unnatural, and Campbell told Glassmire he feared for their client's sanity.

"I will speak to Anderson about this, and by God he will listen!" Campbell said.

The men went back to the front door of the jailhouse and banged their fists on it a second time. After several minutes, it was Mr. Anderson who finally answered their insistent knocking.

"Exactly how long has she been acting like this?" Campbell asked, without preamble.

"I would say she's been in that condition for a week or more," Anderson answered. He made no attempt to ask Campbell how he knew of the housekeeper's odd behavior, because the man's method was obvious: Anyone walking by the jail would have heard her wailing.

"Has she received any attention? Any medical care?" Campbell asked.

"I'd say she's getting all the care and attention necessary," said Mr. Anderson.

"So you just let her lay there on that cold floor all day then?"

"No sir. At night I go in and pick her up and put her on her cot."

Campbell was aghast. What kind of jail were these barbarians running up here?

"She requires immediate medical attention!" Campbell demanded.

"I already told you. The prisoner is getting all the attention she needs."

For a moment, the keening ceased, and Campbell circled back to Stella's window to check on her once more.

"Now you stay away from that window!" Anderson called out after him. "Get away from here! Both of you!"

The men were determined to extract some care for their client, despite the cold-hearted Andersons. They spoke among themselves about what to do next and decided to search out their rival, Leelanau County prosecuting attorney, Ralph Hughes. Over the past few months, Dayton had all but replaced Hughes in day-to-day operations of the prosecuting attorney's office and had been the defense's chief foe at the hearing, but Hughes still held the official title. Campbell knew that when he himself was a prosecutor, if a Manistee sheriff had become as obviously rabid with power as John Kinnucan had, he would not have tolerated it for a moment. He expected the same honorable action from Hughes.

But when they arrived on the doorstep of Hughes's Suttons Bay office they found a sign on the door that read, "Out of Town."

In less than a week the defendant in what was universally agreed to be the most titillating crime in northern Michigan's history would be brought in front of a judge. The matter hadn't even gone to trial yet, and the case still had all the makings of a national sensation: religion, sex, jealousy, murder, secrets, and now, possible insanity. Already, crowds gathered around the courthouse, hoping for a sighting of someone connected to the trial. Every day the newspapers ran stories about the case, even when there was nothing new to report. And yet the sheriff, his cohort Judge Brown, and now even the prosecuting attorney were nowhere to be found.

Where in the blazes had the prosecution's side gotten to?

In the Warszawa district of Cleveland, Ohio, Father Edward Podlaszewski was serving his secret penance by working with the Polish congregants at Immaculate Heart of Mary. After suffering through the humiliation of a trial by his peers at Detroit's St. Bonaventure Monastery, then finding himself banished in shame for thirty days to a tiny church in the foothills of Kentucky's Great Smoky Mountains, Father Edward was now assigned to do the bidding of Father Marion J. Orzechowski.

As head priest of Immaculate Heart of Mary, Orzechowski himself was no stranger to controversy. His current church had been founded in the 1890s by the famous troublemaking priest, Anton Kolaszewski, who had later been excommunicated for his activist efforts. Kolaszewski had caused an angry schism between the city's Polish Catholics and almost every other ethnic group, a rift that Orzechowski, with his management skills and measured way of bringing people together, had gone a long way to finally heal, more than twenty years later. A young wayward priest was a minor inconvenience compared to that.

Still, Father Orzechowski kept Father Edward's past to himself. As far as the other members of Immaculate Heart of Mary were concerned, their new junior priest was simply another man in a long line of young Franciscans who were being trained in their parish.

It would have shocked them to learn that late one afternoon, just weeks after his arrival in Cleveland, when his church duties for the day were complete, the handsome and brooding Father Edward did not retire to his room but was instead seated in a downtown lawyer's office, giving a sworn affidavit in a murder investigation. It would have shocked them even more to learn of that affidavit's contents. "The tongue is slippery," warns the *Rule,* "for it wadeth in the wet, and slide easily on from few to many words; and out of good into evil, and from moderation into excess; and from a drop waxeth a great flood, that drowns the soul." Once Father Edward began to speak, he could not stop.

On May 15th, 1917, I was installed as pastor at Holy Rosary Church, Isadore, Michigan. Within two days after my installation, the pastor next preceding me at Isadore, who remained with me two days after my installation, said to me, "I am afraid there will be a scandal in this parish, because a Sister who disappeared here sometime ago, I heard was buried under the church." He did not know this positively, but he said this was a rumor he had heard. I asked this priest for the details of this occurrence, and he replied, "I do not know any of the details."

Later in that same year, 1917—I think it was in the fall, but I am not positive, nor do I now recollect the month—one of the Sisters of the Order, who was teaching in the school at Isadore, said to me, "There is a rumor in the convent among the Sisters that Sister Mary John [Janina] had disappeared," and she said, "I heard she was buried under the church." She said Mother Superior, and another sister, came down there from Detroit and searched for the remains under the church, but the search was unsuccessful. [S]he told me, too, that the Sisters of the convent in Detroit were praying for her; they had prayers for the dead, so they considered her as a dead Sister and offered prayers for the dead and included her; her name was on the list of the dead Sisters.

I made no investigation of this areaway under the church at that time as I did not believe this rumor, thinking that it was impossible. The Sister who gave me this information was Sister Mary Leoncia; the last time I heard of this Sister she was at Parisville, Michigan, teaching school at that place. This Sister said she had got her information from the Mother Superior at the time this Sister related to me this conversation.

The next thing I heard concerning this matter was from Rev. Father Lempke at Father Skory's house at Grand Rapids, on the occasion of the forty-hours' devotion held at that priest's church during the latter part of May or fore part of June, 1918. I had a conversation with Father Lempke there, and I told him I intended to build a new church at

Isadore, Michigan. Then Father Lempke said to me, "I heard from Bishop Kozlowski that Sister Mary John [Janina], who disappeared at Isadore some years ago, was buried under the church." And he said he thought it would be advisable to remove those remains secretly. He said, "I am not positive of this, but the information I received stated that she was buried there by Mrs. Lipczynska."

I questioned him more about this and he said that he did not know any more about this, but that the rumor that Father Bieniawski was implicated in this was untrue. Then, of course, we spoke about the method of removing the bones. He advised me to do it personally so that nobody would see, then to do it at night and remove the bones to the cemetery.

Father Lempke at this time did not state to me the manner or mode by which Bishop Kozlowski had communicated this information; he did not state whether he received this information from Bishop Kozlowski through letter, by word of mouth, or through the interposition of a third person. I now recollect that he, Father Lempke, also stated at that time that the body was buried under the church under a pile of boards.

The next thing that occurred was this: In the latter part of October [sic] 1918, I commenced to search for the bones under the church in the afternoon, but I had not proceeded far because I thought this task was too gruesome for me; so I informed my sexton of this and said to him, "I received information from a certain party that a Sister disappeared here some years ago and had been buried under the church, and that I heard also that this was done by Mrs. Lipczynska." And then in the evening, in the latter part of October [sic], 1918, the sexton and myself began to search this areaway under the church. I further told the sexton that she was supposed to be buried under a pile of boards.

At this time the boards were not there under the church, they having theretofore been removed, but the sexton said that he knew the precise location under the church where those boards had been.

The sexton commenced to dig in one place but did not find anything there, so he thoroughly examined the ground there and he saw a certain slight elevation, which was about five feet from the place where he first began to dig, and rather loose ground was there; so he thought this would be the place likely where the sister was buried. And after we had been digging for some time with shovels, we having removed about two feet of ground, he struck a bone; it was of the lower limb, the large bone.

This bone was not lying horizontally in the grave, but was sticking up at an angle toward the surface, and we first saw the end of this bone. And then, by degrees, we removed all the bones.

This grave was about three feet deep at the point where the feet rested and the head rested. The length of the grave was about five feet. Both of us dug the dirt out of the grave with shovels, and we used a large fork, one such as is generally used in handling manure, with which to lift some of the smaller bones out, and some of the bones we lifted out with the shovels and other of the large bones we lifted out with our hands.

We did this work between four and six o'clock in the afternoon. Outside it was just around dusk. Under the church it was dark, and we used a lighted lantern in there to see our way about and see into this grave. We did not first uncover the grave so that we could see a completed skeleton therein, but when we came to a bone, we lifted it out; and I did not see whether each bone in the skeleton was connected up in its proper place, as we did not first uncover the skeleton but merely picked out each bone as we came to it.

The skull was in the end of the grave opposite to that in which the feet were; the skull was buried about three feet in the ground, as were the feet. We could not see or determine whether the skeleton was in a reclining or partly sitting position, nor what position the skeleton was in the grave, for the reason that the bones were taken out piece by piece as we came to each one.

We also took out of the grave a handful of fabric. It was very badly rotted and we could not see the color of it or determine the kind of material of which it was composed, and there was in all only a handful of this fabric that was so taken by us from the grave that night. We found this fabric mixed in with the ground here and there, and it was very small and fine.

We also found a pair of shoes in this grave; they were low shoes, something similar to those which Sisters wear or nurses wear. One of these shoes was in the foot of the grave, and the other shoe was in about the middle of the grave. We also found a piece of cord such as Sisters wear about their waist. The cord was about six inches long. We saw no other part of this cord except this one piece of six inches in length. I believe that the full length of the cord is about five feet.

We found no buttons in this grave, nor did we find any pins or clothing fasteners of any kind in this grave. There was no evidence of any other garments, nor any clothing, nor any habit, nor any veil except this handful of fabric to which I have heretofore referred.

Some of these bones were taken out by myself, others of them were taken out by the sexton, and all of them were placed in a box which I had with us near the grave. I did not notice whether there was any hair on the skull that was in the grave. These bones, as we took them out, and particularly the skull, were covered with dirt, which adhered to the bones.

We did not find any jewelry, nor any beads, nor crucifix in this grave. All we found there was put into this box and the box remained under the church that night, being covered up securely by a wooden cover.

It took us about two hours to open this grave and remove the contents thereof. The grave under the church was left open that night, and I was informed that the sexton filled it up the next day. The next day I went under the church there and saw the grave was filled up.

The same night we opened this grave I had informed a Sister of the fact and told her of my finding the bones, and she came and looked at the bones in the box, but was unable to identify them in any way. The Sister was Sister Gastold [sic]. Sister Gastold [sic] wanted to look at the bones because she knew very well Sister Mary John [Janina]. I also informed the Mother Superior there at the time at the school at Isadore of my find, but she did not wish to view the bones.

I have no means of knowing whether all the bones of a complete skeleton were in that grave or taken out of that grave by me and the sexton, as we did not assemble the bones, nor did we count them, nor in any way determine whether all the bones were a complete skeleton.

The night we opened the grave I notified the sexton to make a special box for these bones, which he did the next day; and then the day after he made the box we removed these bones from the box in which they were at the church to this newly-made box, and on that same night [sic] the newly-made box, with these bones in it, was taken to the cemetery and buried there. I did not see the sexton bury this box in the cemetery but he told me he did so, and he told me that he buried it in front of the big cross in the cemetery. I did not know Sister Mary John [Janina] in her lifetime.

The sexton dug the skull out of the grave with his shovel and lifted it up to me, and I told him to throw it into the box we had there, which he did. The sexton did not tell me that night, nor at any time, that there was any break in the skull, nor any marks on the skull. Time after time the sexton, and I, digging with our shovels, struck the bones in this grave, especially the larger ones; and the sexton, in digging for the skull, said to me before he unearthed the skull, "I believe there is a skull there, because it strikes pretty hard there." At this time he was driving the shovel into the earth, and right after that and at that same point, he unearthed the skull. As he said, "I believe there is a skull there," he prodded his shovel at least once into the place where the skull was later found.

The sexton to whom I have referred is named Jacob Flees. I did not notice any discoloration of the earth in this grave except at the point where the bones were, and here and there at that point, the earth was very slightly discolored, that is, slightly darker. This grave was located about eighteen feet from the door and a little to the left of the entranceway. The grave was cross-wise of the church, and the surface of the ground at that point was about five feet from the floor of the church, or maybe less, I rather think it was less than five feet.

I, Reverend Podlaszewski, being first duly sworn on oath, depose and say that each and all of the statements and matters contained in the foregoing affidavit, being pages numbered one to eight inclusive, each page of which is signed by me, are true, and further Affiant sayeth not.

(signed) Edward Podlaszewski
Sworn to before me and subscribed in my presence
this 9th day of May, A.D. 1919.
Robert Fisher, Notary Public
Cuyahoga County, State of Ohio (seal)

Just one day after Father Edward gave his official version of the aberration he had encountered under his church, the local newspaper back in Traverse City made public what those closest to the case already knew: the presumed murderer was showing signs of madness. "Mrs. Stanislawa Lipczynska, held in the county jail at Leland for the murder of Sister Mary Janina of Isadore convent, eleven years ago, may never go on trial. From an authoritative source it was learned today that Mrs. Lipczynska has developed symptoms of insanity, and if an investigation reveals the fact that she is insane, the case may come to a sudden close."

Stella's symptoms, readers were told, included rolling on the floor, tearing at her hair and clothing, speaking in an unnatural voice, and though she was carrying on lengthy conversations with her slippers, she was slinking away from official visitors.

The accused refused food and had to be fed with a tube forced down her throat. The sheriff had observed her dancing about her cell and seemingly playing an invisible violin. For her part, Stella was cognizant enough to meet, finally, with her attorneys and make accusations of mental torture against the sheriff and the "devils" working on the lawman's behalf.

Were her stories true, the sincere physical expressions of a damaged mind, or simply the devious calculations of an unrepentant murderess? The newspaper posed this question publicly; privately, Stella's attorneys were already crafting a legal way to find the answer.

What neither the newspaper reporters nor the accused's attorneys knew was this: the female detective Sheriff Kinnucan had hired weeks ago, sight unseen in Milwaukee, had arrived in Leland, was arrested as planned on a bogus charge, and had been deposited without explanation inside Stella's cell. A second cot was hauled in for her to sleep on. The jailer, Mrs. Anderson, had overheard the two prisoners talking to each other in their native Polish. The lilt of their voices, she said, was that of womenfolk sharing a new friendship. And possibly, a secret.

"They sat on Mrs. Lipczynska's cot many times, facing each other, their heads lowered down, talking," Katherine Anderson said. "Sometimes Mrs. Lipczynska would cry and the other woman would put her arm around her, or lie next to her, and try to comfort her."

The sheriff's secret plan of using a spy to get close to his suspect was apparently working.

A Charlevoix-based judge, the Honorable Frederick W. Mayne, was assigned to hear the case of *People v. Lipczynska.* He had a reputation for strict intolerance of delays and quick judicial decisions. His law library was legendary, and he was known as a careful, intellectually curious judge. He convened the case in Circuit Court in the Leland Courthouse on the afternoon of May 13, 1919.

Howard Campbell and Peter Glassmire were ready for battle, far more prepared for the trial than they had been for the hearing, and were armed with affidavits. The first of these charged Sheriff Kinnucan with illegally keeping them from conferring with their client; another charged the lawman with deviously ensuring that the most important piece of physical evidence, the exhumed skeleton, remained unavailable for their examination. Finally, they argued that their client had descended into "a raving condition," making her unable to assist in her own defense.

Three judicial actions were needed immediately, they demanded of the court, to right these wrongs: Campbell and Glassmire needed to confer privately and at length with their client; they needed access to the bones found under the church; and Stella required psychological care of a professional nature.

As a relative outsider, Judge Mayne had a level of implied objectivity that any local court officer would be hard pressed to claim. Charlevoix was just across the Grand Traverse Bay as the crow flies, but more than seventy-five miles by land. It was in an entirely separate county, and outside the insular villages of the Leelanau Peninsula. He quickly proved his objectivity and in the first few moments of the court session ruled in favor of all three of the defense's requests. In addition, he assigned an interpreter to the defendant, acknowledging that the language barrier could thwart her pursuit of a competent defense. His official decision read in part as follows.

> In this cause it appearing to the Court that the defendant is not in a mental condition where she is capable of pleading intelligently to an Information or conducting her defense and that she may be insane or not insane.
>
> NOW THEREFORE it is ordered that a careful investigation be made to determine whether said defendant is insane or not and to that end the following named physicians be appointed to observe the said defendant so as to be in position to give testimony at the hearing hereinafter provided to wit: Dr. Albert M. Barrett, Dr. A. S. Rowley, Dr. James A. King, and Dr. Joseph Slepica.
>
> IT IS FURTHER ORDERED that, in order that she may be put where she can be observed carefully by competent physicians, that the matter be referred to the Probate Court for the county of Leelanau for the sole purpose of having her committed to the Psychopathic Hospital at Ann

Arbor Michigan for observation and treatment, and for no other purpose shall the matter be referred to the said Probate Court.

IT IS FURTHER ORDERED that no INFORMATION be filed against the defendant until it be first determined whether the defendant is capable of pleading thereto.

IT IS FURTHER ORDERED that this Court shall retain jurisdiction of said case and of said respondent, but that the officers may obtain an order from the Probate Court for a commitment of said respondent to the Psychopathic Hospital at Ann Arbor Michigan to the end that the investigation hereby ordered may be more comprehensive and in furtherance of Justice.

> Frederick W. Mayne
> Circuit Judge

Six days later, on the evening of May 19, while Traverse City's finest female citizens were attending one of the "mass meetings" on social hygiene that were sweeping the country, urging attendees to guard their communities against all of the "moral and health menaces of the day," the tiny Polish housekeeper and accused murderess passed, via automobile, silently through their town.

Stella was escorted by James and Katherine Anderson, the couple her attorneys were certain were two of her tormentors. If their client had indeed gone mad, it was this sadistic couple, alongside the sheriff, that had caused her unfortunate condition. Campbell and Glassmire believed the pair had twisted Stella's mind as if it were a wet rag, tightening and tightening until nothing else useful could be extracted from it, except perhaps by professional psychological means.

It was the Andersons' job to deliver Stella into the care of Dr. Albert Barrett, one of the court-ordered professionals in Ann Arbor. For the next thirty days Stella would be an inmate at the State Psychopathic Hospital, and though he himself had willed it, Howard Campbell shuddered to imagine what she was about to experience there, inside the mysterious brick-walled and antiseptic psychological purgatory, once she arrived.

The image Campbell was left with, as he watched his client exit the jail and be helped into the sheriff's automobile, was of Stella, bone thin and disheveled, huddled alone in the back seat, possibly innocent and now possibly crazy, too. Try as he might, he could not convince himself that, in the months to come, her fate would get no worse than this.

"At the end of the 19th century, Americans with mental illness were not so much diagnosed and treated as managed and sheltered," reports the University of Michigan's Department of Psychiatry, in an article on the history of that organization's treatment of psychiatric diseases. "People with schizophrenia, alcoholism, and depression were housed alongside people with cerebral palsy, epilepsy, and feeblemindedness . . . little effort was made to apply scientific methodology to people with mental illness."

At least one man sought to replace "sheltering" with real treatment, and that was Dr. Albert M. Barrett. The University of Michigan built the State Psychopathic Hospital on Catherine Street in Ann Arbor in 1906 with $50,000 of state money, and Dr. Barrett was installed as its first director. A year later, his facility was examining as many as two hundred patients a year.

"The hospital was among the first of its kind in the nation—one intended to provide diagnosis and research on mental diseases rather than custodial care. It contained state-of-the-art research equipment, including a laboratory in which psychiatrists trained in pathological examination studied brain tissue sent from hospitals all over Michigan." An article circulated around the university further stated, "For the treatment of the nervous system, the hospital is furnished with apparatus for generating all kinds of electric current. Attendants especially skilled in the application of electricity and massage are put in charge of these cases."

If Howard Campbell read those words, his worst fears certainly would have been confirmed. His legal maneuvering had delivered Stella directly into the skullcap of electroshock therapy, a treatment that, in 1919, was in its infancy and looked upon by many as barbaric. By legal decree, Dr. Albert Barrett was now Stella's custodian; his charge from the court was for observation only, and not treatment. At least, not yet.

Despite the primitive nature of the methodology his facility sometimes prescribed, by all accounts Barrett was a compassionate man, deeply interested in his patients. Before the hospital opened he drafted the facility's admission forms, which required far more detail than usually deemed relevant for patients with mental diseases. Barrett believed that family history and genetics played a role in these disorders, that they were not always simply the symptoms of a feeble mind, which was considered a radical idea at the time.

In Stella, Dr. Barrett found a woman whose behavior he deemed "unusually odd." On Stella's admittance form it is reported that she was four feet seven inches tall, and weighed ninety-seven pounds. Was this the violent murderer sent to him from the uncivilized north? Her physical description was recorded thus: "She has a Slavic cast of features. Her skin is wrinkled. There is little subcutaneous fat. The skin of her face shows a number of crusted lesions over the forehead and across the nose. These are caused by the patient picking her face. Her hair is rather thin and of brown color. The eyes are brown."

Stella's respiration was irregular, her heartbeat normal, her pulse between 72 and 85, temperature normal, and blood pressure 120 over 80. "The examination of the nervous system shows nothing pathological except slightly irregular pupils."

With all of the formal diagnostic terms Dr. Barrett surely counted in his vocabulary, "unusually odd" was a pedestrian-sounding observation for the esteemed doctor to make. Still, it accurately reflected what he observed upon her admission May 19, when he found her in a mental state "almost completely inaccessible."

This "unusually odd" behavior that Dr. Barrett observed and documented during the first week of Stella's confinement included the following.

When alone in bed she lay rather quietly with eyes closed as if asleep. If aroused she appeared startled, sat up in bed with eyes staring, gazing slowly about the room, not fixing on anything for any length of time: She then would put out her arms, move them stiffly around, then with fingers in a claw-like position she would pull her hair down over her eyes, pick at her face and then rub her hands together. These movements were executed slowly and very deliberately. All of this time she seemed entirely oblivious to anything around her. Her facial expression during this phase was one of terror.

Her actions then changed. She took the attitude of one fiddling; held her left arm as if holding a violin and with the right hand she picked at imaginary strings. As she did this she made a peculiar rhythmical strumming with her lips. After a brief period she put her fingers to her lips and snapped her lips continuing the rhythmic tones. This soon ceased and she became agitated, jabbering in a foreign tongue; crying loudly with tears running down from her eyes.

She would reach out to the physician, trying to take his hands or pat his arm, and, if permitted, would kiss his hands or sleeve. She then became quieter. Sometimes she would reach under the pillow to get her handkerchief and would wipe her eyes or fingers. She would remain quiet for some time and then would commonly repeat the cycle.

English words were occasionally used. She would call the nurses "angels"; would sometimes speak of "devils." Usually she would end these reactions with the remark in English, "Now I pray, Holy Ghost amen, Holy Ghost amen."

After that first week of observation, Dr. Barrett's diagnosis reverted from one using layman's terms to one pulled from his command of clinical terminology. The State Psychopathic Hospital's newest and most infamous patient was suffering from "A Grand Cycle of Hysterical Manifestations."

This was a much more official-sounding term than *odd* but still, at its heart, medically vacant. *Hysterical* was a label that psychiatrists of the day applied to women in order to describe the female mind gone haywire. Suffragettes, feminists, lesbians, runaway wives, the promiscuous, and the violent of the fairer sex were often labeled as such.

Dr. Barrett came by the diagnosis honestly enough. According to his clinical notes, he first ruled out "flight of ideas, unsound mind, suggestibility, paresis, organic brain disease, arterial sclerosis, mania, epilepsy, retardation, blocking, systematization of a paranoid type, dementia praecox, senile deterioration, pre-senile anxiety, emotional letdown, negativism, convulsions, unclear state of consciousness, and hallucinations." He admitted that his working diagnosis was the only thing left, saying only, "The diagnosis of hysteria cannot be excluded."

Hysterical was the most common psychiatric diagnosis of the day when the doctor, almost always a man, knew something was wrong with his poorly behaved woman patient but had no real idea what it was.

This determination had been made one week after Stella arrived in Ann Arbor. It was May 26; through his process of elimination, Dr. Barrett was reasonably certain that his patient was suffering from hysteria, but he still had twenty-three days of court-ordered time remaining to find out why.

While Stella played her imaginary violin, scratched at her face, and prayed to the Holy Ghost in her hospital room in Ann Arbor, residents in the north anxiously awaited her return. They knew the stakes. Without professionally developed testimony that her mind was sound, there was no defendant. Without a defendant, there would be no trial. The people of Isadore and beyond might indeed never know what really happened on August 23, 1907, on the grounds of Holy Rosary. Without a trial, though, that was a certainty. Everything now swung on whether or not Stella's mind had come unhinged.

"The future of this mystery case that is now all over the land, rests upon the examination being made in Ann Arbor," the newspaper reported. "This is because if Mrs. Lipczynska is found to be insane, she will undoubtedly be committed to some state institution, for permanent keep and treatment. If she is found to be sane, she will be returned to Leelanau County officials, and her trial for the murder of Sister Mary Janina of Isadore convent will be resumed. Continuation of the case, in the event Mrs. Lipczynska is found to be insane, will be practically impossible."

The other particulars, no matter how large they featured in the case, returned to their daily lives. After making his affidavit, Father Edward continued his service to Father Marion Orzechowski at Cleveland's Immaculate Heart of Mary, though he was barred by order of the church from saying Mass. Father Andrew remained in his post as head priest at St. Joseph's church in Manistee, with full privileges. Sheriff Kinnucan met secretly with the female detective he had hired, sent her back home to Milwaukee, and thanked her for a job well done. She would be asked to return to northern Michigan to testify under oath to the conversations she'd had in the jail with Mrs. Lipczynska, if there ever were a trial.

The sheriff and Judge Brown continued to confer on the case. They went over and over the evidence, assembling it into a logical progression for their county's new incoming prosecutor. Prosecutor Ralph

Hughes would soon take a job with the federal government and would be replaced in his post by Clinton Dayton, an attorney from Traverse City. It was Dayton, and not Hughes, who would be prosecuting the case, even if the official swearing in didn't happen for several months.

But the Polish farm families who had organized their lives around their church for three generations were caught in a spiritual form of suspended animation. From the time of Father Edward's removal from Holy Rosary in early February until sometime in late spring, these people had been without a permanent priest. Some in the parish even reported that their faith had been shaken by the experience.

"I don't think we'll have any more church here," said one parishioner. "The church teaches us not to do the very things that we have reason to believe one of the dignitaries has done himself, right here in our midst. A church isn't of very much use to us under such conditions. No, I don't believe we'll have any more church here."

The Felician Sisters felt differently. In the spring of 1919 there were 157 students enrolled in Holy Rosary School, and four Sisters remained in the convent and continued to teach their young charges, even without the leadership of a resident priest. They prayed for the Detroit diocese to send them someone. A general choice, however, would no longer do. They required someone who could lead their community out of scandal and back toward their faithful traditions. The struggle and sacrifice that these pioneers had endured in order to settle this small Catholic village in the wilderness of northern Michigan could not be for naught.

According to a descendant of one of Isadore's original five families, those early struggles had been many and severe. In 1924, Stephan Sbanek sat down with his mother and recorded some of her childhood experiences. She had been an eleven-year-old girl when her family moved to the area from Wisconsin in the late 1800s. "Of the hardships and prevarications experienced by our Fathers and Mothers, about the only thing they possessed was a faith and courage that one does not find in such strong evidence in the younger generations of today," wrote Sbanek, as dictated to him by his mother. "The very first Pioneers here fared almost alike. There were no State roads, only blazed trails from Glen Haven to within three miles of what is now Isadore. There was much to move, and the family and furniture both had to be carried a good deal of the way on the long trip through the forest. The Children weren't the only ones crying, and when at last they did arrive at the cabin the Father had built the winter before, the Mother cried out, 'Oh why did you bring me into this hell!' His answer was, 'Cheer up Mother; some day you'll see a nice Church here.'" A few hard years later, on August 16, 1883, his promise to his wife was realized when Bishop Ignatius Mrak dedicated Isadore's first church building.

By the time Father Edward resigned and Stella Lipczynska was incarcerated in an Ann Arbor hospital, Holy Rosary had stood at the corner of Gatzke and Schomberg Roads for more than thirty-five years. Not since the tiny founding Polish congregation met in farmhouse living rooms to celebrate Mass, scheduling their worship around the unpredictable whims of the weather and the equally random travel plans of wandering Catholic missionaries, had these people been without a priest.

Despite the doomlike prediction of some, the nuns were not the only people who believed that a church here could, and would, continue. Though both Father Edward and Father Andrew before him surely shared culpability for the dire circumstances the parish now faced, the people of Isadore put much of the blame on the fallen woman. Sister Janina's weakness had brought this upon them. In this opinion, they had the support of *The Nun's Rule.* "It was ordained by God in the old law that a pit should be always covered; and if any pit were uncovered, and a beast fell into it, he that uncovered the pit should make it good. This is a very terrible word to a woman who exposes herself to the view of men. She is represented by the person who uncovers the pit. The pit is her face, and her white neck, and her light eye, and her hand if she stretch it forth in his sight. And moreover all that belongs to her, whatsoever it be, through which sinful love might the sooner be excited, our Lord calleth a pit."

While the court was wrangling over punishment and guilt in the murder of Sister Janina, a movement was afoot within the Catholic Church to cover the "pit" back up and bring a new priest to Holy Rosary. Their efforts began with this unsigned letter, that closed with simply "Xto" in deference to Pope Pius, that reached beyond Isadore, beyond their home state, across Lake Michigan to a Polish community on the distant shores of Wisconsin.

Very Rev. Francis Mandl, O.F.M.
Franciscan Monastery
Pulaski, Wis.,

Very Reverend and dear Father,
    The Very Rev. Administrator of the diocese, Rev. Edv. A.
Lefebvre, directs me to write you on a very important matter. It is
very imperative that a Mission be given to the members of Holy
Rosary Church, Isadore (Cedar, Mich.) on account of scandal given
by the late pastor. The Administrator instructs me to explain
conditions so that you may understand what is necessary.
    The late pastor got his housekeeper in trouble, who recently gave
birth to a child. This became known to all the people of the parish
and consequently Father had to resign and is now doing penance.
To make matters worse there, the remains of the Sister Superior
who disappeared eleven years ago, were found under the church
there, and it is now suspected that the housekeeper of the pastor
who was there at that time is guilty of this murder. The matter is
now in the hands of the county officials, and I suppose this affair
has come to your attention through the newspapers. You can
imagine what a sensation and scandal both these affairs have
produced among the people of that parish.
    Could you therefore, Rev. Father, send us a Father who would
take charge of this parish for three or four months, or at least to
give a Mission there as soon as possible. Can you let us know when
we might expect him? One of our young assistants has been sent
there to take charge temporarily of the parish.

> Hoping you may see your way to grant
> this request, I am to remain,
> Sincerely yours in Xto

Later that spring, the prayers of the people of Isadore, Holy Rosary's Felician nuns, and the anonymous correspondent were answered. True to
the needs of the parish, the diocese in Wisconsin did not send just anyone. Rev. Stephen Narloch, a native son born in Isadore on December 23,
1886, and ordained into the priesthood June 24, 1913, arrived home to
lead the very church where he had been baptized thirty-three years ear-

lier. "In 1919 Father Stephen Narloch, a son of the Parish, became the fifth pastor of the church," states a church history. "He turned pessimism into new hope."

In its history, Holy Rosary would see more than forty of its daughters and eight of its sons commit themselves to religious life. The Narloch family alone would ultimately give three sons to the priesthood—Stephen, but also his older brother Andrew, ordained in 1909, and his younger brother Adalbert, ordained in 1925. It was the middle brother, Stephen, who was called to take charge of Holy Rosary at its darkest moment. It would take one of their own to reignite the locals' faith that the church still deserved to lead in matters of the body, mind, and spirit.

Finally, the Church had chosen well. Father Narloch had the natural authority of Father Andrew, the kind nature of Father Leo, and the brains of Father Edward. For moral leadership, Isadore could do no better than looking into the pure, human soul of one of their own.

At the psychological hospital, the depths of Stella's mind continued to be under scrutiny, though her body and spirit were not faring too well, either. After three weeks under the care and observation of Dr. Barrett and his staff, a startling story came to the surface. It did not concern the murder but was offered by Stella to her caretakers as an explanation for her odd behavior and questionable mental state. "Mr. Kinnucan tortured me in that place," Stella told Dr. Barrett. "He was not good to me and it was through him that I lost my health and now I will never get it back."

After Stella revealed some of her mistreatment in the county jail, the clinical notes on her confinement detailed some positive changes in her behavior. She no longer scratched at her face or pulled her own hair, no longer pretended to play music. She expressed an interest in spending time with the other patients and didn't pass the whole of her days lying in bed. She smiled occasionally and even spoke some English words fluently. Other times though, she was quiet and reflective almost to the point of being in some sort of impenetrable trance.

"The oddity of behavior gradually disappeared after the first few weeks, but recurred in fragments in periods in which there could be no question of her being in an unclear mental state," observed Dr. Barrett.

"Even now when she is more consistently better behaved, one can induce very marked emotional episodes, with grotesque behavior, by drawing her attention to some of the incidents connected with her difficult situation."

After Dr. Barrett encouraged her to communicate with him further, his patient's full version of her jailhouse torture at the hands of the sheriff and the spy was, to his horror, finally revealed. Stella told her doctor that on a late April evening, the second night of her incarceration, Sheriff Kinnucan came to her cell alone, and that's when the cruelty began.

"Would you like to see Sister Janina?" the sheriff had asked.

Stella raised herself off her cot. Had the nun come to life again? she wondered aloud. The sheriff did not answer but had just asked her again if she would like to see the nun.

"Yes, I would like to see her."

"All right then, come on," the sheriff said, unlocking her cell.

The two walked to the doorway of a small room at the back of the jail. Sheriff Kinnucan opened the door and pushed Stella inside the darkness. She stumbled in and tried to get her bearings. "I did not see anything but just some bones and two candles," she told the doctor. "The bones were laid out on something long like a table, and the head, the skull, had strings like threads and he came to me and was opening up the mouth and then closing it with those strings. Then I heard the spy's voice behind me shriek out, 'You killed me! You killed me!'"

Fear overtook Stella then, she said, and though the sheriff began yelling out something else, she could not remember, or perhaps never understood, what it was that he was shouting. She did hear him call loudly to the jailor, Mr. Anderson, to shut the door.

"I got scared when he hollered loud to shut the door. I did not know where he was going to put me. There was just the two candles there beside the bones. I was in there about two hours. Afterward, I do not know what did become of me." Stella told Dr. Barrett that she fainted then and woke up the next morning on her cot, fully clothed and alone, inside her jail cell.

Another time, Stella told Dr. Barrett, the spy turned off all the lights in the jail and pulled shades down over the windows. She donned a long black robe and a mask that made her appear to Stella to be the devil, and then the woman stood in the corner of the cell the two women prisoners shared. Eerie-sounding noises emanated from the spy's slitlike mouth and she advanced on Stella, drawing out two bones from behind her robe. "These belonged to Josephine Mezek!" she shouted at Stella. "You must tell me all you know about her murder!"

When Stella professed both her innocence and her ignorance of the crime, the spy, "the devil," beat her with the bones. This torture was practiced on her night after night, Stella said; sometimes the sheriff himself wore his own black robe and participated wholeheartedly in the beatings. Once, he brought along two other men, also in robes and masks, whom she did not recognize, and together the four circled her in her cell chanting, "We are the ghosts of Josephine Mezek . . . We are the ghosts of Josephine Mezek." Another time Sheriff Kinnucan threw her against the headboard of her iron bed so hard that she bruised her side and the injury continued to pain her for many days afterward.

"I had never been in jail before, but at first I was not scared or afraid because I knew I was not guilty. I had a prayerbook and [rosary] beads in jail with me. They were of comfort to me because I knew God will help me. I used them in my devotions, but then Mr. Kinnucan took them away. I was reciting my beads when he came in and he gathered up my books and took a hold of the beads and shook them at me. 'This is not for you,' he told me."

Alone, abused, stripped of her rosary and her prayerbook, Stella told Dr. Barrett that she went crazy, and that was the reason she came to be in his care. She had never experienced any episodes of mental illness before this. Though he was still not convinced that his patient was not simply feigning insanity to shirk a murder charge, he believed her story of the rough treatment she'd received under Sheriff Kinnucan enough to alert her attorneys.

Within days of telling Dr. Barrett her story, Stella was visited in the hospital by an officer from the Washtenaw County Court, which serviced the city of Ann Arbor. This officer took a deposition regarding these allegations, and the one-page document was later filed with the court in Leelanau County by Campbell and Glassmire, Stella's attorneys.

Though Judge Mayne had said in his ruling of May 13 that no further information was to be filed with the court until a determination on the defendant's sanity could be gathered, they felt that these revelations were important enough to defy that ruling.

In the deposition, Stella detailed the repeated beatings, the talking skull on strings, and how she had known from the beginning that Mary Tylicka was not a social worker, and not a criminal, but a spy. She also said that the sheriff had told her that Father Andrew Bieniawski was dead, that her daughter Mary was sick, and that her lawyers had given up and quit the case. "Deponent further says that if she is to be again confined in jail she does not want to be under the charge of Kinnucan nor any of his deputies, that she is innocent of any crime, and that there is no occasion for the treatment she has received while a prisoner awaiting trial."

On June 12, Dr. Alfred Barrett petitioned the court for more time. His deadline to report to the court was fast approaching and he had not yet made a determination. Thirty days was simply not long enough, he argued, to unravel the mind of Stanislawa "Stella" Lipczynska. "Dr. Barrett, of the Psychopathic Hospital, Ann Arbor, who is conducting an examination of Mrs. Lipczynska to determine the status of her mentality, has asked an extension of time to complete his study of her case," the newspaper stated, happy to have news of any kind to report. "Normally, thirty days are sufficient to test the sanity of a patient. However, Dr. Barrett does not feel justified in filing his final opinion until he has had a little more time to pursue his investigation. Affairs in the Sister Mary case have been at a virtual standstill for some time, and will remain so until the alienists decide whether or not the defendant is insane."

The hearing on Stella's mental state that would decide whether there was to be a trial had been scheduled to begin June 24, 1919, but was now postponed until July 10. Patience was again called upon by the spectators, the attorneys, and the court. This virtue was in short supply in Judge Mayne, and he granted the doctor's request but vowed there would be no more delays.

Diagnosis: Sane.

On Thursday, July 10, after a meeting in chambers with Judge Mayne, the four doctors he had selected two months ago to examine Stella submitted the following unanimous determination to the court.

The physicians appointed by you to examine into the mental condition of Stanislawa for the purpose of determining whether or not she is so diseased in mind as to be unable to appear in Court as a defendant on a charge of murder, beg leave to submit their report.

In a final conclusion it would seem that the peculiar mental state of this patient is one that is either a hysterical manifestation or is one that is deliberately assumed by her for her own purposes. To differentiate clearly between these two aspects is not easy as both may merge intangibly into one another and both serve the same purpose, one unconsciously and the other consciously. The purpose of both is to escape from a situation that is painful and one which the personality does not wish to meet.

It is our opinion that at the present time this patient: 1. Understands questions and can interpret her relation to those around her. 2. She is not dominated by ideas not based on facts that compel her to act with uncontrollable impulses. 3. She has the capacity at this time to control her conduct and actions in an orderly manner. 4. There is no evidence that she is intellectually so enfeebled by disease that she cannot choose between right and wrong, or understand the nature of her actions.

From the foregoing we are of the opinion that Stanislawa Lipczynska is not so diseased in mind that she is unable to appear as defendant in the present issue. Her most striking condition is that she suddenly became insane while in prison charged with murder.

Signed, Alfred Barrett, A. S. Rowley, Joseph F. Slepica, James A. King.

Stella's seven-week reprieve from the clutches of the Leelanau County law was coming to a close. On July 29, 1919, she would stand trial for the first-degree murder of Sister Mary Janina. Until that day, she would remain in the Psychopathic Hospital under the clinical eye of Dr. Barrett. During the trial she would remain in custody of county officials.

Though this suggestion was made by the prosecution, it was of a calculating nature—a crafty and strategic move not lost on reporters. "At the hospital she will receive every care, and as her improvement while there has been quite pronounced, it is figured she will be in excellent shape for the trial."

Following the psychological evaluation, though she continued to be housed in Ann Arbor, it was made clear by the court that Stella was back under the legal control of Sheriff Kinnucan, who, the court reiterated, "has the authority to take possession of her whenever he sees fit." The details of her earlier treatment by him were given no notice at all by the court. The affidavit she gave was shuffled aside, just one of the many pages in a court record that was growing to excessive proportions.

Locals greeted news of a trial with a combination of relief and zeal. That someone could get away with murder in their county was unthinkable. That they would be treated to entertainment on a dramatic scale was now a given. Even those who couldn't get a seat in the courtroom could follow it in one of the many newspapers whose editors dispatched their reporters back to northern Michigan.

"Leelanau officials are determined to clear up the mystery to the satisfaction of the public, if it takes a dozen years to do it," one newspaper reported.

By the summer of 1919, only a confession and vengeance would satisfy the public now, and few were willing to wait years to see it.

The Trial

Summer, 1919

> Confession shall be bitter, inasmuch as
> the sin, at one time, was thought sweet.
> On Doomsday our black sins on the
> one side shall sternly accuse us of our
> soul-murder; on the other side stands
> Justice; above us the angry judge. The
> sinner being thus beset, how shall it
> then stand with him? There is nothing
> but that severe sentence—that awful,
> and above all terrible sentence.
>
> —*The Nun's Rule*

"NOT GUILTY."

As scheduled, on the afternoon of July 29, the defendant was brought inside the Leland courthouse and made to stand in front of Judge Mayne. There was not an inch of shoulder space in the gallery. Farmers, farm wives, shopkeepers, and community leaders were squeezed in together with nuns, witnesses, deputies, and priests. For weeks locals had been reading the newspapers and sharing gossip about the tribulations of the suspected murderess, and today would provide many their first opportunity to finally get a glimpse of her.

The spectators' heads turned and leaned in to one another when Stella stood. They first remarked upon her emaciated countenance; she was so thin, they said, that a lock on her cell door would be moot. If she so desired she could turn sideways and slip through the bars.

She was small, too, smaller even than they had expected, and looked so weak and haggard. Her dress hung loosely on her bony form as if it had been sewn for someone far stouter, and the once black fabric was faded to a washed-out gray. Her hair was pulled into a chignon so tight it stretched the skin of her face over each eye socket. The frightening prune-faced woman who had once ruled over the domestic affairs of Holy Rosary so completely had shriveled into a harmless raisin. What kind of threat to public safety was this?

From his elevated post on the bench, it was Judge Mayne who read the charge, answering their unspoken question.

"Stanislawa Lipczynska, late of the City of Manistee, Manistee County, Michigan, you have been charged with feloniously, willfully, and with malice aforethought, killing and murdering one Josephine Mezek, also known as Sister Mary John, and as Sister Mary Janina, of Isadore convent. This charge is contrary to the peace and dignity of the People of the State of Michigan. How do you so plead?"

Stella opened her mouth to speak, but no sound came out. Her two attorneys stood on either side of her, looked down at their tiny client and she up at them, but not one of the three spoke an answer to the charge that now hung in the courtroom. After several moments of silence from the officers of the court, and a crescendo of murmuring from the gallery, Judge Mayne was finally forced to answer his own question, and he entered a plea of "not guilty" for the accused.

Howard Campbell, Stella's lead attorney, then found his voice and found it mightily.

"We move for a change of venue, Your Honor," he said. "Because of the nature of the crime for which respondent is accused and because of the size of Leelanau County and its small population, a person accused as such will be unable to secure a fair and impartial trial as the law and constitution of our State contemplate.

"As example of this, I submit to the court the following: During the examination of the People's material witnesses, particularly Jacob Flees, Sister Mary Hillaria, Sister Mary Veronica, and Sister Mary Antonia, the attendance of spectators was heavy, and the testimony of said witnesses apparently pleased said spectators because of the several applauses given by the audience.

"And, that the newspaper at Traverse City has been made ac-

quainted with our various efforts on behalf of our client, as well as with
the results of these, and said failures to accomplish anything for or on
her behalf have been spread, at large, through newspaper articles circulated throughout the entire district. Said newspaper articles cannot but
have a prejudicial effect against our client and a wholesome effect favorable to the prosecution.

"Each and every effort made by respondent's attorneys for her in
Court has been met with failure. Because of the prejudice now existing
in Leelanau County, Michigan, deponents herein believe that it will be
impossible to secure for our client a fair and impartial trial of the crime
for which she is accused, and so we now make a formal demand for a
change of venue."

As if to support Campbell's argument that there existed a prejudiced
public, boos and groans came immediately from the gallery. Judge
Mayne struck his gavel to quiet the outbursts and then indicated that before he ruled on the defense's motion, he desired a response from the
prosecution. The county's new prosecutor obliged him.

"All the details of this case have indeed been reported here, Your
Honor, but they have been given an even wider circulation in practically
every other county in the state than Leelanau and Grand Traverse," said
Clinton Dayton. "The state newspapers have published many stories
about this case and their circulation is much wider. We would argue
against a change of venue."

This back-and-forth went on for some time, with the defendant
seeming to understand very little of it. She had yet to be given an interpreter for the trial, and though she understood some basic English, the
attorneys and the judge were in full possession of their judicial vocabu-
laries and now used them freely. A change of venue, if granted, would
have certainly caused another delay, and there was still much to do before a trial could begin, including selecting a jury.

And so, late in the afternoon, the judge ruled against a change of
venue, adding one more failure in the long list of efforts by the defense.
"As far as publicity is concerned, there will be a general knowledge of
this case anywhere else in the state," Judge Mayne explained. "Leelanau
is comprised almost entirely of rural districts, with no large cities or
towns. It has been my experience that the residents here know less about
the case than dwellers in large cities. More people have spoken to me

about this case when I've been in Detroit, than right here in Northern Michigan."

Jury selection would begin September 25, and Judge Mayne said he anticipated no problems in finding a dozen willing, capable, and impartial citizens to decide the fate of the woman who had sat mute in front of him throughout the entire day.

When court finally recessed, the defense did achieve one victory. For the weeks leading up to the trial and for the duration of it, their client would indeed remain in the custody of the sheriff's office, but it would be in name only. Stella would rest in the care of probate judge Martin Brown, and not Sheriff Kinnucan, and would be housed in a room at his personal residence and would be attended to by his mother. Should her mental condition worsen, Judge Brown had the authority to commit Stella locally to one of the cottages on the grounds of the Traverse City State Hospital.

Considering all they had asked for and been denied—the most pressing of these the change of venue—this legal win may have seemed small to her attorneys, but it was of paramount importance to Stella. Only she knew what torture she had been subjected to at the hands of the sheriff. Only she knew what the lawman was capable of in the interest of extracting a confession from her. And only she knew if the fragile state of her mind was real, or secretly contrived to escape his grasping hand of justice.

So far, she wasn't talking.

It took more than eleven years, but religion finally entered into the case in an official way. Despite the fact that a Felician nun had been murdered, her body later found under a place of worship by a priest and his sexton, and all indications even pointed to knowledge of the crime within the Catholic hierarchy, religion itself had been strangely absent from both the investigation and the court proceedings. That was, until now. The jury box, of all places, provided its introduction into the formal record.

"Do you belong to the Catholic Church?" each prospective juror, then termed a "venireman," was asked by attorneys for both sides, when they stepped forward. "Do you attend Mass?" and "Have you heard priests or other officials of the Catholic Church discussing the disappearance of Sister Mary or the arrest of Mrs. Lipczynska?" followed.

The defense's concern was that these "insular and superstitious" Polish Catholics might have, in their minds, already tried and convicted Stella with nothing more exact than gossip and innuendo. Conversely, the prosecution worried that Catholics, Polish Catholics in particular, might identify with the housekeeper, feel pity toward her, and acquit.

The final question that probed their religious beliefs was this: "Supposing you thought that by rendering a decision one way or the other, the Catholic Church would be hurt. Would that influence your verdict?" Anyone who answered "yes" was automatically eliminated.

In the end, there were Catholics seated on the jury but none from Isadore. Every address of Leelanau County's sixteen hundred residents was culled for prospective veniremen but that one. Judge Mayne disqualified the whole village from serving. Though women had long been barred from serving on juries, Wayne County, which includes Detroit, had begun allowing women to serve since March of that year. Women would not be called to the jury box in Leelanau County though for a decade.

After more than a week of questioning, five panels of twelve prospects each were randomly selected from three hundred eligible names, and a jury was finally seated. There was not a Pole or a woman among them.

Charged with deciding the fate of Stella were Joseph Bussey, a farmer in Leland; John Shalda, Henry Eckardt, and Bill Wilsey, farmers in Cleveland township; William Challender, a farmer in Suttons Bay; W. C. Ray, a hotelkeeper in Glen Arbor, and John Westcott, a farmer there; Herbert Lindley, a farmer in Bingham; John Young and C. H. Treat, farmers in Empire; John Bright and John Shorter, farmers in Kasson township.

In rural areas at the turn of the century and for some years afterward, everyone worked on Saturdays, including the court. It was assumed that would continue to be the case. But even though he was from another county, Judge Mayne seemed to know what worried the minds of his jury and decided to make a rare exception. Late in the afternoon on Friday, October 3, the judge gazed down upon the dozen men in the jury box. He took in their calloused hands and weathered faces, their clean but battered clothing and the shuffle of their heavy-soled boots. These twelve were all farmers save one, and so without further thought the judge banged his gavel for a weekend recess. For this one Saturday, court would be closed in Leelanau County in favor of something even more important. Potatoes.

"I'm letting you go to your homes over the weekend," he told them, a rare privilege from the punctual judge. "We're going to be starting the real work on Monday morning and I'd like it to be minus any worry on your part for your potato crop. Take care of your fields over the next two days and get everything in order at your homes, because on Monday, you will be sequestered."

While the jury saw to their crops, Sheriff Kinnucan deputized a local man by the name of Levi M. Pheatt, and the staff of Leland's Schwarz Hotel aired out linens, swept floors, and stocked the larder with provisions. From here on out, Pheatt would be in charge of the jury's safety and adherence to the law, and the staff of the Schwarz Hotel, Anna and Blanche Schwarz proprietors, would be in charge of their room and board.

A lodging choice that had been all but closed for the winter, the Schwarz Hotel, more commonly known as the Riverside Inn, was a favorite among summer tourists. An advertisement boasted, "Good Fishing, Boating, Bathing, Summer Sports." A postcard from the hotel mailed in 1910 and featured in *Vintage Views of Leelanau County* further detailed its charms: "The house is large and comfortable with fifty fine, airy rooms. It is open year round, and gives one the solid permanent, homelike comfort that many exclusively summer homes lack. The guests enjoy a bountifully spread table, supplied with seasonable fish, fowl, fruit and vegetables from the great lake and the immediate countryside."

In this trial, "sequestered" meant a private room in the hotel under the watchful eye of Pheatt, and the daily admonishments from Judge Mayne to speak of the case only in the jury room and nowhere else. The "seasonable" food boasted about in the postcard in October would probably have meant canned, frozen, or boiled.

Though the hotel would burn down four years later, the jurors would be well cared for during the trial. They were about to become local celebrities, and even during the usually uneventful jury selection, the courtroom was filled to the brim. If those in the gallery didn't know each other before the trial began, they were now fast friends. Women, especially, were known to pass their entire day in the courtroom, forgoing lunch so as not to lose their seat. After a few days of this, most grew wise and packed a picnic.

"There are some Leelanau residents who put in most of their time listening to examination of jurymen, are present when court convenes and are there to the finish," observed a newspaperman. "Many farmers also find an hour or two a day to listen to the proceedings. They bring their wives in the early morning, go back to their labors and return later in the day in time to hear a bit of the case before supper."

The drama they were expecting to see came initially not from Stella, but from her daughter, Mary Flees. She had arrived from Milwaukee, accompanied by her husband, John, and was among the spectators during jury selection. While many in the gallery clapped, shouted, and even cheered, Mary cried. What set her off was a question posed by the defense to each prospective juror. The twelve men who would decide her mother's fate were each asked this: "Could you, knowing that this woman is a poor widow woman, working as a housekeeper for her living, still give her the consideration that you would a person in a higher station of life?"

Each man answered solemnly that they could do so, and each time their answer brought forth loud sobs from Mary Flees so wrenching that her outbursts moved several of the spectators themselves to tears.

The file on the case was growing. On Monday morning, October 13, Sheriff Kinnucan delivered yet another piece of official paperwork into the increasingly full hands of Judge Mayne. It was a list of people that either the defense or the prosecution might call to testify. On it were written the names of one hundred people, each a potential witness in what was now being called "the most heinous crime in the county's history." At the top this list was titled "100 Witnesses of Isadore." Not counting children, this number made up close to a tenth of the population of all of Leelanau County.

Before a single of these witnesses would be called to testify, Prosecutor Dayton made his opening remarks for the People. In a full courtroom eerily silent except for the simultaneous intake of breath at his revelations, Dayton vowed to prove the following.

"That Sister Mary Janina was killed in the basement of the Isadore church Friday, August 23, 1907, by Mrs. Lipczynska, the respondent.

"That the nun was going into the basement of the church to obtain some paper flowers contained there in a box, the flowers to be used for decoration of the school, which was to be blessed.

"That the respondent struck the nun on the head with a blunt instrument, knocking her unconscious.

"That the respondent hurriedly dug a grave eighteen inches deep in the basement of the church, the grave being shorter than Sister Mary.

"That the nun was placed in this grave, her knees doubled up, and that, still alive, she was buried, her body being covered with earth.

"That the respondent had been jealous of the nuns and had called them, 'priest's wives,' and names unprintable.

"That the respondent has made a full confession of just how the alleged murder was committed.

"That the respondent has told how she feigned insanity since her imprisonment, and that she told certain persons beforehand that she was going to feign insanity.

"That the secret of the alleged crime has been known by church officials since it was committed."

Spectators shuffled in their seats and turned to look at one another as the prosecutor paced up and down in front of the jury box. The women forgot all about their picnic lunches sitting untouched on their laps, though the noon hour was long past.

Poor Sister Janina had been buried alive, they whispered to each other, and the Church had perhaps even known about it all along.

"I remember the 23rd of August, 1907. I was pastor of Holy Rosary Church at Isadore. On the morning of that day I was at home, 'round the school, 'round the premises, 'round my bees, my barn, my pheasants, alligator, foxes, and rabbits."

The first witness for the People, a familiar face to many, was Father Andrew Bieniawski. Dressed in the traditional black cassock that reached almost to the floor, he strode to the witness stand, shoulders back and head held erect. His implied message was this: no shame shall be attached to me, nor to my station, by this trial or by what I reveal.

"My name is Andrew Bieniawski," he announced to the room, smiling. "I live in Manistee and have resided there since 1914. Prior to that time I resided at Isadore."

After repeating that he had been seeing to the outdoor chores, the priest detailed his fishing trip on the afternoon Sister Janina disappeared, his arrival home, and the worrisome news of the nun's disappearance. He told of the search he and the other Sisters had made for the missing sister that evening, and of subsequent searches organized in the days to come. He told of enlisting the help of county authorities and that of his own parishioners. He detailed his trip to Detroit and the tireless work of the private detective the priest had hired with his own money.

For two hours Father Andrew testified without interruption, not once deviating from his arrogant bearing. When he was finished, he folded his hands and settled them on his knees, lifted his chin a fraction, as was his habit, and gave a measuring stare to the spectators.

Judge Mayne indicated to Stella's attorney, Peter Glassmire, that he could cross-examine the witness.

"Father," Glassmire asked from his seat, almost casually, "it was stated by the prosecution that enmity existed between the defendant and Sister Janina. Did you ever observe any enmity between the housekeeper and the Sisters?"

"No, never," Father Andrew answered. "The Sisters had their own table and rooms."

"They ate and slept and taught in the convent?" Glassmire asked.

"Yes."

"Did you ever hear this defendant say anything detrimental to the character of Sister Janina or the Sisters?"

"Not before she disappeared."

"Well, what did she say after she disappeared?"

"That she was ungrateful for all the care we had shown her and the solicitude about her health, that she was ungrateful if she intended to go and didn't tell us, that she went so quietly and made so much disturbance."

If Glassmire had been trying to make the point to the jury that Stella and the nuns were on good terms, he failed. Instead, the impression they had was this: even the defense knew that division existed among the women of Father Andrew's household.

In his redirect the prosecutor made an effort to get into the record that the Isadore nuns had an established history of receiving ill treatment at the hands of Stella. And, more important, that they were afraid of her. In 1905 when the first school and convent burned down, the Sisters had nowhere to live and were temporarily housed in the rectory. The prosecution had obtained information that this was an unsatisfactory arrangement.

"Didn't they object to going to your house because they were afraid of Mrs. Lipczynska?"

"We object!" the defense shouted. "Immaterial and incompetent."

"And didn't you have to assure them that they wouldn't come in contact with the defendant before they would go there? Didn't one Sister complain to you about the conduct of Mrs. Lipczynska toward her, and didn't you go to Mrs. Lipczynska and make her go and ask the pardon of this Sister, on account of Mrs. Lipczynska offering her personal violence?"

"We object to that as immaterial and incompetent and they can't impeach their own witness," the defense reiterated.

"Question withdrawn," Dayton said.

And with that, Judge Mayne recessed court for the day. The trial would reconvene first thing the next morning, when the People would continue to present their case.

Stella went back to Judge Brown's house, and her attorneys went to their makeshift offices in the courthouse to review their case. The spectators went home to their families and their farms and their fencepost gossip.

When everyone else had left, Deputy Levi Pheatt accompanied the jury on their silent walk back to the Riverside Inn. They were barred from talking with each other about the case, and so, even in the "solid permanent, homelike comfort" of the hotel, were left with their own thoughts.

Seared in their minds had to be the image of Isadore's Felician Sisters, their convent burned, with no place to turn for shelter but the domain of the defendant. Out of the fire these desperate Sisters went, as the prosecutor had just detailed, and directly into the angry heat of Stella's frying pan.

A Sister lost, and then found.

While Father Andrew had already detailed the former, the first witness to testify the next morning told the gruesome details of the latter. In the first two days of testimony, the beginning and end of the search for Sister Janina were revealed, with the middle portions of the story left for the remainder of the trial.

Jacob Flees, Holy Rosary's sexton, took the stand, and both his language and his posture could not have been more different than Father Andrew's. By the time Jacob was hired as sexton, it was Father Edward Podlaszewski who was priest at Holy Rosary, and Father Andrew had already been transferred to St. Joseph's in Manistee.

"Father Podlaszewski was the parish priest at Isadore when I commenced work there. I did go into the basement, looking for bones. Father Podlaszewski went with me," Jacob Flees said. The courtroom had gone completely silent. Even the autumn wind that had been battering the windows quieted, making the room feel like an eerie bubble, stationary in time.

"It was about three o'clock in the afternoon and I had a lantern. I had a spade with me and I dug. I kept shoving the spade in the ground. I dug down about eighteen inches and I struck something which sounded like a stone, and we thought it was a stone. I dug out a little more dirt, and then I handed Father Podlaszewski the spade, and put my hand down there so I could feel what it was. I pulled it out and it was a bone.

"After we got about so deep he throwed down the shovel and I kneeled down alongside and commenced feeling around and commenced picking out some of those bones, and I picked them out and handed them to him and he put them in a box.

"I found bones like rib bones, back bones, and so forth. It was in the shape just the same as a human person would lay. The head was south, and the skull rolled in onto the ribs, and I picked that up and handed it to him. The bones were in an up and down position, just the same as if a person were doubled up, with the knees drawn up."

Here Jacob lifted his own knees to his chest and circled his legs with this arms. Just the sound of his rustling clothes was almost deafening in the quiet.

"The general appearance of those bones was as if the person was throwed in on their back."

Later, Jacob said, he built a proper wooden box for the bones and, at Father Edward's direction, filled it with the bones and buried it in the cemetery adjoining the church school. This second grave had been directly in front of a large cross marking the center of the cemetery.

"Why didn't you notify the officers that you had put some bones over into the graveyard?" Glassmire asked him.

"I thought it was the priest's place to notify them. I did all this in the dark of the night, so nobody could see me, and I never on my part told anybody."

"You wanted to keep it an absolute secret?"

"Yes, sir."

"Was there anything said to you by Father Podlaszewski, placing it upon you as a secret?"

"Yes, sir."

"When did he mention that you should keep it a secret?"

And here it was as if Jacob did not hear the question. He had other, more pressing details of his dark work with Father Edward on his conscience, and it was these that he wanted to share with the court.

"I did not strike that skull in any way with my shovel or spade," Jacob said, his voice rising. "I never seen a crack in this skull. I don't know whether it was there or not. But I *did not* take this skull out of the grave with my shovel and lift it up and show it to Father Podlaszewski. And he *did not* tell me to throw it from my shovel into the box."

If a crack had been found, Jacob intimated, it had been made by the instrument of death wielded by the killer, and not by his own innocent garden tool. All else about the crime remained a mystery to him, but of that he was certain.

The People's next witness was Father Edward Podlaszewski, and much would be revealed before he would leave the stand—key parts of the defense's strategy, the reason for Jacob Flees's uncharacteristic and seemingly random outburst, and even Prosecutor Dayton's contention that the church itself was an accomplice to the murder after the fact. All of this from one passive and humiliated priest.

"I formerly lived at Isadore in this county," Father Edward stated softly, his head down and his narrow shoulders slumped. "I was pastor of the Rosary church. While I was there, I made a search for a skeleton under the church. I made the search in company with Jacob Flees. I found the skeleton under the church."

In a quiet voice that was sometimes little more than a whisper, Father Edward recited his version of what he and Jacob had done underneath the church late that fateful autumn afternoon. His revulsion at the prospect of the task before him was evident even now, a year later, and he could not seem to make eye contact with the attorneys, the judge, the jury, or any of the spectators.

"I first left the search to Jacob. I went home to my house and remained there over half an hour when he came to me and told me that he had found a bone. I went with him to unearth the rest. I discovered the shoes and some of the leg bones, and after that I didn't do any unearthing, only I took the bones from Mr. Flees as he handed them to me and I put them in the box.

"They were taken out with a big fork. They were lifted up in order to get the amount of dirt—we thought there might be some flesh adhering to those bones, therefore we used the fork. The rib bones were mostly handled by hand.

"The skull was discovered after we viewed the rib bones. I did not see the skull when Mr. Flees first discovered it, not the first moment. I just saw it when he handed it over to me. I told Mr. Flees to be very careful not to disturb those bones and we viewed the entire torso as it lay in the grave.

"Preparations were being made to build a new church at Isadore. I made the preliminary steps in 1917 and had the plans made in 1918, the blueprints. I even bought some brick for the new church. It was to stand on the same place where the present church stands. There was to be a basement to the new church that would necessitate excavating there."

Glassmire stood for the defense's cross-examination, waving a mysterious document above his head. More paperwork to add to the reams already generated, and continuing to grow. He held the document in

front of the witness's face, shuffling through the handful of pages. This
was the notarized affidavit the priest had made almost five months earlier when he was posted at Immaculate Heart of Mary in Cleveland.

"What is this here?" Glassmire said, pointing to something at the
bottom of each page.

"That is my signature," Father Edward answered.

"You swore to this paper, everything here, didn't you?" Glassmire
asked.

"Yes, I did, but of course I did not know what you call it when one
swears to it. I gave the facts upon which the affidavit is based, and I was
asked if the contents were true, but it is not extensive enough. I did not
tell everything there. They asked me to make the affidavit, but I was at
the time mentally unbalanced."

Glassmire then read directly from the document.

"After my installation, the pastor next preceding me at Isadore remained with me over two days and said to me, 'I am afraid there will be
a scandal in this parish because the Sister who disappeared sometime
ago, I heard was buried under the church' did you so swear?"

"Yes, I did say that Father Lempke was the first who told me that."

"Was that the first that you heard anything about it?"

"Some of it. I did not intend to deceive anybody in this affidavit. I
was mentally unbalanced at the time."

"I say," Glassmire scoffed, "when you were making preparation to
testify here today, you knew you had made this affidavit, didn't you?"

"Yes, but at that time when I was making it, I didn't know that it
would be an affidavit. I was told only that a party wants information."

"You don't mean to say that you could not be relied upon to make a
true statement, do you?"

Here the prosecution objected, and their objection was sustained by
Judge Mayne. When Special Prosecutor Parm Gilbert got up to redirect
for the prosecution, he established that this mysterious affidavit had
been commissioned by the defense, and not by the prosecution. Not
only that, but it was also useless as far as the court should be concerned
because it had been given under what the witness himself termed "mental distress."

Even though it wasn't stated publicly, everyone in the room knew
the cause of that mental distress—his love affair with his teenage house-

keeper and her resulting pregnancy. This, the spectators, the judge, the witnesses, and the attorneys all knew, was the reason Father Edward was no longer in Isadore. It was the reason he would never again say a public Catholic Mass, why he hung his head on the witness stand, and even why the whole sordid mess had ever come to light and necessitated a trial in the first place.

So shameful was his sin that, even though it was common knowledge, nowhere was it entered into the extensive court records. The murder of a nun could be made public, but not a priest's sexual indiscretions. Which was the only explanation for why nothing was said, either, about the smallest bones found with Sister Janina's remains.

If he knew about the pregnancy Prosecutor Dayton did not say, and he only danced around the edges of Father Edward's indiscretions.

"You said there were certain influences brought to bear upon you. What do you mean by that?" he asked.

"Well, mental distress I believe I said," answered Father Edward.

"Was that explained to the man who took this affidavit?"

"No."

Finally, the affidavit was read aloud to the court in its entirety. The exact passage that all this legal wrangling had been getting at was this: "The sexton dug the skull out of the grave with his shovel and lifted it up on the shovel and showed it to me, and I told him to throw it into the box we had there, which he did. I did not see any break in the skull, nor any mark on the skull. [But] time after time the sexton and I, digging with our shovels, struck the bones in this grave, especially the larger ones; and the sexton, in digging for the skull, said to me before he unearthed the skull, 'I believe there is a skull there, because it strikes pretty hard there.' At this time he was driving the shovel into the earth, and right after that he unearthed the skull."

Even in a small-time rural courtroom in the early years of the twentieth century, a first-degree murder conviction depended only upon proving that one person had killed another without justification and with "malice aforethought." In order to get a jury to convict, however, sometimes other logical elements needed to be proven: the triptych of means, motive, and opportunity. If a piece of evidence as central to the prosecution's case as the victim's skull had been roughly treated when it was exhumed, the defense might be able to eliminate the first of those three elements. Or, if not eliminate means completely, at least instill reasonable doubt in the minds of the jury.

In this matter, it was Father Edward's word, made under "mental distress," against Jacob's, made right here in the courtroom. It was still early in the proceedings, but already the defense was losing ground.

By the time of the murder trial, Father Edward's religious career had taken on a distinctly transient quality. Since his comeuppance at St. Bonaventure Monastery only six months previous, he'd been sent to the hill country of Kentucky, to downtown Cleveland, Ohio, and to upstate New York. It was from New York that he had come back to northern Michigan for the trial. His wish was that while he was visiting, he could secure a post back in the area.

Father Edward also thought he might board at the Isadore rectory in the weeks before the trial started. He could visit with his former parishioners if they'd have him, and perhaps the current priest, Father Narloch, might even see his way to letting him say a public Mass.

The leaders of the Catholic Church, however, had other ideas. The same men who had sat in judgment of him at St. Bonaventure had already contemplated the possibility that Father Edward would want to participate publicly in his spiritual homecoming, and this could not be allowed. When Father Edward arrived at Holy Rosary, he found a letter waiting for him.

"The Bishop instructs me to write that he considers it unwise for you to say Mass in Isadore and therefore does not grant that permission. If you can secure some other priest to live with where the circumstances of your case are not known, the Bishop will give you permission to say Mass privately. With best wishes, I am, Chancellor A. Fitzpatrick."

Father Narloch abided by the church's wishes, and not only did Father Edward not say a Mass, he didn't even spend a single night in Isadore during his visit or, for that matter, ever again. During the trial he stayed at the same address as the jury, the Riverside Inn in Leland. Father Edward took his meals not with the jury, of course, but at another location important to the proceedings: Anna Brown's house, Judge Brown's mother.

There, seated at the old woman's dining room table, for at least two meals a day for weeks on end, were these three diners: probate judge Martin Brown; Father Edward; and Stella. No transcript exists, of course, for the discussions that took place over Anna Brown's potato stews, beef roasts, and baked squash pies that were the standard autumn fare of the day. There is, however, one brief but telling mention of this arrangement in the court transcript. "I took my meals at Mr. Brown's house perhaps three weeks or so," Father Edward testified. "While there I have talked some about this case. Since I was brought back, I have taken some interest in it."

That statement was on par with a human lung saying it took some interest in air. The case was Father Edward's past and present, and would help decide his future. The same could be said for Stella and, in a less crucial way, for Judge Brown.

If Father Edward and his dining companions spoke in depth about the case over these meals, each could certainly have held up their share of the dinner conversation. The priest, sitting on one side of the table, had found the skeleton, and the judge, sitting on another side, had sifted through the grave for the smaller bones and the personal trinkets the priest had missed. Both men thought that the housekeeper, seated on the third side of the table, possessed the murderous impulse that had set them digging in the first place.

No mention is made of a fourth diner, the cook. It is not difficult to imagine that Anna Brown preferred to take her meals alone, in the kitchen.

Backward from the murder the prosecution marched. How the diggers knew where to look was almost as important to their case as what they were looking for. On Wednesday, the court did its best to tread down the case's overgrown trail of confession, gossip, and secrecy that had led to the discovery of the murder. That this trail had been blazed by none other than holy men and pious women made for a capricious judicial excursion.

The first guide on the court's travels was Sister Mary Antonia, Mother Superior of the Felician Motherhouse in Detroit.

"Isadore parish is part of that province; it is part of my duty to supply them with teachers and I have been doing so since 1914. I knew Sister Janina," the Mother Superior testified.

Prosecutor Dayton questioned her further, asking first how she found out that the nun had been murdered.

"I received this information in the fall of 1915, at Detroit, Michigan. Sister Veronica came with Sister Pius to Detroit. They were both members of the Milwaukee province. They said that Bishop Kozlowski came to their convent and he told them that, inasmuch as he knew, Sister Janina did not leave the convent as it was related before, but she was killed by a woman and buried under the church at Isadore. That was the first I heard of the location of the remains of Sister Mary Janina. The very first time. It was not very long afterwards before I imparted that information to Father Lempke."

"Why did you tell Father Lempke about this?" Dayton asked.

"Because he was our priest, the convent's priest, and I thought he should know it and could, perhaps, do something with the remains."

Throughout the investigation, the hearing, the many court motions, and now the trial, most aspects of the murder of the nun had been followed, examined, and detailed, but now there was something new to consider. Sister Janina had not been given a funeral service. It took her order's spiritual leader to finally point this out. Whatever fate awaited the woman in the defendant's chair, Sister Janina's had already been decided by a higher authority, and she was waiting for mortals to put her remains properly to rest. Despite two graves, she had not been given a proper religious burial.

Following this path further back, Prosecutor Dayton called another nun, Sister Mary Pius, to the stand. Had she indeed heard Bishop Kozlowski talk about the murder and burial of Sister Janina? he asked.

"He came to our convent at Milwaukee to settle some matters and we entertained him, Mother Veronica and I. That was the last Thursday of July, 1915."

"State whether he gave information or made a statement there relative to where the bones or remains of Sister Mary John was."

"I should exactly state his words?"

"Yes, if you can Sister. Just what he said."

"Well, he said that Sister Mary Janina didn't leave the convent, but was killed by a woman on the premises; she was the woman that struck the sister on the head and buried her under the church."

The prosecutor would not have the opportunity to depose either Mother Veronica or Bishop Kozlowski, however. Mother Veronica was confined to the convent with ill health and high blood pressure, and Bishop Kozlowski was dead.

During that meeting in Milwaukee, Sister Pius said the Bishop had complained to them of a severe pain on the side of his neck and an overall feeling of malaise. I am not well, he told them. Nine days later, he was dead, struck down by an abscessed boil that ruptured and released its poisoned pus directly into his bloodstream.

The Mother Superior's poor health and the Bishop's death were inconvenient for the court. It meant that the conversation the Bishop shared with the two nuns could be considered hearsay and stricken from the record, despite its obvious usefulness to the prosecution. Judge Mayne pondered this and ultimately ruled in favor of the defense.

"The entire answer may be stricken out," he told the attorneys. And to the jury he said, "Gentlemen, the answer I have stricken out is not in the case now and you will not consider it. It is withdrawn from your consideration. It arose by reason of a misapprehension of the question on the part of the witness. It is not receivable, so, gentlemen of the jury, you will disregard it."

The prosecution, however, simply went at the conversation in another way. Prosecutor Dayton questioned Sister Pius only about what had been said directly to her.

"Did Bishop Kozlowski give *you* the information—make a statement as to the bones of Sister Mary Janina being buried under the church at Isadore?"

"He did."

"Did he state that her bones were buried under the church?"

"He said they were."

"Do you know whether Sister Veronica is a Sister in your Order?"

"She is in the Motherhouse."

"Do you know whether she repeated this information to Sister Antonia at Detroit?"

"She did."

"Were you present?"

"I was."

The meeting between the nuns and the bishop was now back in the court record and firmly established in the minds of the jury. Still, there was at least one more step backward in the trail of the murder that was yet to be traveled. That step would attempt to answer the questions that remained. How had the Bishop come to know about the nun's murder in the first place? How did he know that the killer was a woman? And how did he know that the victim had been buried under the church?

The prosecution next called Father Lempke to the stand. He might not have been the link between the killer and the now-deceased Bishop Kozlowski, but they would show that he was the link between the Bishop, the Sisters of Milwaukee, and Father Edward.

"I am pastor of St. Joseph's church and chaplain for the Felician Sisters at Detroit, Michigan. I have been such chaplain since October 1st, 1909. Mother Antonia is now the Mother Superior of the Felician Order there. I know Father [Edward] Podlaszewski, who was priest at Isadore. I have known him at least four or five years. I recall seeing Father Podlaszewski in the spring of 1918, at a forty hours devotion."

"State whether at that time or on any other occasion you gave Father Podlaszewski information relative to the bones of Sister Janina being under the church at Isadore."

Here the defense objected. Though the prosecution certainly had a reason for calling Father Lempke, it was lost on the defense. Judge Mayne said he understood their confusion, agreed that the testimony was not proceeding in the most logical fashion, but that he was still determined to allow Dayton and his team to prosecute Stella as they saw fit. He explained his decision this way: "In his opening statement the prosecuting attorney stated that there was a confession, and that by means of that confession he expected to show certain things. The prosecuting attorney said that he would connect the respondent directly with this matter. I am permitting him to begin at the date of finding these remains and placing it backward, instead of beginning at the other end of the story. Assuming that the prosecution is correct, that he can show these things, I am taking that for granted and I am permitting this testimony which would otherwise not be relevant. I have done so because in a mass of testimony of fifty or more witnesses, in the preparation of counsel for the people, they must necessarily have analyzed the situation and have formed a definite plan or system, and I didn't want to disarrange that plan or system by requiring them to follow what I might think was the most logical way of presenting the testimony, and I take their word that they can connect the respondent with this information."

In other words, the prosecution might have been proceeding clumsily, and not laying out their case the way Judge Mayne himself would do it if he were trying the case, but they were well within the bounds of the law, and he would let them reveal their case the way they saw fit.

Judge Mayne looked at the witness and motioned for him to answer the question, which, by now, had been all but forgotten by everyone but the judge. Dayton asked Father Lempke again whether he had told Father Edward about the bones under the church.

"On that occasion I told Father Podlaszewski that I heard the remains of Sister Janina were buried under the church."

"Did you refer to the building of the church in any way in that statement to him?"

"I did."

"In what way?"

"That the remains there would be found and we, not having sufficient proof to our minds to find the perpetrator, wanted to avoid all the trouble."

"Did you, in the same conversation, give him information as to the sources of information or from whom you obtained it?"

"Yes."

"And what did you say to him about that; what source did you name to him, if any?"

"I told him then that we received the information from Bishop Kozlowski. That I received the report directly from the Felician Sisters. From the Superior, Mother Antonia. I know nothing of the information except what the Superioress told me. I know nothing nor do I pretend to know anything of the manner in which Sister Mary Janina met her death."

The prosecution turned its attention then from the inner lives of nuns and priests, to the flights of fancy of either a very confused, or a very calculating, young woman. Next on the witness stand was Stella's daughter, the delicate and outwardly grief-stricken Mary Flees.

It had been Mary's boisterous weeping that disrupted the trial during both jury selection and the opening statements, but she had been gaining more control of her emotions as the trial wore on. By the time she was called as a witness, Mary took her seat, sat down dry-eyed and silent, and faced the gallery. Her first words were to Judge Mayne.

"Will you please give me an interpreter, dear Judge? I can't talk English."

"If you can't understand, we will try it, but first we will see," Judge Mayne answered. "Mrs. Flees, where do you live?"

Mary Flees stared back at the judge but made no attempt to answer him. He waited a moment, then tried another question.

"You went to school at Isadore, didn't you?"

She again said nothing at first, then decided to speak.

"Your honor, please give me an interpreter."

"She may have an interpreter," the judge said.

"Well, she testified in English right along at the hearing, at the examination," Prosecutor Dayton pointed out. What he didn't say was that her reactions so far to court testimony, given in English from her seat in the gallery with the rest of the spectators, had been frequent and quite obvious. She understood plenty.

"Yes but sometimes I don't understand," Mary blurted. "Sometimes I say yes when I should say no."

"Well, I will take care of you if you say no when you ought to say yes," the Judge told her. "There will be no advantage taken of you at all."

"Will your honor be so kind as to give me a Polish interpreter?" she asked again.

Judge Mayne surveyed the first few rows of the gallery. His eyes stopped on a farmer sitting in the front row.

"Do you talk English and Polish?" he asked the man.

"Yes, sir."

"Well," the judge told Mary, "you may have an interpreter. Swear him in."

To his surprise, Leelanau potato farmer and trial spectator Frank Blosvick was now the official Polish interpreter for the most complex and sensational murder trial in the region's recorded history. As luck would have it, he was uniquely qualified; he attended Holy Rosary, knew the local variations of the parish's speech patterns and had even done chores for the church before Jacob Flees was hired as sexton. With this new and familiar aide at her side, Mary opened her mouth to speak and didn't close it again for almost two hours.

"I live in Milwaukee," she began. "I have lived there about nine years. I lived at Isadore before going to Milwaukee. I am married. My maiden name was Mary Lipczynska. I am a daughter of the respondent. I remember August 1907. I was living at Father Bieniawski's house at Isadore. Father Bieniawski and Susie Bieniawski and my mother was living in the same house with me. Sister Janina was in charge of the convent and of the school. I knew all the Sisters well. I think I was seventeen at that time. I remember the day Sister Janina disappeared. No one told me to ask for an interpreter."

If this last statement made either Judge Mayne or Prosecutor Dayton suspicious of what was to come next, neither made any mention of it. Mary next told of Father Andrew's fishing trip, of waving good-bye to them as they left, and of returning to the rectory with her mother, repeating much of what other witnesses had already said.

"I don't quite remember how long we were in the kitchen after the fishing party drove away; half or three-quarters of an hour."

"Were you sworn on the examination?"

"Yes."

"Wasn't this question asked you?"

"Yes."

"Do you know any better today than you did when you were examined on the examination?"

"Yes, I know."

"You also gave testimony before Justice Nelson down in the probate courtroom the day before the examination, didn't you?"

"I did."

"And then it was all called to your mind at that time, wasn't it?"

Mary gave a long answer in Polish. When she stopped to take a breath, everyone in the courtroom who didn't speak fluent Polish looked directly at Mr. Blosvick.

"She says she was never bothered about it because she knew it was a fake and it didn't hurt her and she didn't bother her head about it."

Prosecutor Dayton waved another document in the air, shoving it at the witness much the same way he had done days earlier to Father Edward.

"This is an affidavit you made in Milwaukee to Sheriff Kinnucan, isn't it?"

"Yes, I did."

"And you told him that you and your mother were sewing, fitting sleeves on a dress?"

"Yes, sir."

"Now, going back to the time that your mother was helping you fit the sleeves, she left you after the sleeves were fitted, didn't she?"

"Yes, she left me."

"When did you see her again?"

"I heard her. In the kitchen."

"How is it you say that *now*, and yet never said that before when you were sworn? I read to you now from your affidavit which has been marked Exhibit 6: 'I, Mrs. Mary Flees, further depose and say that from the time my mother, Mrs. Stanislawa Lipczynska, left the sewing room at one-thirty p.m. on the day in question, I did not see her again until four p.m. that day when she came back to the sewing room, and during that period I didn't know, and can not say, where my mother was.' Did you swear to that?"

"Yes."

"Isn't it a fact that you did not know where your mother was after she left your room until about four o'clock that afternoon?"

Mary looked at her mother, seated directly in front of her at the defendant's table, and smiled. She answered Prosecutor Dayton's question, but tears spilled down her cheeks and she kept her gaze on Stella's face.

"Yes, I know where Mama was. Sure, I ain't *seen* her. I heard her. She was working."

"Didn't you tell Mr. Kinnucan that you didn't know where your mother was from the time she left the sewing room until she came and asked if you had seen Sister Janina?"

"I don't remember anything."

"You don't remember anything about it? Your talk with him?"

"I don't remember anything."

This back-and-forth between a weepy girl, married but yet just in her late twenties, and the respected prosecutor of Leelanau County went on for another half hour. No matter how he phrased the question, Dayton could not get Mary to admit that she had told the truth to Sheriff Kinnucan but that she was lying now. She even refused to admit that she had told two different versions of what happened that afternoon. She was sewing and was concentrating on that; she did not speak good English and might have misinterpreted the questions; she was young and inexperienced in the rules and regulations of the court.

"I signed my name to that," she said, indicating the crumpled papers in the attorney's clenched fist, "but I didn't know what I signed."

The Felician Sisters in the courtroom looked back and forth at one another but made no comment. Many of them knew Mary Lipczynska Flees from before she was married, when she was part of the Holy Rosary household. The girl was willful then and apparently little had changed. "She, then, who moveth her tongue in lying, maketh of her tongue a cradle to the devil's child," states *The Nun's Rule*, "and rocketh it diligently as a nurse."

Dayton did not hide his feelings; he was furious. In her earlier testimony, Mary's recollection of the day had given her mother ample opportunity to kill and bury Sister Janina. Without her, his case was significantly weakened. If the jury believed that Mary had heard her mother working in the next room all along, Stella couldn't have committed the murder and she would be acquitted.

To add insult to injury, in the past two hours of testimony Mary Flees had made him look like he couldn't best even a frivolous, immigrant girl who spoke only broken English. Amazingly, she'd done all this with a good-natured, if sad, veneer of naïveté. It was maddening.

"I want to introduce in evidence this affidavit, number six for identification, because it has been demonstrated that she is an adverse witness and it shows that her testimony has been changed."

Judge Mayne then delivered one of the first rulings against the prosecution. The affidavit was not admissible for now, but he would take its contents under advisement.

After their perceived loss on almost every issue that they'd battled over with the prosecution, thanks to Mary the defense had won back a bit of hard-packed legal ground.

 ❧

Privately, Dayton must have wanted to take Stella's lying daughter out to the proverbial woodshed, the way any sensible parent did with their back-talking children. Publicly, he would take his satisfaction in the specter he was about to let loose in the courtroom. Whereas yesterday's drama had been unforeseen, Dayton settled himself at the prosecution's table on Thursday morning, quite certain, almost cocky, about what was to come. Since being elected to his first term in 1894, he had been Lee-lanau County's prosecutor four separate times, his legal reign interrupted only by Hugh's election. That man's exit from the position before his term was served was evidence that Dayton was the man for the job. "By those who do not hold themselves amenable to law he is feared," wrote one local historian. "Every detail of a cause is given its due prominence and the case is argued with such skill, ability, and power that he rarely fails to gain the verdict desired."

This skill and ability Dayton was about to unleash inside the Leland courtroom to great effect. He was quite sure that the defense, not to mention that lying Mary and her murderous mother, weren't going to like his tactic, not even one little bit.

As the gallery filled with spectators, they quickly began murmuring among themselves as they filed to their seats. Once everyone was settled, the talk grew louder. There was something new in the courtroom: a long table situated directly in front of Judge Mayne. Next to it were three wooden boxes, two of which were covered with short planks. The judge pronounced the court in session and invited the prosecution to call the day's first witness. Dayton recalled Holy Rosary's sexton. Special Prosecutor Parm Gilbert stood to conduct the questioning.

"Now Mr. Flees, I want you to look over these boxes here. Are any of these boxes the ones that you put the bones in, that you've already told us about here?"

Jacob Flees did as instructed, then looked back at his questioner.

"I know of these two boxes being brought over from Leland," he said, pointing to the boxes with lids. "Those little boards were placed over them for covering at Isadore. The open one with the gravel in it was brought here by me and Mr. Brown. We dug up twelve shovelfuls of dirt and screened that. Then we had about a half of a shovel full of gravel and that is in that other box there now."

Jacob was asked to step down and Probate Judge Martin Brown was called up to take his place. When the witnesses changed, so did the attorney for the prosecution, and Dayton stood and replaced Gilbert at the front of the courtroom.

"After the bones were dug up," Dayton asked Judge Brown, "did you go back and examine the grave and what was in it more particularly?"

"I did."

"And what did you find in doing that?"

"We found several articles; a wooden cross with an image on it, a small metal cross, a spool of thread, a scapular, a thimble, a ring, and some buttons."

"And where are these items presently?"

"In that box there."

Judge Brown was released back to his seat and the prosecution recalled Mother Superior Mary Antonia. Again, as the witnesses changed, so did the prosecution, and Gilbert was now poised to conduct the questioning. He had something shiny in his hand, and he passed it to the Sister on the stand.

"I wish, Mother, you would examine this ring and say whether that it is or is not like the rings nuns receive when you take your final vows."

The Mother Superior took the tiny ring in her hands and held it up to the light. She looked carefully at its inside and then handed it back to Gilbert.

"It was made of the same kind as our rings are made," she said.

"Is the inscription in your ring the same as in the other ring?" Gilbert asked.

"The same, yes, sir."

"Do you know whether those rings were made especially for those who took their final vows at that time?"

"They were made especially for our whole class of twenty-two sisters."

"What I mean is, can a nun go into the market and buy a ring like that?"

"No, they were made specially."

"When this ring is given to a Sister taking her final vows, what is she expected to do with it, under the rules of your Order?"

"She should wear it for her whole life. Until her death." The Mother

Superior barely got this final sentence out before she began to weep openly on the stand. *"Jezus Moj Wezystko!"* she cried out in Polish, reciting the inscription engraved on the inside of the ring she'd just handled; then, translating, "Jesus My All."

After Mother Antonia had composed herself and vacated the witness stand, the purpose of the long table sitting empty at the front of the room was finally made clear. It had been brought into the courtroom for the display of the skeleton, and for the prosecution to finally prove that a box of bones was all that remained of Sister Mary Janina.

Months earlier at the hearing to decide whether or not there would be a trial, the defense had argued that the prosecution had failed to show corpus delicti, or that a crime had been committed at all against the once missing Sister Janina. Even now, days into the trial, the defense still did not acknowledge that this had been proven, and it was one of the strategies they planned to use on behalf of their client. A strategy soon to seem ill advised.

"An awesome undertone, accentuated by the rattle of human bones, hummed in the crowded court here today," a newspaperman would later observe.

At Special Prosecutor Parm Gilbert's direction, Dr. George Fralick and Dr. James Slepica, the two local physicians and Leelanau County's official coroners, walked to the front of the courtroom, reached into the boxes with their bare hands and assembled the earth-soiled remains on the evidence table.

The spectators in the gallery sat rapt, leaning forward on their benches until their chins almost touched the backs and shoulders of the person in front of them. The room was completely silent except for the sound of each soiled bone being laid in its rightful place among the others on the table.

At one point, Dr. Fralick held up one of the recovered shoes, untied the laces, and turned it upside down. Small bones, dirt, and a plume of dust poured out onto the table. When he got to the skull, Dr. Fralick settled it in its rightful place at the top of the neck bones, turning it sideways so that the sightless eyeholes pointed directly at the defense table, and Stella.

Heads in the gallery turned from the boxes, to the doctors, to the table, to Stella. If the spectators were expecting her to break down, faint, tremble, or display any sign of her earlier psychosis, they were disappointed. A flush could be seen in her hollowed-out cheeks, but she sat up straight and defiantly returned the skeleton's vacant stare.

Though he still had other orchestrations in his conviction strategy for the jury yet to hear, this was Prosecutor Dayton's longed-for moment of judicial crescendo. Here was the murder trial of the decade, and he had just invited Death into the proceedings, and then displayed its awesome power for all to see. Moments earlier the holy ring the Mother Superior had handled seemed quaint and tinged with meaning; now its glint was more in keeping with light bouncing off the Grim Reaper's scythe. A skeleton in their midst changed everything, and the prosecutor knew it.

Dayton strutted back and forth at the front of the courtroom, putting himself between the spectators and the table. He paused before calling his next witness so that everyone could get a good look. Nothing, he surely believed, could trump the bones now laid out on the table. Mary's perjury the day before had come as a surprise, and he had been unprepared for it. There would be no surprises today, he had told Gilbert earlier, but in that supposition, he was again mistaken. This time, though, the bolt from the blue would be in his favor.

"Judge," said a female voice from the gallery, "may we have a moment with our Sister?"

With every pair of eyes upon her, Mother Antonia stood and faced Judge Mayne. The entire row where she had been seated was filled on both her right and her left with brown wool and black veils and busy hands working over rosaries. Some had been reading *The Nun's Rule.* "Let everyone attend to their own business and not meddle with that which is another's," it advises. On this, they struggled.

Some of the nuns were from the Felician Motherhouse in Detroit, but many were local. Holy Rosary School had been closed all week so that the nuns who taught there could attend the trial.

"Of course, Mother," Judge Mayne said, nodding. "Please, do as you will."

The judge had granted permission for this highly unusual request without hesitation. He could have denied the Mother Superior's request outright, he could have called a recess, he could have delayed her request until the end of the day, or, at the very least, he could have sent the jury out of the room temporarily. He did none of these things, and whether he intended it or not, by his swift grant of permission he was standing with the prosecution in their argument that this was indeed Sister Janina.

In the present day, such a request alone might be cause for a mistrial; in Judge Mayne's courtroom, however, it was the high drama everyone had been waiting for.

At the judge's nod of assent, Mother Antonia and sixteen of her Sisters stood and filed silently to the front of the room, circled the table where the skeleton lay, and clasped each other's hands. Their shoulders heaved with silent weeping, and Mother Antonia led them in the recitation of their ritual prayer for the dead. It came out as a quiet chant. The rest of those in the courtroom—attorneys, lawmen, farmwives, and the jury—watched in silent awe. The defense watched in horror.

At the end of their lives, Felician nuns are supposed to be given a special burial ceremony by their order. In the convent's public room, the Sister's body would be laid out in an austere pine coffin atop a bed of wood shavings. The evening before her burial, composer Gregorio Allegri's choral masterpiece "Miserere"—music so powerful it was once deemed by the Vatican only to be played on the week leading up to Easter and even then only in the Sistine Chapel—would fill the room where her body was on public display.

Misereme mei, Deus: secundum magnam misericordiam tuam, the convent choir would sing in Latin. *Et secundum multitudinem miserationum tuarum, dele iniuitatem meam.* Have mercy on me, O God, according to thy great mercy. And according to the multitude of thy tender mercies blot out my iniquity.

A procession of clergy, the deceased nun's fellow Sisters, and finally relatives and friends would file past; her pallbearers would be selected from among these fellow Sisters, and her coffin would follow the procession into the convent's chapel for a recitation of Vespers for the Dead. The following morning, a Requiem Mass would be said for her, and as the chapel bells tolled out the end of her physical life, the faithful would walk to the cemetery and lower her body into the ground. When her grave was covered and marked with a small white cross, the Felicians would offer her a moment of silence, then help her to heaven by singing the Salve Regina in Polish. *Witaj Krolowo, Matko milosierdzia, zycie, slody-czy I nadziejo nasza, witaj!* "Hail, holy Queen, Mother of Mercy, our life, our sweetness, and our hope."

Not one of these rituals had been observed for Sister Janina at the end of her life. There had been no singing, no praying, no chapel bells. By surrounding her now and praying over her ruined remains, Mother Antonia and the sixteen members of her order tried their best to remedy what had thus far been a woefully inadequate entry into eternity.

It was not only the spectators who held their breath as the Sisters prayed, but the officers of the court did, as well. Prosecutor Dayton would later say his thoughts were focused not on eternity, but rather the here and now. A chasm had been crossed, but as far as he was concerned, it was an evidentiary leap that had been made, and not a spiritual one.

Though he would put doctors up on the stand next, to swear to the identity of the skeleton, the Sisters' simple prayer for the dead had firmly established what the defense had argued against and medical science could only guess at—that the skeleton was Sister Janina's. The defense wouldn't dare argue against corpus delicti, now.

"We examined a collection of bones," Dr. Fralick recalled, when his turn came on the stand after Judge Mayne called for a lunchtime recess. "They were taken out of a box in the front hall of the jail. That box, marked Exhibit F, appears to be the box. I examined those bones to see whether it was a human skeleton. I found it was almost a complete skeleton of a person. Of a woman. That is determined by the shape of the pelvis."

Missing, Dr. Fralick said, were two ribs and possibly some small bones of the wrist, hand, ankle, and foot that he did not attempt to assemble or count. Some of the latter were in the rubble dumped out of the recovered shoes. Death had been caused by a fracture to the skull.

"It was a fracture inward and upward through a portion of the temporal bone across the groove of the middle meningeal artery, in the neighborhood of one and one half inches in length." To illustrate, Dr. Fralick pointed to a corresponding place on his own head, between his temple and his eye.

"It showed more prominently inside than outside the skull. That would indicate that there was a force applied to the outside. A force that could have been made by a dull instrument. The meningeal artery supplies blood to the membranes covering the brain. When a fracture of that kind is made, the artery is ruptured, and the result would be a hemorrhage. It would bleed and form a clot between the skull and brain, a pressure which would cause unconsciousness, and if not relieved, finally death. Death would not be immediate. Unconsciousness might be immediate as the result of this kind of blow, but death would not."

For several more minutes the doctor droned on. He detailed his method of measuring the bones in order to determine the woman's height in life. He discussed the possible degree of curvature of her spine, the way the human spinal cord fit through the neck bones, and the way arteries delivered blood and oxygen to vital organs. The science behind his pontificating was beyond the schooling of most in the room, but even the doctor's lengthy medical-speak could not obscure the horrid truth of Sister Janina's death. The farmers, laborers, and housewives in the room, some nearly illiterate, now heard evidence that the prosecutor had been right: the nun had been buried alive.

With its next series of witnesses, the prosecution attempted to show that it understood just how murder could have happened in Isadore, right in sight of the very farm people who had packed the courthouse every day. From hard science, the prosecution turned its attention to the shifty-eyed study of local gossip.

On Friday, classes at Holy Rosary School were canceled again, and all sixteen Felician Sisters who had prayed over the skeleton the day before returned to court. Seven of them would be called as witnesses for the prosecution.

The substance of their testimony did not concern matters of the soul, however, but rather matters of the heart. In any other circumstance, the idea that nuns would be sources of knowledge about a clandestine romance between one of their own and a priest would be scandalous; here, though, so much had already been revealed that the Sisters' words made just one more disclosure in an already shocking trial.

The first of these witnesses was the sixty-one-year-old Sister Mary Nepomucine, who had twice traveled by train to Leelanau County all the way from her posting in Pittsburgh: once more than a decade earlier to help search for Sister Janina and now to testify at the trial of her accused murderer. A nun for forty-three years, Sister Nepomucine had helped raise the orphaned Sister Janina when she first came to live in the Motherhouse in Detroit.

"I knew Sister Janina from childhood," she told the court. "I knew her in Detroit when she was accepted and I knew her when she was with me in Buffalo and I knew her when she was with me as a child in Detroit. I knew her when she took her final vows. I never saw her again after she was sent out to the Isadore school."

The elderly nun told how she had traveled by train to Isadore after Sister Janina disappeared to help search for her. During her stay, she was introduced to Stella. It was soon made clear to her that the housekeeper did not much care for the missing Sister.

"I heard Mrs. Lipczynska talk while I was there about Sister Mary Janina. In my presence. I talked with her in the garden there."

"Tell us what she said," urged Dayton.

"Well, she said that Janina wasn't very good, very religious," Sister Nepomucine said.

"Did she say anything against her character?" the prosecutor asked.

"She did."

"Did she say anything about her relation with the priest?"

"She did."

"What was it?"

"That very often Father Bieniawski used to be too confidant with her. That very often Father Bieniawski used to speak with Sister Janina more than he ought to."

"What do you mean by 'too confidant,' Sister? Do you remember whether Mrs. Lipczynska used that particular word?"

"Well, it was the same meaning."

"Do you speak Polish?"

"I do."

"State whether or not the conversation with her was in Polish."

"In Polish."

It is possible that by using the English word *confidant* the nun meant *intimate*. The words are similarly spelled in the Polish language, with the former spelled *konfidant* and the latter spelled *konfidencjonalny*.

The prosecution's next witness was Mary Gatzke, Mike's older sister. She and Stella had been friends for years, she said, and when the house-keeper worked for Father Andrew, the two women visited at her kitchen table as often as three or four times a week.

"I remember her talking about the Sisters. I heard her talking always about that when we were together. She would call them some names and she would call Sister Janina some names."

"Well, go on and tell us what she said."

"She said that the priest was no priest; he was no more than a man and the women were his wives. She called [Sister Janina] names. She called her a slut."

"Anything else?"

"She said something worse. A worse name than that."

"We would like to have it. I know it is very disagreeable to you, but just what did she say? What did she call her?"

"She said they were whores."

When the din in the courtroom died down and Judge Mayne had re-stored order, Prosecutor Dayton called up church sexton Jacob Flees's wife, also named Mary. She said that she had also heard Stella denigrate Sister Janina.

"This is what she said and how she said it: I was at vespers and I stepped out of the church and Mrs. Lipczynska was on the front steps and she said like this—that the Sister wasn't worthy to walk upon this holy ground. That she was such a light character that she let Father Bi-eniawski and the doctor in her cell. That nuns weren't allowed to do this, even on their dying bed, but Sister Janina was so low that she let Fa-ther Bieniawski and the doctor in her cell."

Throughout the day, witness after witness testified to the ire the housekeeper regularly directed toward Sister Janina.

Church neighbor and Isadore postmaster Jake Rosinski: "The house-keeper said that Sister is not worthy of being called a Sister. Father Bi-eniawski was always going to Sister Janina. That he goes there so often and that she had his suppers cooked but she had to always wait and the kettles get all burned and they are harder to clean. She said he always had something to do with that Sister Janina."

Sister Leonissa, who taught in Isadore before Sister Janina arrived: "She said that Sister Janina would not fulfill her duties and that she was very angry with her. That she could just shake her from temper. She did not know what to do from anger at her sometimes. She said Sister Janina was no good as a nun and it was God's blessing that she disappeared. She said that the Father would go over to the school too often. That Sister Janina was too intimate with Father Bieniawski."

Sister Innocencia, a nun from St. Joseph's who knew Stella in Manistee: "Once at a recreation hour in the evening, Mrs. Lipczynska came over to the porch and asked whether we Sisters knew of Sister Janina's disappearance. We said we did not, and she began to tell how foolish it was, instead of giving the dog Sister Janina's shoes to smell, they gave it Sister Colletta's, and that's why they couldn't find her."

And finally, in an omen of what was to come, the prosecution called another member of the Holy Rosary parish and a church neighbor, Helen Strang. Helen had been a friend of Stella's and was one of the only people from Isadore to visit her in jail after she was arrested. Like most of Holy Rosary's neighbors, Helen spoke fluent Polish, and it was in this language that the following exchange occurred.

"I went into the jail to see her and she said, 'Listen Helen, what is all the people up to, blaming me in this way?' The people is making so much complaint about this and putting everything over her—you know—that she killed Sister Janina. And she said that God would never bless the people at Isadore, they make such a complaint about this crime. And I said 'Auntie,'—I call her Aunt, you know—'you can't blame the people, they didn't done anything to you. The people didn't give this out—he gave this out. It comes by the priest, you know?'"

"And what did she say?" asked Dayton.

"She said, 'Yes Helen, it seems if the secret of the confessional is coming out, it will be the end of the world.'"

By now, it was late in the afternoon, and the prosecution could have ended for the day, but Dayton instead wanted to leave the jury with even more evidence against Stella, and called one more witness who would exact "a terrific blow," against the defense, according to the newspapers.

Spectators watched as a stranger, a woman no less, walked to the stand and was sworn in. By its geography, Leelanau County was a hard-to-reach place, especially from the west by boat over the wide and sometimes treacherous Lake Michigan, but also from the north through the wilds of the Upper Peninsula and then the unpredictable currents of the Straits of Mackinac. Strangers were a novelty; women strangers traveling alone were unheard of. And yet, here was one walking right in front of them and settling herself on the witness stand.

"My business is investigating," said the large-framed woman. She testified in English, though her words were heavily accented with her native Polish. "I live in Milwaukee and I work for the Wilson Detective Agency."

Private detective Mary Tylicka told the court that in April she had received an assignment to report to work in Leelanau County later that month, working with Sheriff Kinnucan and Judge Brown on a ruse they were planning as part of a criminal investigation. She was to be arrested on a phony charge and locked up in the same cell as the defendant, and while there she would attempt to gain her cellmate's friendship. Her charge was to extract a confession out of the woman if she could. The witness was here in court to report making a thorough success of her challenging assignment.

"I remained in the jail six days, during which time I had talks with the respondent about the disappearance of Mary Janina and what became of her," Mary Tylicka explained. "I had these talks on different occasions and she told me what became of her on the 28th day of April, in the afternoon."

"How did she come to make this statement to you?" Dayton asked.

"She began to cry and say, 'Well, I went to confession and confessed my sins,'" the detective answered.

"You were hired to get a confession from this woman?" asked Dayton.

"I was hired to come here and get what I could. I represented myself to her as Mrs. Dombrowski. I said I was a social worker from Detroit."

"What were you put in jail for and what did you represent to her you were put in for?"

"I was put in jail for violating the laws. She knew it. She had seen it."

"What was the violation?"

"I had been running around the rooms, pretending to conduct an inspection, and one of the deputies had told me to get away from there and I did not, and when I kept on, he got indignant and locked me up." This scene had been played out in full view of Stella, she added.

"Did the respondent ask you to do anything for her?"

"Yes."

"What did you say?"

"I told her, 'If you want me to do anything for you, first tell me what and tell me all.'"

"What did she tell you?" Dayton asked.

"She said, 'I went to Father Nowak in Milwaukee and confessed my sins and done my penance. My sins were forgiven and so why do they bother me now? I am not guilty anymore because my sins are forgiven.'

"Then she says, 'Yes, I killed Sister Janina. I first stunned her, then I went out into the garden and looked for a spade and dug a hole under the church and dragged the body to the hole and put the Sister in the hole and covered her body partly with earth. As I was trying to cover the head, the head would always rise. I was trying to cover that head three or four times. I put three or four shovels of ground on the head but the head would never stay down. Then I took the back of the spade and knocked the Sister on the head three times with all my might.'

"I says, 'Is this true?' She said, 'Yes. Please believe me now. I have told you just exactly as I have told it in confession to Father Nowak. That is all I can say now. I can't bear to talk about it.'"

Mary Tylicka's voice had been the only sound in the courtroom as she detailed Stella's confession, but with these last words the place erupted in a cacophony of human sounds, though none of them could have been said to be words, exactly. The nuns clutched each other and sobbed. Many of the other spectators gasped loudly in unison, one large inhale of breath that seemed to suck every molecule of oxygen from the room. The attorneys for the defense were on their feet, objecting, and Judge Mayne pounded his gavel until some may have believed it was about to splinter. Only the jury was silent, though they looked from one to the other as if seeking some steadying point.

The stranger's words, while outlandish, had a certain ring of truth to them. Many in the immigrant Catholic parish believed strongly that God's laws will always trump man's, and absolution from a priest was more powerful than anything the court might decide constituted justice. If Stella had sincerely confessed her sin, even if it were murder, and been given absolution and a religious penance, she could very well have believed that she was no longer guilty of the crime.

That she would travel across Lake Michigan to go to confession was not out of the realm of possibility, either. Her daughter lived there, and she might have gone for a visit, and decided to confess while she was there, to a stranger instead of to a priest she knew. It certainly would have been easier than confessing to Father Andrew.

For a full ten minutes the shock reverberated through the court and Prosecutor Dayton watched it all with a sense of delicious satisfaction. Judge Mayne finally regained control of his court and the questioning resumed.

"Now, what did Mrs. Lipczynska say to you the next day?" Dayton asked the detective.

"She said, 'Are you angry with me because I have confessed to you this crime?' I said, 'No, I am not angry.' Then she repeated the very same story right over as she had told it to me the day before. She said that when she confessed her sins, Father Nowak said to her that he can't give absolution right now. He said, 'I have got to see Bishop Kozlowski. You stay here in the church until I return.' She stayed there about fifteen or twenty minutes or one half hour, it was not long, she said, because the distance was not very far where the Bishop lives. Father Nowak returned and gave her absolution."

The confession had been made to the detective on Monday, April 28. On Tuesday, April 29, Stella told Mary Tylicka about receiving absolution. The next morning, Wednesday, the defendant woke up, took her breakfast as usual, then returned to her cell. She looked out the window, and Sheriff Kinnucan just happened to be walking past.

As Mary Tylicka watched, Stella's face turned purple and she shook her fist at the sheriff and yelled an insult at him. "*Pais krew!*" the housekeeper blurted out in Polish. "You dog's blood! You think you are wise, but I am just as wise! I will lead you out into the field and leave you there. You people think I am not wise but I am wiser than you are. You will not know where you are at!"

That afternoon, the detective testified, Stella went insane.

By the time Mary Tylicka was released from the witness stand, it was late in the day on Friday. Evening was settling over Leland, the windows of the courthouse were black squares against the white interior walls. Prosecutor Dayton looked over each face in the jury box, and then over at Stella. The composure she had shown all through the trial was finally dissolving. The rosy flush that colored her cheeks at the sight of the skeleton had turned ashen. Her ridged posture was slumped down, and somehow even the tight coil of her hair seemed disheveled.

Dayton walked back to his table and turned to face Judge Mayne. "The prosecution rests."

Although the chilly and bright days of mid-October spread pink, gold, and a deep scarlet over the hardwoods that dotted the hills of Leelanau County, all the vibrancy had drained from the defense. It was a dark weekend for Stella and her attorneys. Judge Mayne canceled court on Saturday, giving Howard Campbell and Peter Glassmire until Monday morning to solidify their defense strategy.

As a rule, the defense has the option to present their case first in a murder trial, and it may have been a mistake for them not to exercise that option on behalf of Stella. Their decision to reserve their opening statement may have allowed them to see the prosecution's case, but it afforded the same opportunity for the jury. And, unlike Campbell and Glassmire, the jury heard the prosecution's case without being privy to the defense's theory on the crime. Every legal strategist will recommend against this tactic in ninety-nine cases out of a hundred. Whether *People v. Lipczynska* was this one case where it worked remained to be seen.

However, if ever there had been a time in this trial for the defendant to change her plea, it was now, but Stella maintained her innocence. By Sunday night the defense had finalized their plan and it was this: Admit that the remains shown in court were indeed those of Sister Janina, but say they had not been buried under the church immediately after the crime, only much later and for nefarious reasons. This constituted a clear case of "spoliation of evidence," and the court should look upon it with the harshest of views. The defense also would contend that the defendant's alleged confession was obtained through fraud, coercion, and torture and was therefore inadmissible. They would express outrage over the inhuman treatment the defendant had been subjected to at the hands of Sheriff Kinnucan and his allies, and would again point out the Polish/English language barrier.

"We will show that the authorities practiced upon the respondent the most inhuman, cruel treatment ever accorded a human being incarcerated and awaiting trial," Glassmire roared in his opening statement for the defense. "We will show that a detective beat her, pulled her hair, and smothered her cries with a pillow. We will show that the authorities took away the respondent's rosary and prayerbook. We will show that their efforts culminated in their displaying a skeleton in open court here, within three feet of the respondent, a display sufficiently startling to threaten any well-balanced mind."

Titillating the spectators, Glassmire added one other promise: The defense would also put Stella on the stand to testify on her own behalf. By presenting their defense after the prosecution rested, instead of directly following the opening arguments, Campbell, Glassmire, and Gaffney were now in a life-and-death game of catch-up. Presumption of innocence is one of the most precious rights a criminal defendant has; presenting the reasons for that innocence before the prosecution has an opportunity to argue against it is another. For reasons unknown, the defense had squandered one of their most precious resources.

When Stella's attorneys did present her case, their first witness was not a representative of the law in Leelanau County, Stella herself, or anyone even remotely familiar to those gathered. As their opener, the defense called a lowly public servant from a neighboring county, a woman germane to the case only because of a series of coincidences.

Blanche Srsinska, the probate registrar of Manistee, happened to have an office near St. Joseph's rectory, happened to speak fluent Polish, and happened to be available the day Stella was arrested. In what Campbell and Glassmire believed would be a boon for the defense, she also knew the law and had a well-developed sense of fairness.

"When she was arrested, the officers found that Mrs. Lipczynska could not speak English fluently and so Mrs. Srsinska was brought in as an interpreter," Glassmire explained. "She was asked to interpret a list of questions about Mrs. Lipczynska's life and these were typewritten on a slip of paper. Miss Srsinska lifted the top sheet when told to obtain Mrs. Lipczynska's signature and found a blank affidavit underneath. We shall show that she realized the significance of this and refused to advise the respondent to sign, explaining that the authorities then could fill in anything they desired above the signature and call it a confession. We will show that the Leelanau officers then consulted and said, 'If she won't sign that, we will get it some other way.'"

With Miss Srsinska on the stand, the defense hoped to tell this story of hypocrisy and deception by those supposed to uphold the law, in the young woman's own words. If the way in which their first witness was received by the court was any indication of how the remainder of the trial would play out, they were already in trouble.

"I have been register clerk for seven years in all," Miss Srsinska said, by way of introduction. "I recollect the respondent being brought up to the probate office in the courthouse in Manistee, the first of last March. Mr. Kinnucan was there at the time. I talked with the Sheriff before the respondent came into the office and also at the time she was there."

"Will you tell us what that conversation was?" defense attorney Glassmire asked.

"To which we object as incompetent, immaterial, and irrelevant," Parm Gilbert stated for the prosecution, before Miss Srsinska could tell a word of what she'd observed. "We assume that it refers to matters mentioned in the opening statement of the defense concerning some alleged signature of the respondent. No document has been offered and any testimony inquiring about it is an entire waste of time."

"Mr. Kinnucan took that paper away!" the defense protested. "He does not now know where it is and it is for that reason that the paper itself is not introduced."

"The objection is sustained," said Judge Mayne to the attorneys. "I see no materiality or relevancy in the testimony. It is purely a collateral matter." And then to the jury, "In making this ruling I will say that this paper does not enter into the case at all directly or indirectly and that it is as though it never had been taken."

After traveling the fifty-plus miles from Manistee, Miss Srsinska left the stand, having offered the court little more than her name and profession. While the prosecution had been able to get an engraved nun's ring, shoes filled with bones, and an entire skeleton entered into evidence, it seemed the defense was having difficulty getting Judge Mayne to consider so much as a piece of paper.

If the court would not sanction the value of a probate registrar, perhaps they would look more favorably upon yet one more holy man. As their next witness, the defense called Father Timothy Koback, a priest from a church in Suttons Bay who had visited Stella in jail. When Father Edward had been removed, and there was no priest from Isadore to attend to Stella, another Leelanau County priest had been called into service.

"How did you come to make that visit?" Gaffney asked him.

"Mr. Kinnucan called up at six that morning and asked me to come over to the jail here and see Mrs. Lipczynska. I went into the cell with her immediately upon arriving at the jail. She was lying on the bed. This detective woman was there administering medicine to Mrs. Lipczynska. She seemed to be taking it willingly. I requested the detective to go out and she went, and then she rushed in again.

"I left the cell and told Mr. Kinnucan that he would have to get her out or that I would not go in. He could make his choice. He deliberated for five or ten minutes. He told me that he was in a quandary and did not know what to do. If I went there alone then anybody else could go in and claim the same privilege to be alone with her in the cell. He thought about it a while then went and got Mrs. Tylicka out. Then I went in."

"Did the respondent make any reference to Mrs. Tylicka?" Gaffney asked.

"Yes sir; she said that woman put into her cell was a spy."

A day before, the "spy" had made a convincing witness for the prosecution. Now, her story was being called into question. Mary Tylicka had sworn under oath that while the two women were locked together in the same jail cell, Stella had confessed to murdering Sister Janina with a garden spade. This confession, she said, had taken place on April 28. But according to Father Koback, only a day or two later Stella already knew that Mary Tylicka was a spy, put in her path to extract just such a confession.

The authenticity of that confession now hinged on when Stella had learned her cellmate's true nature. If it had been after April 28, the confession might indeed be real; but if before, Detective Mary Tylicka had probably made it all up. The spy had already told her version of those last three days in April. Now, it would be Stella's turn.

It began as more autobiography than testimony. Speaking in broken English, heavily accented with her native Polish, Stella's unwavering voice seemed out of place with the haggard shell that contained it.

"I am Catholic," she began. Following this first label she assigned to herself, Stella went on to detail her life in Poland, her arrival at Isadore, and her work as a housekeeper. She was born in Posen, in German Poland, in 1869. Her husband died when she was in her late twenties and when her daughter, Mary, was only ten years old. On his deathbed, her husband made Stella promise him that she would never remarry. After he died, she brought her daughter to America, visited distant relatives in the Polish settlement of Isadore, and was hired to be Father Andrew Bieniawski's housekeeper sometime in the year 1900. She kept her promise to her dead husband and deemed herself now bound not to a man, but to her daughter and to the church.

"I remember the first time Sister Janina came to Isadore. I became well acquainted with her. She was a good Sister. There was never any trouble between Sister Janina and me. I did not find fault because Father Bieniawski would visit the convent and stay late for meals. I did not at any time say that Father Bieniawski was too intimate with the Sister. I was always good friends with the Sisters. I never said anything bad about any of them. I did not call them bad names as some swore to here. I did not say that Sister Janina and those other Sisters were just whores to the priest or anything like that. I was to confession just once in Milwaukee, at Christmas time. I confessed to Priest Barron. I never saw anyone called Father Nowak. I never confessed to any such person."

Every unflattering statement made at trial thus far about her was categorically false, she said. She was not a gossip, she did not begrudge the time Father Andrew spent at the convent or even pay much attention to it. She did not use those foul words to describe Isadore's Felician Sisters, she did not kill the nun or ever once even raise her voice in anger. She did not know a priest named Father Nowak, did not confess to him, and so could not have received absolution from Bishop Kozlowski for something she did not do.

Her neighbors, her friends, Isadore's remaining Sisters, and the Sisters who visited from Detroit were all lying. It was just an average, pious, happy household that she ran in Isadore, albeit one that required her unrelenting labor to keep up.

"I took care of the house, cooking the meals for Father Bieniawski and the family, and took care of the flowers, the garden, the animals and fowls. I did all kinds of work. My daughter and the Priest's sister and the boy, everybody around the church helped. I did the work for all those people, the washing and the ironing and scrubbing and sweeping and cleaning.

"Sister Janina taught my daughter to play the piano and sing. I used to take stuff over for the Sisters. If they came to the kitchen and said they needed anything, I gave it to them. I continued to live there after the disappearance of Sister Janina until I went with Father Bieniawski to Manistee. I lived in Manistee until I was brought here by the sheriff."

Whether she had intended to or not, Stella provided her attorneys with the perfect segue into the next two elements in their defense strategy: the inhuman treatment—torture they called it—she'd received at the jail, and the resulting coerced, and therefore unreliable, inadmissible, and false, confession.

"The first nights in jail, I was alone. Afterwards, that woman was brought over. I had a prayerbook and beads with me. They were taken away. Up to that time I used them in my devotions. They were of comfort to me because I knew I am innocent and God will help me. Then Mr. Kinnucan took them away. I was reciting my beads when he came in and he took hold of the beads and shook them and said, 'That is too strong for you.' He took my prayerbook."

"Did anyone come there and tell you that her name was Mrs. Dombrowski?" the defense attorney asked.

"Yes, Mary Dombrowski."

"What did this Mrs. Dombrowski say to you while she was there?"

"She would pretend to be a friend of mine. She said that the priests and the Sisters sent me to jail. She told me that my lawyers had quit me, and that Father Bieniawski was in prison for fifteen years, and that my daughter was dead, and Father Bieniawski's sister was in the hospital. I knew she was a spy the minute she came in."

"How long did the detective woman stay in the jail?"

"I do not remember because she tortured me so that I can't. She got a hold of my hair and pulled out a handful. She took a dipper and beat me on the head with it. She choked me and beat me. She hurt me—it still always hurts in my side."

"Did this Mrs. Dombrowski ask you if you wanted to see Sister Janina?"

"Never."

"Did Mr. Kinnucan ask you that?"

"Yes."

"What did you say?"

"Yes. I thought Sister Janina came to life again."

"What was done then, if anything?"

"It was in the evening. I was ready to go to bed when he came. The spy was there. I do not know what time of the night it was, but it was dusk, and the lights were lighted. I went through a little room and Mr. Kinnucan opened the door and pushed me in there. I did not see anything but just some bones and two candles. I got scared and could not see."

"Did you see the head or the skull?"

"Yes. He had it on strings like threads and was opening up the mouth and closing it again. I was in there about two hours. I remember the spy was with me the next day. I was so sore and sick. I wondered only what was to become of me."

"In talking to this spy, did you ever tell her about your life?"

"No."

"Did you make a confession as the spy—Mrs. Tylicka—says you did?"

"No, it is not the truth. That is a lie. I never confessed to her and I never at any time told this spy that I was going to pretend that I would be crazy. Never! I never said a word to her because I was as afraid of her as I am of *fire*."

"I want you to say now, Mrs. Lipczynska, whether you killed Sister Mary Janina or not."

"No."

"Do you know anything about how or why she disappeared?"

"The people said that someone took her away, and the Sisters said so, too."

Though she became emotional at the close of her testimony, Stella had done herself some good on the stand. She was a credible witness, the newspapers reported, some even calling her "excellent."

"Gaffney aimed his questions to refute testimony of prosecution witnesses," reported the *Traverse City Record-Eagle*. "In this the defense was successful to a marked degree. Mrs. Stanislawa Lipczynska is slightly haggard from the strain of tedious court sessions, yet apparently unshaken in her confidence that her attorneys and the evidence will clear her of the murder charge."

Stella had told the court that she had no memory of her two-and-a-half-month stay in the State Psychopathic Hospital, no memory of working with that facility's famed director, Dr. Albert Barrett, and no memory of her odd behaviors that led to her commitment.

For these details, the court would hear directly from Dr. Barrett himself, who would be called as a rebuttal witness by the prosecution the very next morning.

"At first her conduct was very abnormal," Dr. Barrett stated to the court. "She acted very strangely and talked strangely. After a few weeks her conduct changed and she began to be a more normal person. And, while at first she seemingly could not understand English and only spoke a few words in that language, toward the latter part of the time she was there she understood ordinary conversation, talked comparatively fluently in English, and seemed to have reached a fairly normal stage."

"Now doctor, did you think she was insane?" asked Prosecutor Dayton.

"I did not think she was insane," Dr. Barrett answered. "It was my opinion that the symptoms she showed were those of simulation."

"Explain to the jury what you mean by 'simulation'."

"I mean that she assumed an abnormal state of mind, showing certain symptoms which were not what an ordinarily healthy person would show, and yet were not those which were usually in evidence in a case of insanity of any kind. It was as if a person were trying to act as you *think* a person would act who is insane. I do not think the experience she is said to have gone through with the jail would produce the symptoms she exhibited."

One more doctor was called to the stand by the defense on Wednesday, now the eighth day of the trial; this man had knowledge not of the human mind and brain, but rather of the skull bones that encased it.

Days earlier when Dr. Fralick took his finger and traced a line on his own head to illustrate where Sister Janina had received her fatal blow, he was representing her cause of death as fact, and not simply as one country doctor's opinion. The defense now would put forth the esteemed Dr. Ludwig Hoektoen to take issue with Fralick's assumption.

Attorney Campbell had found Dr. Hoektoen in Chicago, and he was a courtroom wonder. Dressed in the latest fashion, he had an air of the scientist, the entertainer, and the dandy, all rolled into one man. A pathologist born in Wisconsin to immigrant parents, his own mental cavity was soon shown to be exceedingly large. Dr. Hoektoen was the closest thing 1919 had to a celebrity pathologist, taking his studies in England, Sweden, Prague, and finally Chicago.

He was a pathologist at that city's famed Cook County Hospital, the chief physician for the county coroner's office, and a professor of pathology at Rush Medical College. When he took the stand, the skull was handed up to him by Peter Glassmire to use in his testimony.

"I am a physician and professor giving 'especial attention to pathology," Hoektoen sniffed. "I study bones of the skeleton and have testified in cases involving fractures of the skull, etcetera."

"Did you examine the remains and if so, what did you find?" asked Glassmire.

"I examined it as a pathologist," he said, obviously fond of this word and proud to attach it to himself, "yesterday afternoon, in the room here just behind this one. Dr. Fralick and a deputy were present. The bones were in a fair degree of preservation. I examined the different bones of the skeleton, paying special attention to the skull. I saw this skull yesterday and heard the testimony of Dr. Fralick and his description of how he sawed and severed the skull. I examined the skull to determine whether or not there was a fracture on the exterior, and also whether or not there was a fracture on the interior. There is an exterior fracture."

"Did you know whether that fracture was caused before or after death?"

"Yes, I know. It was caused after death."

"Why do you say that, doctor?"

"Because there are also recent cracks in the skull—I take it for granted that it is twelve years since the person died. In my answer, I assume that to be true. Assuming that this person met her death twelve years ago, the fractures now appearing were not produced before death. It is plain that this fracture that you see here and here"—and the doctor pointed to a place on the skull—"was produced when the skullcap was taken off. There can be no question about that."

Defense Attorney Frank Gaffney sat down, satisfied. Prosecutor Dayton rose to have a go at this learned man from the big city. The prosecutor had seen the skull many times for himself, and knew every crack, scratch, stain, and irregularity on it. Known by an observer as being "gifted with a spirit of devotion to wearisome details," he planned to use this trait to his immediate advantage.

"On the inside of the skull, this same crack that shows on the outside, is discolored, isn't it?" he asked Dr. Hoektoen.

"No."

"Show me that."

Here the rural prosecutor and the urban doctor both bent their heads down over the skull and examined it closely. The doctor turned the thing over in his hands, running his fingers over the offending crack.

"You say there is no discoloration there do you?" Dayton asked again, his voice incredulous. It became obvious to the jury that the two men were looking at the same place on the same object and seeing two very different things.

"I do."

"I would like to have the jury, each of them, examine that, right now."

"And *I* would like to point it out to them," Hoektoen demanded, seemingly perturbed that this legal bumpkin would dare question his expert opinion.

"I want each of the jury to look at that. Let them look at it, doctor. Hold it so each of them can see if there is any discoloration there," Dayton instructed.

Dr. Hoektoen stepped down from the witness stand and, carrying the two parts of the skull in his hands, he was guided, politely and almost gingerly, to the jury box by the prosecutor. Dayton had seen the dark mark there, and he wanted to make sure all twelve men on the jury saw it, too. Stella might have stifled her anger long enough to appear reasoned during the trial, but even she couldn't hide the stain inside her victim's skull, he believed, and he wasn't going to let this pontificating doctor hide it away, either.

It took several minutes, but Dayton got his wish; each juryman let his eyes linger over the skull before the doctor moved on to the next and then the next. Some backed away in their seats, some ran a hand over it, some glanced at it and closed their eyes. Finally, Hoektoen was seated back on the witness stand. He looked as if the trip to the jury box and back had sapped some of his bluster, but the prosecutor wasn't finished with him yet.

"Now doctor, how black does an area have to be before it's discolored, according to your idea?"

"Well of course this is a question that each one can form his own opinion about."

"Answer the question, doctor."

"I am trying to answer it! My claim is that this crack is not what we call a discoloration."

"I didn't ask you that. I didn't ask you what you claim. I am asking you how dark it has to be before it's discolored."

"Before it's definitely and clearly discolored it must be of a distinctly different color from the main color of the rest of the inside of the skull."

"Yes. Now, you claim that in that crack that it is not distinctly different in color from the rest of the skull?"

"Yes I do. I don't think I have examined any skulls where the person has been dead for ten years. I don't remember any. What I have said about these cracks are simply opinions of mine. They can't be anything else but opinions."

Dayton had taken on one of the defense's star witnesses, a professional man they had probably paid a handsome fee to for his expert testimony, and moved him from an arrogant "there can be no question," to fully backing off with "they can't be anything else but opinions" in one turn on the stand. In the process, the prosecutor had maneuvered the damaged skull so close to the nose of the jury, he could be almost certain that they smelled a conviction.

The trial was nearing its end, with only legal housekeeping details and stray facts to be swept up into the record in the waning days of the airing-out of Isadore's secrets. The final leavings presented to the jury were these.

What had been cruelly displayed was not a full skeleton, the defense contended. Dr. Hoektoen said that as many as fifty bones were missing, including a piece of the breastbone and a rib. There were also items found under the church that were unexpected: men's fingernails and dog's bones, for example. This must mean, they argued, that when Sister Janina died she had first been buried somewhere else, for reasons unknown, and her bones later dumped into the grave uncovered in the dirt basement of the church. The bones of a fetus were never entered into evidence, not by the defense or the prosecution, and it is unclear if what some called dog bones were really evidence of Sister Janina's secret pregnancy.

Doctors for the prosecution did not argue for or against the curious items found with the bones but rather sought to explain them away. The theory they presented to the jury was that most of what was missing from the skeleton were the smallest bones of the feet, wrists, and hands, and these had simply decomposed in the dozen years that Sister Janina had been buried. And, they said, Holy Rosary Church was surrounded by farms, and most had dogs. Of course their bones were bound to be buried just about anywhere. No explanation though was forthcoming from either side for the fingernails. Perhaps they belonged to those who had exhumed the body, broken off in the considerable effort to bring it out of the ground.

The prosecution did put up a Dr. Rollo McCotter, a University of Michigan anatomy professor, and if Dr. Hoektoen had a shred of sway left with the jury, this new medical witness quickly disposed of it with the simplest and most nonsurgical of tools—his pocket jackknife.

"You can clearly see that all the dirt and discoloration on the skull can be scraped off," he told the court, taking out his jackknife and demonstrating. "But there is a dark area that extends over an inch that cannot be scraped off. It is only noticeable on the interior of the skull. It is a real stain of the bone. If a fracture of a bone occurs before death, we have the circulation still going on; the portion of this fracture that is stained was made before death."

Next, both sides turned their attention to the ground beneath the church and the lumber pile. In the years between Sister Janina's disappearance and the discovery of human remains, many searchers had looked for the missing nun under the church, and no sign of either a nun or a grave was ever found, the defense pointed out. At one point, rods had even been poked deep into the earth, and they sunk in cleanly, without encountering any obstruction.

Yes, the prosecution agreed, searches there had been many and fruitless for one obvious reason: no one looked under the lumber pile, and that's where the nun was buried. There was no record of a single search after the lumber pile was removed, until the secret one undertaken by Father Edward and Jacob Flees.

The tiny defendant was either a simple and innocent housekeeper caught up in circumstances beyond her understanding or control, driven temporarily mad by a cruel sheriff and those faithful to him, or a mean-hearted fanatic who could measure out a fatal punishment to a member of her own household, for sins real or imagined, and then feign insanity well enough to intrigue even the very best doctors for several months.

The courtroom audience had several of their variations on these choices. Perhaps Stella had simply experienced an attack of anger that she could not control, killed Sister Janina, and even though she had not confessed to the crime in court, regretted it now. In her own mind, she was no longer guilty since she had confessed to a priest. If anyone besides the Sisters had read it, they would have found that *The Nun's Rule* even addressed such a loss of temper. "Let the heart cool, and thou will rightly judge the sin to be loathsome and foul which seemed to thee fair; and that so much evil comes of it, that if thou hadst done it while the heat lasted thou wouldest think thyself mad for having intended it. This is true of every sin."

But whatever the impetus for the crime settled on silently by the courtroom audience, the defense certainly hoped the jury would believe that Stella was simply an innocent church housekeeper, caught up in aggressive law enforcement tactics.

"Mr. Kinnucan came over and asked me if I wouldn't like to see Sister Janina," Stella explained when her attorneys recalled her to the stand. "I told him I wanted to see Sister Janina. I thought she read about all this in the paper, that I was in jail, and she came to release me. I thought she was alive again."

"But then you knew she was dead, didn't you?"

"I didn't know. I didn't know anything. I've lost my health and I will never get it back. I don't remember all they done with me."

For the first time, Stella lost her composure and made no attempt to stop her grief. She wept openly on the witness stand for several minutes, and no one came forward to comfort her, or to help her back to her seat.

Glassmire watched his client grieve, and for once remained uncharacteristically silent. He looked around the courtroom, from the gallery to the jury, to his co-council. There might not ever be more sympathy for Stella's plight than he hoped he sensed right then at that moment. He looked up at Judge Mayne. "The defense rests, your honor."

Judge Mayne took the words *speedy trial* in the defendants' list of rights not as a guide but as immutable and unchangeable law; he had a reputation of making certain that every defendant who appeared in his courtroom had full access to this unalienable right. His trials were not usually drawn-out affairs, and in comparison this one had gone on particularly long. For this defendant in particular, he must have felt like there was no time like the present. Without so much as a short recess, he used the waning hour of the day, Thursday, to instruct the jury. With a sincere and solemn seriousness, he turned and spoke to the twelve men seated to his right.

"In this, as in every case in which a person charged with a crime is on trial, the respondent, by this I mean the accused, is presumed to be innocent of the offense charged until she is proven guilty by evidence which satisfies your minds of her guilt beyond all reasonable doubt. This presumption of innocence extends to each and every essential element of the offense with which the respondent is charged, and continues and abides with her during the entire trial, including your deliberations in the jury room until you are convinced by the evidence in the case to the contrary beyond all reasonable doubt.

"All evidence received must be received and considered by you in the light of this rule of law as to the presumption of innocence. This is your duty as jurors, that the respondent may have the full benefit of this presumption and rule of law."

It was the jury's task now to "harmonize" any conflicting testimony and decide questions of fact. When all circumstances, facts, exhibits, and witnesses were contemplated by each man in his own mind, he was then to deliberate these with the other jurors, Mayne said. They could consider the outward appearance of the witnesses while they were on the stand, the opportunity they had of knowing the facts, their bias or prejudice if any, believing or disbelieving as they saw fit. The judge then singled out one particularly unusual witness. The bloodhound.

"I have been practicing law a great many years, and been on the bench, and this is the first case in which I have ever known a bloodhound or other dumb animal to be brought in as a witness." The jury's task here, he said, was to determine if the dog had been given a true scent and, if so, possessed the ability to follow it.

Judge Mayne detailed the People's case and the defense's, stressing that Stella denied all wrongdoing and knowledge of the crime and professed her complete innocence. Her alleged confession was something that the jury must decide the veracity of. Before they could accept the confession as fact, they had to determine whether it was voluntary, whether it was true, and whether it had been made by a sound mind.

An involuntary confession, he told them, made by an impaired mind, could not be received by them for any purpose. A true confession, however, must be assigned the most importance possible by the jury.

"You and I have a grave responsibility, gentlemen," the judge said at the close of his instructions. "I have endeavored to the best of my ability to see that a fair, impartial trial was awarded to the respondent. It is now for you to retire to the jury room, deliberate, and arrive at a verdict.

"I want to say this: That it is entirely immaterial in this case what the opinion of the public may be. You are here as searchers after truth, and the field of your investigation is the testimony in the case, and you are to take that testimony back with you to the jury room, and in your minds you are to search for the truth carefully, cautiously, and deliberately, and when you arrive at the truth you are to render a verdict. The public expects that. That covers it, I think, gentlemen."

Again an important date for Stella fell, coincidentally, on a Friday, the day of the week her countrymen had, for generations, seen as particularly unlucky. At 5:45 p.m. on Friday, October 24, 1919, the twelve veniremen retired to the jury room to begin their deliberations.

No doubt Judge Mayne approved of the way the jury used their time; just nine hours after he sent off his dozen truth seekers, they announced to their guard at the door that they had reached a verdict. The judge, the attorneys, Stella, and her keepers were roused from their beds. Court was convened again at the bleary hour of 4:30 Saturday morning.

A rainstorm slashed at the courtroom windows, and though the building had been packed to bulging throughout the dramatic weeks leading up to this moment, regardless of the weather, few now braved the inconvenient hour to hear how the story turned out. The gallery was strangely empty; even Father Andrew and Mary Flees were absent. Stella's only companion was one of her attorneys, Howard Campbell. Her host and guard, Judge Brown, was also in attendance.

When all were seated, Judge Mayne silently nodded his cue to the jury. Foreman John Westcott stood.

"We find the prisoner guilty of murder in the first degree," he stated.

Stella looked at Howard Campbell for clarification. "I no understand," she said to him in a faint voice.

"They say you killed Sister Janina," he explained, putting his hand on her bony shoulder.

"I no kill Sister Janina," she said, through tears, as one of the guards from the jail came forward, helped her up, and led her out of the courtroom and back to her cell.

Later, Foreman Westcott revealed that it had taken six anonymous polls of the jury to convict. The first of these was nine to three for conviction; four more were eleven to one; the sixth and final ballot was unanimous. Whoever the one holdout had been, his name remained secret.

"It is the sentence of this court, Mrs. Stanislawa Lipczynska, that you are sentenced to the Detroit House of Correction, at hard labor, for the remainder of your natural life."

Judge Mayne had bested even the time efficiency of the jury; he took only four hours to decide Stella's sentence and convened court again at 8:30 in the morning of the very same day. It was the first life sentence

Frederick W. Mayne had meted out in his twenty-plus years on the bench.

For the announcement of her punishment, all of Stella's supporters who had been absent for the reading of the verdict now gathered around her. Her attorneys Howard Campbell, Frank Gaffney, and Peter Glassmire leaned in close and explained the meaning behind the dread words of the judge. They promised to appeal. Her daughter, Mary, threw her arms around her mother and sobbed into the embrace. Father Andrew and his sister, Susan, approached, too. Susan lavished affection on the housekeeper, and the priest murmured a few words in Polish to her, then turned and walked from the courtroom.

Through all this Stella's face held on to a single expression—resolve. It was as if every emotion that one would have expected a condemned woman to show was instead borne on the faces of those closest to her. There was one more label besides "guilty" that would be bestowed upon her, this time by the court of public opinion. Her new moniker was "the iron woman."

"Thus has the soul of the murdered Felician Sister, Mary Janina, been avenged in the eyes of the laws of men," the newspaper reported in the afternoon edition on Saturday, October 25, 1919. "Still, there was no evidence of deep feeling on the face of the iron woman."

By Monday, October 27, another shocking local story knocked Stella off the front page of the newspaper. A well-known local farmer had committed suicide by hanging himself in his barn. William Groesser, fifty-two, devoted husband and father of nine children, ate the noon meal with his family, walked out to his barn, climbed the ladder to his haymow, tied one end of a rope to a barn rafter and put a slip noose in the other end, placed it around his neck, and jumped to his death.

On the surface, the farmer's suicide and Stella's conviction had absolutely no relationship. The headline in the paper read, "Despondent Farmer Takes His Own Life," and perhaps it was as simple as that. Potato prices had plummeted, and many farmers were facing financial difficulties. Privately, however, the talk began. Suicide was rare in northern Michigan, almost unheard of at the time; no man would leave a wife with nine children to raise alone, except under the most calamitous circumstances.

It was telling, some said, that his suicide had come just hours after Stella's conviction. Did he know something? Did he have regrets? William Groesser had been among the audience at her trial. His family would say little, only that he was "despondent because of business troubles and other discouraging circumstances." Some suggested the circumstances had something to do with Sister Janina's murder.

"This farmer belonged to a private club that was fiercely anti-Catholic," relates local researcher Jack Sweeney. "The club members, informed of the nun's death, organized a plan to discredit the church. This is just opinion, and nothing more."

Perhaps, the rumors went, his anti-Catholic activities had gone too far. With his death went any opportunity to pursue the theory further.

Rumors were one thing, a conviction from a jury and a sentence from a judge were quite another, and on Halloween Day, Stella boarded the Pere Marquette train at the Traverse City station with Probate Judge Martin Brown and his mother, Anna, as her escorts. The city was in the throes of its harvest parade and costume procession. Ballerinas, kings, witches, and knights made their way through the same streets as Stella and the Browns. She was bound for the women's prison at the Detroit House of Correction, they to the annual street fair.

Those waiting for any parting words of culpability were left unsatisfied. Stella made no public statement after her conviction or in the week before she left the region that had been her home for the past nineteen years.

"There were those who expected that when the full weight of the law fell upon her, she would say something, and it was expected by certain Leelanau officials that what she would have to say might involve other parties. The attitude of Mrs. Lipczynska, however, since sentence was imposed has been the same as her attitude throughout the trial. She is stoical, displays little emotion, talks freely with her jailers, and seems to be enjoying life to the fullest extent."

By early evening, Stella arrived in Detroit. While trick-or-treaters were knocking on doors in search of sweets, Stella walked through the front gates of the Women's Prison. The "iron woman" was fifty years old, reached not even five feet tall and weighed less than a hundred pounds. Like the oft-quoted verse from the book of Matthew, she was the eye that had offended thee, and she had been plucked out, though over time her exit would do surprisingly little to lift the great heaviness that still settled over the four corners of Isadore.

The story simply became known as "the tragedy," and speaking about it in polite company was frowned upon.

Back at his post in Manistee, Father Andrew may have tried to forget his time in Isadore; tried to forget the trial, and the ire he'd inspired in the members of his former parish, and finally tried to forget even the scandal that was begun, consciously or not, under his leadership. Perhaps he was successful in this; more likely he was not.

What he absolutely could not forget was the image he conjured in his mind of his tiny and loyal housekeeper, dwarfed inside the iron bars and brick walls of prison. He remained, he told anyone who'd listen, convinced of her innocence. "I will not relax my efforts to find the guilty party."

The same force Father Andrew had put into looking for Sister Janina when everyone else had given her up as lost he now devoted to gaining Stella's freedom. His first efforts were directed to her attorneys. While he said he didn't blame them for her conviction, their work was not finished; the priest demanded that Campbell and Glassmire follow the case upward, to a higher court.

In 1920, this could only mean the Michigan State Supreme Court; there was no other court of appeals at the time that separated the circuit court from the state's highest court. A trial conviction, if appealed, went directly to the Supreme Court, and this was the course that Father Andrew now demanded.

His forcefulness was unnecessary. A week after Stella arrived in Detroit to begin her life sentence, Howard Campbell and Peter Glassmire were already drawing up the papers not only to appeal her conviction but to have their client released on bail until the Michigan State Supreme Court could hear their arguments. That secrets of the Catholic confessional had been invaded, and its sacred privileges cast aside and ignored, would be their charge.

"Our client denies her guilt, disclaims any connection with, or knowledge of, the crime and contends that her conviction is based upon hearsay and incompetent testimony," Glassmire said in his brief to the Supreme Court. "Sister Janina was brought to her death unlawfully, but there is no legal evidence to bring this crime home to our client. The circumstances point clearly to a different agency of death and any testimony that occurred between our client and her alleged priestly confessor is hearsay of the worst sort."

Bail was a long shot in an appeal of a murder conviction, and it was denied; the case, however, would be heard. Stella's attorneys were given almost a year to prepare to plead, the second time, for the freedom of their client. They would argue their case before the state's Supreme Court justices in the state's capital city of Lansing, on October 14, 1920. In the meantime, Stella would remain in prison.

Campbell and Glassmire and a new attorney, Charles Withey of Flint, who specialized in Supreme Court cases, were quite clear on the ways in which Judge Mayne had erred in presiding over Stella's trial; what they needed now was an alternate means of death. If Sister Janina was not killed by Stella with three brutal whacks of her garden spade, even though they were challenging the legalities of her conviction the justices would still want to receive a plausible explanation for how the Sister met her death.

The theory they came up with was this: Sister Janina had encouraged love affairs with as many as two men, and she was pregnant. There is no evidence that Stella's attorneys were aware that fetal bones had been discovered with Sister Janina's remains, but the rumor that the nun was pregnant was widespread. They would argue that Father Andrew had enjoyed intimacies with her, and that Dr. Fralick was trusted with fixing the problem that their love affair had created. They would tell the Supreme Court justices that Sister Janina left the convent of her own free will on the day of the fishing excursion, and she hid in the swamp until she could meet up with the doctor or his emissary. Someone came and spirited the nun away, then arranged, or perhaps even himself performed, an abortion that went horribly wrong, and Sister Janina died as a result. Only later, their theory went, were her remains dug up from some unknown grave and moved to the dark place under the church.

"It is the theory of the defense that Sister Janina was discontented with her lot as a nun, and that her conduct as such had not been satisfactory, and that she entertained the purpose, prior to her disappearance, of leaving the convent. Her relations with men may be legitimately subjected to critical examination, and that instead of being murdered on the convent premises by our client or anyone, she left voluntarily."

A pregnant nun was even more scandalous than a murdered one, but that is exactly what they planned to argue when their opportunity came to stand before the seven men who made up the premier word of law in the Great Lakes State.

From the anonymity of her prison cell, Stella found a way to continue to profess her innocence. In personal letters on prison stationery stamped with the words "Do not send Fruits, Candies, Clothes, Toilet preparations, or any other articles to inmates without first getting permission as they will not be passed," she wrote, in her native Polish, to Father Andrew.

Jan. 9, 1920

Reverend Priest and Pastor,

I am writing to ask, Reverend Priest, to right away answer and inform me further of the unlawful verdict handed out.

I ask you Priest to be so kind and refer the case up to the highest court as they did not give me time to speak. I would like to get just a couple words, please Priest. I have such worry, and unjust treatment, and am being uncared for, and I get miserable.

I know that you are busy with your work and other things, but I beg you greatly for a couple of words on how it happened.

I kiss the hand of my Priest.

Always thoughtful,
Stanislawa Lipczynska

Dec. 11, 1920

Reverend Priest and Pastor,

I am very nervous and legs are swollen and the hands also. I do not know what it is that these hands are paralyzed, dead and stiff. I don't get any rest and those brutes in Leland were killing me, so that I cannot remain in health.

Here we have good weather. Snow I cannot see. Shortly I anticipate being with the children of Jesus Christ and the Mother of God. I beg every day so that I quickly get released from Jail. In the yard I work hard but I have good security and something to eat. I lack for nothing but I cannot help myself and cannot understand what the criminals did to me. The innocent to be stuffed down and taken my health away instead of lawfulness.

I beg you Priest for a picture of St. Anthony, with justice and moral work you serve Lord Jesus.

Greatly I pray to the Lord Jesus and the Mother of God, to quickly act so that I can be with and see my children. For your support, my Priest, I kiss your hand and request your prayers.

> Always,
> S.L.

Inside the women's section of the Detroit House of Corrections, Stella would have the opportunity to worship and pray, and have her prayer-book and her rosary kept with her in her cell. She would have to work in the prison gardens, but as she notes in her letter, the once gaunt prisoner would not lack for nourishment. On the contrary, the Department of Corrections utilized college-educated dietitians to plan nutritious meals, and they took some pride in their work. Good food helped keep prison problems manageable.

A menu from the prison for the month of November 1920 shows the women dined on breakfasts of "Fried Corn Meal Mush, Stewed Prunes, Bacon," and "Fried Salt Pork, Fried Potatoes, Buttered Toast"; lunches of "Lima Beans and Pork, Syrup, Onions, Corn Bread, Chocolate Pudding" and "Beef Stew with Vegetables, Rice Pudding"; and dinners of "Beef Hash, Pickles, Beans" and "Cold Meat, Vegetable Soup, Baked Pork Sausage, Brown Gravy." At each meal, there were bread, butter, coffee, cream, and sugar available. And potatoes. Even here in the southern part of the state, far from the endless potato fields of Leelanau County, there were always potatoes. Fried potatoes, mashed potatoes, boiled potatoes with brown gravy, and baked potatoes with the skin on.

So prevalent, in fact, were potatoes that one dietician's report on inmate nutrition criticized the prison kitchen for peeling them too often. The matter even caused a controversy among the members of the state's prison commission, remarked upon by one of the wardens, Harvey Jackson.

"Again, mentioning the subject of potatoes, specifically the ones that are served in their jackets, this is not done because the inmates do not like them so well. From what information I can gather, the food that has been served has been sufficient and appears to be giving entire satisfaction, and the physical condition of the inmates will bear out this statement."

Stella's physical condition certainly did. According to records of her incarceration, she had gained almost fifteen pounds by the time her case came before the Michigan State Supreme Court. The wan seventy-five-pound bruised murderess was now a healthy eighty-nine-pound clear-eyed inmate, popular with the guards and known for both her good appetite and her fervent expression of her Catholic faith.

Stella's case was finally coming before the court again. At their allotted moment, the defense took no time at all to work up their ire; with their first righteous words they came out raising Cain against what many held so dear—the church, the court, even female virtue.

"Concerning the case of The People versus Stanislawa Lipczynska, the Court has transgressed and trampled underfoot every principle of justice of a right and fair trial," said Charles Withey, in his opening statement. "The whole thing has its inception in the alleged confession to Father Nowak. The Court will take judicial knowledge of the fact that no better organized institution exists than the Roman Catholic Church. Its skill and competency in that direction is historical; and yet with all the information available from that organization and the State to back it, the prosecution still failed to call this priest to testify to a fact that, if it existed, would be the cornerstone upon which the whole superstructure of the prosecution would rest."

So many questions had circled in the aftermath of Stella's trial, yet not one official representative of justice—not the judge, not one attorney from either side, not any member of the jury—had asked this one: Why hadn't Father Nowak been called to testify?

The prosecution had traced each intricate step in the chain of the accused woman's guilt more carefully even than Tom the well-bred bloodhound had traced the alleged victim's scent. Backward in time the attorneys had traveled, from Sheriff John Kinnucan, to farmer Joseph Miller, to Joseph's daughter, Martha, to Father Edward and Jacob Flees, to Father Lempke, to Detroit's Mother Superior Mary Antonia, to Milwaukee's Mother Superior Mary Veronica's assistant Sister Mary Pius, to Bishop Kozlowski, to Father Francis Nowak, and finally to Stella, alleged confessor of the dreaded deed.

Besides Father Nowak, only one of these links in the evidentiary chain of the confession had escaped the prosecution's subpoena—Bishop Kozlowski—and he had the very best of alibis: he was dead. Father Nowak was still very much alive, still saying Mass and taking confession in Wisconsin, just a one-day steamer ship's ride away, on the other side of Lake Michigan.

By using only the logic of conjecture, its possible that the prosecution decided that by not calling Father Nowak to the stand, they were able to convict the confessor without actually having to officially open the sacred door of the confessional. If Mary Tylicka, the spy planted in the jail, was believed—and the jury obviously did believe her—then Stella herself had broken the bonds of the Catholic confessional by revealing herself in a moment of weakness. Every other living witness besides Father Nowak who knew of the substance of that confession was called by the prosecution not to defy the Church but rather to verify the truth of Stella's jailhouse admission.

On the day he delivered the defense's arguments for setting aside the verdict, something gave Charles A. Withey an optimistic view of the way in which his words had been received by the justices. Perhaps it was that Chief Justice Joseph B. Moore had specifically asked him if the case had been "sloppily tried," but on October 15, 1920, the second day after he'd put forth the case, Withey wrote the following letter to Father Andrew:

Dear Father,

I was in Lansing the night before last and yesterday and argued the Lipczynska case in the Supreme Court. I had the undivided attention of all seven of the judges from the beginning to the end of my discussion, which occupied exactly one hour, all of the time which was allowed us by rule. The indications were all extremely favorable, but of course those things are sometimes deceptive, but I feel thoroughly confident that we will win. For this work and the money expended I make no charge as I think you have paid enough.

One week after Withey's letter arrived in Father Andrew's hands, the Michigan State Supreme Court adjourned, and the newspapers remarked that the judicial body had done so without making a decision on several important matters, including the Lipczynska case.

Nearly two months passed, still without word. Then in mid-December Withey's sources indicated that a ruling would be made before the end of the year. He communicated this news in a second letter to Father Andrew, dated December 17, 1920.

My Dear Sir:

I suppose that you are disgusted by this time at the delay of the Supreme Court for not deciding the People against Lipczynska. I have information that they will convene on the 21st for the purpose of handing down opinions and I trust that the above case, as well as some others I have there, will be among the ones favorably disposed of.

Watch the Detroit Free Press on that date and you will probably see it. If it says "Reversed" that means we win, and if it says "Affirmed" that means we lose, but I think that is impossible.

Yours truly,
C. A. Withey

"Affirmed."

Withey's instincts were right about the date but wrong about the outcome; on December 21, 1920, what he thought "impossible" came to pass. The Michigan State Supreme Court affirmed the first-degree-murder conviction against Stella. Their decision, in part, read: "The defendant has had a fair trial; she has been convicted by an impartial jury. We find no occasion to disturb the verdict. Her conviction is affirmed."

As far as the Michigan Supreme Court was concerned, justice had already been served in the "hamlet of Isadore." In their nineteen-page opinion they asserted that Stella had been given a fair trial, that she had been well-represented by counsel, and that the prosecution's theory of how the crime occurred was sound. They unanimously believed that Sister Janina had been struck down by the defendant who, though small in stature, was also a "Polish woman accustomed to outdoor work." Stella followed the nun to the basement of the church, killed her in a fit of jealousy, rage, religious fervor, or a combination of all three, moved a pile of lumber away, dug a grave, buried her victim, and then replaced the lumber. Life in prison was a fitting and fair punishment for such a heinous act, the decision stated.

As to the defense's charge that the confessional had been violated, the justices were unconvinced. It was not Stella's jailhouse unburdening that they identified as the deciding factor in her conviction, but rather the affidavit Father Edward had made in Cleveland that was entered into evidence by the defense. In this document Father Edward detailed how he had come to learn of the secret grave; in the process, Stella's confession was revealed. By submitting that affidavit to the court, the defense had thought they were casting doubt upon the forensic evidence and showing that the skull could have been fractured not by Stella's spade but by a tool used later by Jacob Flees. This backfired, and despite the courtroom admission by Father Edward that the affidavit had been made under "mental distress" the document worked in the prosecution's favor. If anyone had broken the Catholic confessional, the Supreme Court justices said, the defense had unknowingly done it themselves. Stella had also shared her confession in the jail and done so quite willingly.

"The privilege of the confessional is the privilege of the penitent and if the penitent waives such privilege to the extent of giving evidence of what took place at the confessional, he or she cannot complain of evidence which goes no further than to establish the facts proven by him or her." In other words, Stella's attorneys should not complain that their own statements had later been used against their client.

To Father Andrew, the decision came as a solid blow, but not a final one. The Michigan State Supreme Court had not stopped his crusade to free his housekeeper but only served to slow his progress; he would just have to find some other way of securing Stella's freedom. The priest still had his own questions about the whole affair, even after all this time. He was not certain Stella was innocent, only that she had suffered enough.

It's possible that Father Andrew felt twinges of regret during his reflections on "the tragedy." His intimacies with the nun could have driven Stella's murderous urges. His mission now was not to find out what had happened that August day all those long years ago; his mission was obtaining Stella's freedom. If he were unsuccessful in this effort, the regret, he told a confidant, would surely kill him.

Father Andrew's first idea was to discredit the jailhouse "spy," Mary Tylicka, and he made an inquiry into her background. By now Father Andrew was temporarily posted in Bay City, and so he paid a visit to the local police superintendent to assist him in this effort. This spy was a rough character, Father Andrew told the police officer. Her own employer at the detective agency had acknowledged that much, and perhaps she had been involved in unrelated nefarious activities that nonetheless should be pointed out.

Superintendent George Davis was willing to help Father Andrew find out if this were true, and wrote a letter on the priest's behalf to his equal in Milwaukee. The priest's theory, as far as Mary Tylicka's hometown police department was concerned anyway, proved to be a dead end.

February 1, 1923
Mr. George V. Davis
Supt. Of Police,
Bay City, Mich.

Dear Sir:

Replying to your letter of the 23rd requesting criminal record of Mrs. Mary Tylicka, beg to advise that we have no record of her in this office under that name. If you have any further data regarding this woman, kindly advise me, and the same will be given my prompt attention.

Yours very truly,
J. G. Laubenheimer, Chief

Epilogue: Forgiven

Winter, 1923

> Hope is a sweet spice within the
> heart, which spits out all the bitter
> that the body drinketh. But she that
> openeth her mouth, with much talking,
> and breaketh silence, spits out hope
> entirely, and the sweetness thereof,
> with worldly words, loseth spiritual
> strength against the fiend. Hope keeps
> the heart sound, whatever the flesh
> may suffer or endure.
>
> —*The Nun's Rule*

THE CHILDREN OF HOLY ROSARY CHURCH, almost a hundred in all, braved the cold and came to call at the rectory at the appointed hour. The door opened, and their priests and his holy visitors came outside and joined the gathering of their youngest charges. Together, they formed a magnificent procession; girls in lacy pinafores and Sunday school shoes, wrapped snugly in their best wool coats; boys in miniature dark suits and starched shirts; priests in ankle-length black robes; and at the front, their Bishop dressed all in white.

The children's parents and grandparents joined in, and this serpentine line of the joyous faithful soon wound its way all around the new brick church until the building was fully encircled. The Bishop, the Right Reverend Edward Kelly, had come all the way from Grand Rapids for the occasion. He moved slowly along the line and paused several times to bless the object of their celebration: the new and unbelievably magnificent red brick church that stood at the four corners of Isadore and stretched sixty feet in the air. The thin winter sun radiated off the church's crown—a copper dome.

"Each brick is dedicated to the worship of God for all time," Bishop Kelly would say, and then he would move on, pause, and say the blessing again. "Each brick is dedicated to the worship of God for all time."

Set inside these sturdy bricks were more than a dozen stained glass windows. There was Baby Jesus in the manger. There was the Crucifixion. The Resurrection. Subjects in prayer and in spiritual ecstasy. These windows were more beautiful to the humble eyes gazing upon them than any master's painting hanging in any big city museum or gallery. At first glance, the windows told the story of Christianity itself; but the parishioners all knew the other story behind this obvious one. The other story of the windows mirrored Isadore's own, filled, as it was, with sacrifice, hardship, uncertainty, and finally triumph.

As part of the new church's design, Father Stephen Narloch had decided, with his parishioners' enthusiastic blessing, that the building would have thirteen Franz Xavier Zettler windows from the famous German glassmaker, made exclusively in his Royal Bavarian Art Institute in Munich. Zettler, for a time, was the Vatican's favored stained glass artist and had pioneered a technique that involved painting the religious scenes on large sheets of thick glass using a three-point perspective that made the Bible stories seem to come alive. The colors too were more vibrant than those used by other glassmakers; the special paint ingredients were kept secret by Zettler and rumored to be of divine inspiration.

Though the cost of the windows was exorbitant for the time—$1,500 apiece plus hundreds more to ship them to America accompanied by the German glaziers who came along to install them—Holy Rosary found the money and the windows were ordered just as World War I raged across Europe. They were completed early in 1919 but could not be shipped to Isadore until much later for fear they would be destroyed in the skirmishes at sea that continued sporadically even after the war ended. Instead, they were buried in Germany under several feet of sawdust; when the Allies finally triumphed, each window was carefully dug up, cleaned off, packaged, and shipped to northern Michigan. These were the windows now reflecting the pale winter light of the solstice.

The procession moved forward again and stopped finally at the church's massive front doors. Someone flung them open, and the people of Isadore strode inside, jubilant, and took to the pews to worship in their new church for the very first time. Visiting holy men led the service. By coincidence or by design, each knew the trials endured by these immigrant farm families and faithful worshippers in order to arrive at this place, in this building, on this day.

Father Casimir Skory of St. Adalbert's in Grand Rapids said the Solemn High Mass. It was at a Forty Hours' Devotional he'd planned and hosted that Father Lempke had told Father Edward about the bones once buried right below where the worshippers now stood. Father Skory's assistant was the recently ordained Father John Gatzke, another man intimately familiar with Isadore's history. Michael Gatzke, Sr., was his father, and he grew up with the rest of the Gatzke clan, in the farmhouse right across the street.

Holy Rosary's own priest, Father Stephen Narloch, sat off to the side, unable to contain a smile. If he would just allow himself, he could take some pride in the fact that he had been able to accomplish what Father Andrew, Father Leo, and Father Edward had not. But pride, of course, was a sin, and not part of his humble nature. Not even with his older brother and fellow priest, Andrew Narloch, sitting nearby.

The old church had been torn down and hauled away, and this new and majestic testament now stood in its place. For three long summers the Isadore farm families had hauled in fieldstone from their cleared land to be used in the new church's foundation. Local stonemasons labored for two full years to set the stones properly and then set to work on the brick, using mortar mixed by the willing hands of less skilled, though no less committed, parishioners.

The Romanesque church with granite footings squaring off the fieldstone and the gleaming new copper dome, as yet free from tarnish, could shelter as many as five hundred people thanking God together inside the building's sturdy walls. Bishop Kelly sat off to the side too, with his assistant, Father Timothy Koback, of Suttons Bay. Father Koback had visited Stella in jail and comforted her when her own priests were unavailable. That was only four years ago, but it could have been forty or more for all the pause it gave him, or anyone, now.

And finally, the Solemn Dedicatory Sermon was preached in Polish by Father Ladislaus Krakowski. "God and my Lord, long have your faithful servants whispered here in sacred moments."

Father Krakowski once made a special trip to Manistee just to interrogate Father Andrew about the missing nun. How he had learned of the secret grave was now known only to him, and he would not speak of it, to anyone, ever again. At the close of his sermon, seventy boys and girls of Isadore came forward to have the priest administer their confirmation.

So momentous an occasion was the celebration of this first Mass in Holy Rosary's new church building that the Catholic Church's newspaper, the *Catholic Vigil,* sent a reporter to cover the event.

"He recalled the hardships and trials of the early settlers," the Catholic reporter wrote, after listening to Father Krakowski's sermon. "How they labored not only to gain a livelihood for their body from the unsympathetic forests and unyielding hills, but how they strove to provide for the spiritual nourishment of their souls, and now, at last, they have accomplished their design.

"The new church is the best in this part of the state. Not only Isadore, but all of Leelanau County is proud of this church. Both the people of the parish and their pastor deserve unstinted praise in this undertaking."

Father Andrew had not attended nor been invited to the dedication of the new church. While Isadore triumphed over its sordid past, he remained embroiled in it. His actions on behalf of Stella were not looked upon fondly by the Catholic Church, and he was moved around frequently, from Manistee to Saginaw, Bay City, and Standish, as well as other smaller parishes, and finally to Mackinaw City.

Age had tempered some of his harshest traits but not his determination in the face of what he regarded as wrongdoing. These not-so-subtle sanctions from his diocese did nothing to end his campaign for Stella's freedom, and he continued to revisit the evidence in Sister Janina's murder. Time had given the man perspective, and he was not as convinced of his former housekeeper's innocence as he had been during the trial. Still, he worked just as diligently to free her; she had confessed and been punished, and it was unjust to ask more of any mortal than that.

The case simply would not leave him, even sixteen years after Sister Janina was murdered, despite his efforts to put it in the past. In this regard at least, his mind had been functioning more as a detective's than a priest's. The same year that Bishop Kelly visited Isadore to bless Holy Rosary, Father Andrew handwrote these notes on the back of a 1923 Eastern Clergy Bureau Coupon.

1. Doubtful character of the evidence.
2. Undisputed record in regard to the conduct of the sheriff's detectives in coercing the alleged confession.
3. The fact established by affidavit that among the bones exhibited were those of the fetus, which evidence was not permitted to go to the jury.
4. Generally that in view of the doubted character of the proof, the woman has suffered enough.
5. As bearing on the probable force of evidence, the situation at the convent that afternoon involves the overpowering improbability of one woman being able to kill another and dispose of the body by burying her in broad daylight and in such surroundings and in the length of time.

Sister Janina had been pregnant when she was killed; the lawmen knew it and purposely kept this information out of the official record. Father Andrew knew it too, and kept the fact to himself as well. He does not write about "a fetus" as if the unborn child were an anonymous castoff but rather says "the fetus," suggesting some knowledge of its existence. His motive to participate in keeping Sister Janina's pregnancy out of the court record was obvious: he was the father of her doomed baby. If the nun's pregnancy was germane to the case, and even was somehow the motive for the nun's murder, the opportunity to use it in court was long past. Father Andrew would need to find another way to secure Stella's freedom. He turned, finally, to the foreign and secular land of politics. Perhaps Stella could be pardoned.

Unfortunately for the priest, the parole or pardon of any of Michigan's incarcerated criminals was an incendiary issue in the mid-1920s. After a successful stint as Michigan's attorney general from 1916 to 1921, Alexander Joseph Groesbeck was elected governor in November 1921 and subsequently served three terms. In his term beginning in 1924, one of his highest priorities and the platform that helped him coast into office the third time was prison reform. A Republican, Groesbeck spearheaded a movement to rebuild the state's crumbling prison infrastructure, improve the functioning of the prison commission, and upgrade conditions for inmates, from menus to medical care.

His efforts were seen as humane and needed by some, but there were those in his own political party who sensed weakness and watched closely for an opportunity to challenge him in the next primary when he was thought to seek a fourth term. Having a reputation for being soft on crime has never been a good political strategy, and his prison reforms were viewed by some as exactly that.

Under these constraints, only well-protected people with high-up connections dared to request a pardon or parole from the governor. A powerful Catholic Bishop from Detroit would be one such connection; he just might be able to broach the topic successfully.

By the time the parole issue became controversial, Stella had served nearly seven years of her life sentence. An August 27, 1926, article in the *Detroit Free Press* helped heat this political stew to boiling for Michigan's governor. "Alex Groesbeck has paroled 7,500 or more convicts since his election," the newspaper reported, quoting a Saginaw judge. "He has literally let loose upon the people of Michigan an army of robbers and killers. Why, nobody knows."

That the judge had released only those figures to the public, with nothing to compare them to, did not halt the uproar. A deluge of incoming mail and telephone calls from constituents washed into the governor's office, each missive protesting what many saw as an "easy on crime" mind-set.

The complaints inspired the state's powerful to take a meeting; the gubernatorial primary was only weeks away, the November 1926 general election bearing down on them, too. On August 28 Governor Groesbeck, the five members of the State Prison Commission, and assorted hangers-on met inside the Hotel Downey to strategize. It was a matter of perception, the men agreed. The public must be made to see what these frightening-sounding numbers truly meant.

On August 29, the *Free Press* reported corrected parole figures provided by William Porter, chair of the Prison Commission under Governor Groesbeck: "During the five years from 1916 to 1920, inclusive, the entire population of the three prisons was 10,833. During that time Governors Ferris and Sleeper issued 4,912 paroles, which was a trifle more than 45 percent of the prison population. During the five years of Governor Groesbeck's administration from 1921 to 1925 inclusive, the total population of the three prisons was 19,533. Of this number 7,638 were paroled, or 39 percent."

Groesbeck had indeed paroled more prisoners than anyone who'd held the state's highest office previously, but that was only because the prison population had grown, and not because he was releasing robbers and killers to prey on an innocent public. In his previous position, Groesbeck had been a judge on the state's Supreme Court; he was not soft on crime.

In a private letter to the Saginaw judge who was quoted in the *Free Press* article, Porter expressed his exasperation at the airing of a political matter in public and invited the judge to inspect prison records if he so desired. "If you have any doubt about it, I will be very glad to go through the records with you or any representative that you may send here and you will find that they are correct to a man."

And to a woman.

On November 2, 1926, Fred W. Green won the election to become Michigan's thirty-first governor; Alex Groesbeck's six-year reign was over. It was into this flaming pot Father Andrew and Stella's other remaining supporters tossed their request for her freedom. They could only hope that her last chance wouldn't be burned in a political firestorm.

These secular politics were unfathomable to Father Andrew, and so he returned to those he knew well, even if he hadn't always been welcome within: the politics of the Catholic Church.

Stella's champion reached out to his Bishop.

Detroit Michigan,
December 21st, 1926

Right Reverend Michael J. Gallagher,

Efforts are being made by prominent persons in Detroit and elsewhere to interest Governor Groesbeck in the pardon of Mrs. Stella Lipczynska, unjustly convicted of the murder of Sister Mary Janina at Leland, Leelanau Court, Michigan. This can be brought about before Christmas if I can secure your cooperation.

Will you not kindly sign the enclosed letter and mail same to me without delay.

Respectfully yours,
A. Bieniawski

Hon. Alexander J. Groesbeck, Governor
Lansing, Michigan

My dear Governor;
    May we intercede for the parole or pardon of Mrs. Stella Lipczynska, now serving a life sentence at the House of Correction, Detroit. Since her incarceration, she has conducted herself in a highly edifying manner and we believe there is a reasonable doubt of her guilt. Her steadfast devotion to her religious duties week after week, is indicative of deeply spiritual motives wholly incapable with the crime of which she was adjudged guilty. I respectfully recommend executive clemency in this case.

Cordially yours, Michael J. Gallagher, Bishop

December 24, 1926
Mr. Fred Jeanette
Commissioner of Pardons,
Lansing, Mich.

Dear Sir:
    In addition to the facts presented to you personally in case of Mrs. Lipczynska, I beg to call your attention to the following:
    The anonymous letter, proved to be written by the missing Sister's physician, who admitted on the witness stand that he was calling on her for several months twice or three times a week treating her for a cracked rib, was written on Sept. 12, 1907, while the sister disappeared on Aug. 23, 1907.
    The letter, the reduced photographic copy of which is herewith enclosed, states plainly that she was not murdered, but "slipped quietly away" and if she was alive on the 12th of Sept. she could not have been murdered on Aug. 23rd by Mrs. Lipczynska but was being detained or sheltered somewhere by the writer of this letter,

or at least he knew where she was at that time hiding. The writer was also Coroner of Leelanau County.

The purpose of the letter was to stop our searching efforts, assuring plainly that, "you probably won't find her and she don't want that you should."

The writer of said letter must have been in communication with the missing Sister's relatives, because although her brother promised to come, he never showed up and never explained the reason why he did not keep his promise, but instead of him, the anonymous letter arrived, which we thought at that time was written by somebody in the family of the missing Sister.

I enclose Dr. Fralick's own statement under his signature, written to Dr. Ramsdell of Manistee, that the bones are all present, with the possible exception of two twelfth ribs.

Dr. Hoektoen of McCormick's Institute, Chicago, Ill. Established the fact that there were 52 bones missing, while there were some other bones mixed among them, not belonging to the skeleton. Two small ribs were present.

The hair which was found was of red color, while the Sister was dark complected, hence the hair was not mentioned by the prosecution until we found it out after conviction.

No safety pins, no buttons were found, no clothing, but a few inches of shreds, to be more exact, one half size of human palm as Martin Brown told me at the time he called to arrest Mrs. Lipczynska, while the Sisters wear very heavy woolen garb, the sample of which you have seen.

The outside woolen garb of the Sisters takes about seven or eight yards besides the underclothing they wear and black woolen veil and a stiffly starched white linen bonnet. None of these were found.

Submitting these few important details for your intelligent consideration, I ask you to present them to the Governor and pardon the unjustly suffering woman.

Respectfully yours,
A.B. (Andrew Bieniawski)

"I would have kissed the dust from her shoes. But I can't talk anymore. Please don't ask me."

After serving more than seven years in prison, Stella had learned a valuable skill—English. On New Year's Day 1927, she walked out of the Detroit House of Corrections a free woman. Governor Alex J. Groesbeck paroled her as his last official act in office. She would not be pardoned for her crime, but she would be free.

Seven years before, he had been serving as the state's attorney general and helped argue the prosecution's case against her to the Michigan State Supreme Court, which ultimately affirmed her conviction. Now, he must have believed she was either innocent or no longer a danger to the people of Michigan. It was either compassion, second thoughts, spiritual intention, or something else equally subjective that guided his hand as he signed her parole papers.

It turned out to be an element of Stella's character, and not any language barrier, that held her tongue in public this time. Despite her present command of the English language, Stella was no more forthcoming about the murder, or her part in it, than she had been when she spoke mainly Polish. When Stella left prison, she went to a halfway house in Detroit for women parolees. Her parole card states she was to remain at the facility "indefinitely." She stayed for thirty days and then was turned over to the care of J. Zimmerman, in Milwaukee, Wisconsin, one of the lay leaders of the Catholic Diocese there.

In Wisconsin, Stella was reunited with her daughter, Mary, her grandchildren, and her son-in-law, Joseph, and she took her secrets with her, and out of Michigan. She never made another public statement about the case. In April 1931, she was officially removed from probation, considered to be fully rehabilitated, a rare prison success story.

Detroit House of Corrections' Women's Prison Warden, Captain Edward Denniston, wasn't as shy with the press about her release as Stella herself was. In her time under his care Stella's nature had softened, and her new nickname reflected this change. From the "Iron Woman" moniker that had seemed so apt during her murder trial, she was now "Old Stella" to the warden and the guards. They used the term almost affectionately.

Captain Denniston said he had come to know his infamous prisoner quite well, was impressed by her devotion to her religion, and felt compelled to make public his belief that she had earned her freedom.

"I have seen many prisoners come and go from here, but never have I seen one to whom I thought was more deserving of executive clemency than Stella," he said.

Besides her family, Father Andrew, and the prison warden, Stella had other supporters. The Felician Order in Wisconsin either believed in her innocence or forgave her for her crime. A month after she left prison for murdering one of their own, the Felician convent in Milwaukee hired her on as their cook. She was fifty-six years old; she worked for them for more than thirty years.

Stanislawa "Stella" Lipczynska died in Milwaukee, Wisconsin, on January 21, 1962, having never revealed anything more about the mysterious murder of Sister Janina, at least not publicly. She was ninety-two. Her obituary celebrated her as the "dear mother" of Mary Flees, mother-in-law of Joseph Flees, and further survived by five grandchildren, twenty-two great grandchildren, two great-great grandchildren, two sisters, one brother, as well as additional family still living in Poland.

Stella is buried in St. Adalbert's Cemetery in Milwaukee and now lies next to her daughter and her son-in-law, who died separately many years after she did. Before Stella was interred, her final church, St. Alexander's, held a funeral service for her, held her body in state, said a private rosary with family and friends, and finally said a public parish rosary for her.

Hail, Holy Queen, Mother of Mercy, our life, our sweetness, and our hope! To thee do we cry, poor banished children of Eve.

Like Stella, Father Andrew and Father Edward were also posted far from Isadore in their later years. Both remained in the priesthood until they died, although just as their parish ministering styles differed greatly, so did their fates.

After delivering his tearful testimony inside the Leland Courthouse, Father Edward was sent out of the area to New Jersey. From the safety of boarding at Judge Martin Brown's house, and the strange camaraderie that developed around the judge's mother's dining room table, Father Edward was hidden away as an assistant pastor at St. Joseph's Church in Passaic, New Jersey. His head priest, Monsignor Monteufeel, soon shipped him north to Bayonne, New Jersey, to be dealt with by another Monsignor, Father Swider. Father Swider sent Father Edward back to Passaic, but this time to another church, coincidentally named Holy Rosary.

There Father Edward found himself again, finally, in a Polish-speaking parish. Under head priest Father Stanislaw Kruczek, he served for many years as assistant priest, though he was still not allowed to say Mass publicly. He must have continued to miss Michigan, because on March 2, 1923, he wrote to the Gaylord, Michigan, Diocese to inform them of his whereabouts and to ask if he could ever come back to the Midwest.

"I am with Father Kruczek where I arrived this very day. I have written to Bishop Scollard of North Bay, Ontario, for a position but I have not heard from him. Might it be possible to reinstate me in the diocese?"

For eleven years the answer to his question was no. Then, in 1934, while he was visiting acquaintances in Milwaukee, a development was made clear that would finally allow him to serve back in Michigan.

"Father Podlaszewski dropped into our Chancery Office a few days ago and filled out the enclosed questionnaire," a priest at St. Francis Seminary in Milwaukee wrote to the Gaylord, Michigan, Diocese. "He was ordained June 24, 1909 by Bishop H. J. Richter. At the present time he is assistant at Holy Rosary parish in Passaic, N.J. He changed his name to Polan."

With this new anonymity, Father Edward was allowed back in the Midwest, and acquired the patronage of a Michigan priest, Father Joseph Koss of St. Stanislaus in Ludington. Father Koss tried to intercede with the Gaylord Diocese on Father Edward's behalf.

"His case is a matter of record. His repentance and the fact that he paid heavily may not be on record. I'd like to do something for this unfortunate priest who has been away from the Diocese for 20 years. So far, the Bishop has been unapproachable in the matter. Now, this priest is helping the priests in Milwaukee. Might it be possible to reinstate him in our Diocese? I beg Your Excellency to show him mercy."

In 1945, Father Edward was allowed to serve as assistant priest to any of the churches in Grand Rapids, Michigan, that would have him. Sometime after that, he disappeared from the Gaylord, Michigan, Diocese records.

Almost two decades passed without historical mention of Father Edward. Then, in 1962, a Yale doctoral candidate in law, who was also a Jesuit priest, happened upon Father Edward's unfortunate history in his legal studies, and wrote to the Custodian of the Archives for the Arch-diocese of Detroit to inquire further. His letter asked:

In the cause of research for a doctorate in Law I am writing on the status of the clergyman in American Civil Law and have to discuss the problem of the priest-penitent privilege in the law of evidence.

In People v. Lipczynska the Court record states that the Defendant, a former housekeeper of the parish, charged with having murdered a nun, stated on the witness stand that her identity was discovered because a Bishop Kozlowski broke the seal of confession.

The Court records are not too clear but apparently what happened was: the defendant murdered the Nun. The defendant then went to confession to a Fr. Nowak, in Milwaukee, who told her she must see Bishop Kozlowski in order to obtain absolution.

Some time later Bishop Kozlowski told a Father Lempke that the body of the nun was buried beneath a parish church. Father Lempke related this to a Fr. Podlaszewski, the pastor of the Church, who exhumed the body—and the scandal broke.

It occurred to me that there might be some evidence in the archives that the penitent approached Bishop Kozlowski outside of confession. If there is any such evidence I would appreciate learning of it.

Thank you very much for your kindness. Since this is the only instance in Anglo-American law in which a priest or bishop has been formally charged with a violation of the seal of confession, I am extremely anxious to "track it down."

Sincerely, Rev. Francis Conklin, S.J.

It took two months, and the return correspondence did not answer his question, but the Jesuit law student did get a response from Michigan. The note was curt and to the point: "The only information in our files is that Father Podlaszewski left the Diocese of Grand Rapids," answered a chancellor responding for the Detroit Diocese. "We have no official word where he is."

After the trial, the Supreme Court case, and Stella's eventual parole, Father Andrew had a more respected role in the church, certainly, than Father Edward could claim, though he, too, was frequently moved around by his superiors. It's probable that the gossip surrounding his involvement with Sister Janina, and his continued efforts on behalf of Stella, did not please those in power at the diocese. From Manistee to Saginaw to Standish to Bay City and finally, in the 1940s, to Mackinaw City, he moved.

In Mackinaw City Father Andrew found his forever home and even had the opportunity to dedicate a new church building. Groundbreaking ceremonies for St. Anthony Church were held in November 1958, with Father Andrew performing the honors. On July 3, 1959, he said the church's first Mass.

The years sanded down the roughest edges of his nature and relaxed the broad shoulders that had always been tense. The voice that had been used only to lecture and criticize was heard to say kind words more often than not. The tightly clenched jaw would even sometimes let the corners of his aging face curve into a smile.

After serving as head priest for more than twenty years at St. Anthony's, Father Andrew died March 22, 1964, at the age of eighty-nine. His headstone in the church cemetery calls the man once so feared and despised in Isadore simply "Our Beloved Pastor."

Though people who live and worship in the village will not say her name out loud, Isadore has not forgotten Sister Mary Janina. Her death and the myriad scandals that surrounded it are today referred to as just "the tragedy." In 1998, a well-researched, heavily illustrated, and lovingly compiled book about Holy Rosary School was published by the parish to celebrate the school's centennial. Not even here, in the only historical record of the school where she was teaching when she was murdered, is the event that still silently permeates the area's history detailed. On the contrary; though every priest, every other nun, every missionary, and even the school's janitors are all honored and mentioned by name, Sister Mary Janina is nowhere to be found within its 175 pages. According to the editors of the volume, time in Isadore leapt from 1904 to 1919 with only this statement: "The succeeding years proceeded relatively uninterrupted."

That is true only if you don't count the convicted murderess who faked insanity, the female spy, the jailhouse confession, the skeleton assembled in front of a jury in the old Leland Courthouse, the Michigan State Supreme Court appeal, a governor's clemency, and a local farmer's suicide. The years indeed passed relatively uninterrupted except for those events.

There are a few occasions worth mentioning when Sister Janina's story has been brought to mind, however. The first of these takes place on a rather unlikely, and public, stage. Literally. While Isadore might be ashamed of their infamous nun, Broadway doesn't appear to be. On May 18, 1976, a play based loosely on Sister Janina's murder opened on Broadway at the Little Theatre. A Yale School of Drama graduate student and playwright, Milan Stitt, wrote *The Runner Stumbles* after a suggestion by his then-wife. She was a Traverse City native and had been told stories of a love affair between a priest and a nun, and also of the housekeeper's trial. After Stitt completed an early version of the play, he visited the Leland Courthouse and read the trial transcript. As recently as 2007 the play was again produced on Broadway, this time in the Beckett Theatre on West 42nd Street.

In *The Runner Stumbles* the main character is Father Rivard, a Catholic priest banished to a remote parish because of his abrasive ways. He falls in love with a nun who is a teacher in the small convent school there, the naive but enthusiastic Sister Rita. A rigid and meddling housekeeper, Mrs. Shandig, also plays in the drama. The nun is murdered, Father Rivard is charged with the crime, and the story is revealed in flashbacks the priest experiences while in jail and during the trial.

Though *The Runner Stumbles* received some enthusiastic reviews from drama critics in New York City, news of its production was not as well received by some in northern Michigan. The notoriety attached to the play inspired the *Traverse City Record-Eagle* newspaper to run a six-part series about the actual case, written by local historian Larry Wakefield and titled "The Missing Nun." A June 4, 1976, Letter to the Editor by Traverse City resident Mrs. Robert Seeberg expressed the opinions of many.

"I was a very small girl living in Leelanau County at the time when this sordid affair happened. I still remember the gory details. I am sure that the editors of your paper could have written an article that would have contributed to something educational and uplifting about this area. There is surely much that could be presented in the paper of the early days of this region."

Days earlier, another resident, Esther Saxton, shared similar views: "Why would a newspaper find a story that has happened some sixty years ago so newsworthy to give full page coverage? I am referring to your series on The Missing Nun first appearing Monday, May 24. A newspaper is a publication devoted basically to current news. This story was laid to rest years ago and should be allowed to stay there forever! You were correct in stating that the people of this small community care; they care very deeply. Why hurt them by bringing back the ghosts of the past."

These correspondents could not have been pleased when, three years later in 1979, "the tragedy" was elevated to the silver screen. "Excellent human drama," was the general consensus about director Stanley Kramer's version of the screenplay Stitt adapted from his play. The production starred Dick Van Dyke in a rare dramatic role as Father Brian Rivard, Kathleen Quinlan as Sister Rita, and Maureen Stapleton as Mrs. Shandig. *Variety* said the movie "ultimately emerges as more than melodrama because director Stanley Kramer puts equal emphasis on the priest and how he grapples with his love for God and this woman in his life." Critic Roger Ebert said the movie contained "interesting performances."

In his *Chicago Sun-Times* review, Ebert described the movie's plot. "The love affair between Van Dyke and Quinlan is developed pretty obviously: They're isolated, they're thrown into each other's company, slight friendly gestures and a shared sensibility grow into affection, and then there's trouble. The town is filled with gossips, of course, and in Van Dyke's own household there's a menacing presence in the person of the loyal housekeeper, old Mrs. Shandig . . . who is depicted as such a classic textbook case of repressed sexual hysteria that we immediately suspect she's capable of violence."

The movie revived interest in the true story of Sister Janina, Father Andrew, and Stella, but that interest was short-lived.

Then in 1989 a brief but powerful electrical storm surprised Leelanau County and put Sister Janina's memory back in the pages of the local newspaper, and in the minds of villagers. Curiously, the storm seemed to affect only Isadore and was centered inside *Cmentarz Kalwaryi,* Holy Rosary's cemetery.

It was late in the day more than seventy years after Sister Janina's anonymous grave had been dug up, and storm clouds were threatening. The way that Isadore sits at the crest of Schomberg and Gatzke roads, with little to obscure the miles of farmland that fall away in every direction, makes for a spectacular view. Standing in the cemetery one can see the weather coming. By 8 p.m. that evening it had started to drizzle. There had been a funeral service that morning, and sexton Richard Nachazel wanted to get the coffin in the ground and buried before nightfall. His labor was cut violently short when one of the ancient cedar trees that sheltered the cemetery's oldest headstones suddenly exploded.

Even in its more recent history, grave digging is not always a fully safe endeavor in Isadore. Nachazel, who held the same title in 1989 that Jacob Flees claimed in 1918, barely escaped this task with his life.

"A bolt of lightning nailed that cedar tree and I saw it blow up," he said. The force of the strike burned holes in the grass, broke tombstones apart, toppled them over onto one another, and even snatched the garden spade out of the sexton's hand. Fingers tingling, he found it a few minutes later, lying on the ground fifteen feet away.

The happening was dramatic enough, especially considering the cemetery's odd history, that a local newspaper sent over a reporter. The reporter brought along a camera and took photographs. These show the splintered trunk of a cedar tree, scattered evergreens, and fist-sized chunks of ragged granite tossed randomly like a handful of dice in some meteorological game of chance. The big cross in the center of the graveyard—a ten-foot metal crucifix that one might logically fear would function as a giant lightning rod in weather like this, the cross that can be seen from farther away than any other marker and that had once guarded the second secret grave of Sister Mary Janina—was untouched.

The special date of the storm was not remarked upon by the reporter but is worth mentioning here; it was the evening of Memorial Day. Only minutes earlier dozens of people had been gathered together inside the fence surrounding the old cemetery, honoring their dead.

No one in the group would have come expressly to visit Sister Janina; according to court documents and newspaper reports she is no longer buried at the foot of the large cross. After the trial, some sources say that her remains were released into the care of her fellow Felicians. They supposedly took their Sister away from Isadore and gave her a traditional ceremonial burial. Some say she rests in the cemetery next to where the Detroit Motherhouse once stood, in the company of her family of Sisters. It's satisfying to think of her finally surrounded by religious acceptance, an orphan no more, at peace with eternity.

But these reports, like so much of Sister Janina's previously reported history, simply may not be true. In 1936 the Felician Motherhouse outgrew its Detroit location and moved to Livonia, Michigan, where it stands today. Sister Elaine is the order's historian, and according to her private files, Sister Janina's remains were not reclaimed by the Detroit Felicians. She is still buried in Isadore, interred in Holy Rosary's cemetery. Some helpful locals say the cemetery's plot map is so convoluted it is almost useless. Sister Janina is there, they say, in an unmarked and child-size grave. On this plot map there are two curiously labeled cemetery squares directly in front of the cross. One says "old well pit" and one is simply labeled with a question mark.

Traditional Polish death customs call for certain remains to be interred separately in the cemetery, off to the side and away from the other graves. Murder victims are among these. In Isadore's *Cmentarz Kalwaryi* there is such a section, but the markers are so small and so timeworn the names and dates engraved upon them are completely illegible. Perhaps one of these flat gray place-markers once marked the Sister's third, and final, grave. Or, maybe she is in the spot labeled with a question mark, or in the old well pit. If so, it is impossible to determine by sight alone.

A walk through the grounds in the small cemetery, with its ancient evergreen boughs that drape over the back fence and the still-majestic Holy Rosary Church towering overhead, is both a spiritual and a historic endeavor. More than a century after Sister Janina's death, one lingering element in "the tragedy" is that no one seems to want to claim her. Not publicly, at least. Her fate has been left to be decided by actors and playwrights, by her God and by history.

"I am a person who is a nun, not a nun who used to be a person," the fictional Sister Rita states passionately, in a scene from the movie. Perhaps this simple declaration is just what the real Sister, the blood and flesh and bone Sister Janina, has been trying to say, all along.

CAST OF CHARACTERS

SISTER MARY ANGELINA—Teaching nun who lived and taught school with Sister Janina and who, along with Sister Mary Josephine, was the first to discover her missing.

MOTHER MARY ANTONIA—Mother Superior at the Felician Motherhouse in Detroit. It was she who told Father Lempke the rumor that Sister Janina was buried in the basement of the church in Isadore. She testified at Stella's trial and led her fellow nuns in prayer around the exhibit of skeletal remains in full view of the entire courtroom.

CHIEF WILLIAM ASHTON—Traverse City police chief in 1907, he made a clandestine visit to Chicago to stake out the home of Sister Janina's brothers, but found no evidence she had taken refuge there. He also conducted a background check on Mary Tylicka at the behest of Father Andrew Bieniawski but found no criminal record.

DR. ALBERT BARRETT—First director of the State Psychopathic Hospital, which opened on Catherine Street in Ann Arbor in 1906 and was selected with caring for up to 200 mentally ill patients. Dr. Barrett was one of four physicians selected by the court with determining whether or not Stella was sane enough to stand trial for the murder of Sister Janina.

FATHER ANDREW BIENIAWSKI—Born in Warsaw, Poland, on November 24, 1874, and priest at Isadore's Holy Rosary Church from 1900 to 1913, he served with Sister Janina and was rumored to be both her lover and the father of her unborn child. Father Andrew was shuffled around to Manistee and Standish following his ouster from Isadore and eventually settled in Mackinaw City at St. Anthony's Parish where he served from 1928 to 1961. He died in 1964 at the age of eighty-nine.

SUSAN BIENIAWSKI—Father Andrew's younger sister. She was unmarried and lived with him in Isadore, and accompanied him on the fishing trip the day Sister Janina disappeared.

SHERIFF MARTIN BROWN—Sheriff of Leelanau County from 1901 to 1902 and 1905 to 1908. He was sheriff when Sister Janina disappeared and, along with his deputies, investigated the case to no avail. By the time Sister Janina's remains were found, he was a probate judge and again involved himself in the investigation. He was present at the arrest of Stella and led the initial interrogation of Father Andrew. He also supervised the removal of the nun's remains.

HOWARD L. CAMPBELL—Lead defense attorney for Stella, hired by Father Andrew. A former prosecutor of Manistee County, years after the trial he maintained that he always believed his client was innocent of the murder of the nun.

DETECTIVE J. R. CASTLE—Detroit-based detective affiliated with the Pinkertons hired by Father Andrew to find the missing nun. He spent a week in Isadore and found no clue.

PROSECUTOR CLINTON L. DAYTON—Prosecutor of Grand Traverse County in 1920 and the man who tried the case against Stella, along with two additional special prosecutors brought on for the trial.

DR. GEORGE FRALICK—Sister Janina's physician and one of two coroners of Leelanau County in 1919. He treated Sister Janina for tuberculosis and probably knew of her pregnancy.

JACOB FLEES—Isadore native and sexton of Holy Rosary Church from 1917 to 1919. Along with Father Edward Podlaszewski, he exhumed the remains of Sister Janina in the fall of 1918. He was a cousin of Joseph Flees who married Stella's daughter, Mary.

JOSEPH FLEES—Husband to Stella's daughter, Mary Lipczynska. They married October 18, 1910, and moved to Wisconsin. Joseph and Jacob Flees were cousins.

MARY LIPCZYNSKA FLEES—Stella's daughter. She lived in the Holy Rosary rectory with her mother, Father Andrew, and Father Andrew's sister, Susan, and later married Joseph Flees. Testifying at her mother's murder trial, she contradicted statements she had given to law enforcement.

BISHOP MICHAEL J. GALLAGHER—Bishop of the Detroit Diocese from 1918 to 1937, he personally requested clemency for Stella from Governor Alexander Groesbeck in 1926.

MARY AND MIKE GATZKE—siblings and neighbors of Holy Rosary Church. Each testified at Stella's trial that she gossiped about Sister Janina's light character.

PARMIUS C. GILBERT—Special prosecutor in Stella's trial.

PETER T. GLASSMIRE—Member of Stella's defense team.

GOVERNOR ALEXANDER JOSEPH GROESBECK—Michigan's attorney general from 1916 to 1921 and governor for three terms from 1921 to 1926. Known as a prison reformer, his last official act in office was paroling Stella.

THEODORE GRUBA—Chore boy at Holy Rosary Church in 1907. He, along with Susan, was with Father Andrew on a fishing trip the day Sister Janina disappeared. He later moved to Canada.

SISTER MARY JANINA, A.K.A. JOSEPHINE MEZEK—Born January 24, 1874, in Prussia to John and Josephine Mezek, she immigrated to Chicago with her parents and two brothers. A third brother, Joseph Mezek, was born to her parents after they immigrated. She was orphaned in 1884 and was placed in a Detroit convent orphanage. She became a nun in 1901, went to Isadore to teach at Holy Rosary School in 1906, and disappeared a year later. In 1918 her remains were exhumed from the dirt-floored basement of Holy Rosary church.

SISTER MARY JOSEPHINE—Teaching nun who lived and taught school with Sister Janina and who, along with Sister Mary Angelina, was the first to discover her missing.

SHERIFF JOHN KINNUCAN—Sheriff of Leelanau County from 1917 to 1920. Interrogated sexton Jacob Flees and assisted with the exhumation of Sister Janina's remains from the church cemetery. Led the investigation that resulted in Stella's arrest for murder and was later accused of torturing her in the Leland Jail.

SHERIFF WILLIAM KITTLE—Antrim County sheriff in 1907 and owner of Tom, a renowned bloodhound. He and his dog made several searches for Sister Janina in the early days after her disappearance.

BISHOP EDWARD KOZLOWSKI—Bishop of Milwaukee from 1914 to 1915. He reportedly heard of Stella's confession directly from Father Nowak and passed the information on to the Detroit Felicians. He died August 6, 1915.

FATHER LADISLAUS KRAKOWSKI—Priest of St. Stanislaus Church in Bay City from 1913 to 1917 and enemy of Father Andrew. Father Krakowski threatened Father Andrew with the secret of the missing nun as early as 1914 when he visited him in Manistee.

FATHER JOSEPH LEMPKE—Priest of the Felician Motherhouse in Detroit in 1919. He passed the rumor of Sister Janina's secret grave from the Detroit Felicians to Father Edward at a chance meeting at a Forty Hours' Devotional.

STANISLAWA "STELLA" LIPCZYNSKA—Longtime housekeeper for Father Andrew and accused killer of Sister Janina. She was arrested, tried, and convicted in 1919, the Michigan State Supreme Court upheld her conviction in 1920, and she was paroled New Year's Day, 1927. Stella was born in Poland and immigrated to the United States with her daughter in 1900. After her release from Detroit Women's Prison she moved to Wisconsin and worked as a housekeeper and cook for a Felician convent for three decades. She died January 21, 1962, at age ninety-two.

JUDGE FREDERICK W. MAYNE—Charlevoix-based judge who presided over *People v. Stanislawa "Stella" Lipczynska.*

JOHN, EMIL, FRANK, AND JOSEPH MEZEK—Sister Janina's father and three brothers.

JOSEPHINE MEZEK—Sister Janina's name before she entered the convent; she was named after her mother who was committed to the Illinois Eastern Hospital for the Insane in 1884, just after her husband, John, died in a traffic accident, making her daughter an orphan.

MARTHA MILLER—Teenage housekeeper hired by Father Edward Podlaszewski in 1917 when he became priest at Holy Rosary. A love affair between the two resulted in an unplanned pregnancy, Father Edward's eventual ouster from Isadore, and his loss of privileges to say Mass in public. After she gave her baby up for adoption, Martha moved back with her parents, remained unemployed and unmarried, and died in 1921 of tuberculosis.

FATHER STEPHEN NARLOCH—Native son of Isadore ordained June 24, 1913, and priest assigned to Holy Rosary after Father Edward was removed. Under his tenure a Romanesque brick church was erected in place of the original more humble wood building. That church still stands today in Isadore and celebrates three Masses a week.

FATHER FRANCIS NOWAK—Wisconsin priest that Stella supposedly confessed the murder of Sister Janina to. Stella denied this and for reasons unknown Father Nowak was not subpoenaed to testify at her trial.

FATHER LEOPOLD OPRYCHALSKI—Well-loved priest who served in Alpena, Manistee, Bay City, and Isadore. He was directed by the Diocese to change places with Father Andrew after Father Andrew was forced out of Isadore by parishioners unhappy with his stern ways and inability to find Sister Janina when she disappeared. Father Leo, as he was called, was the first to alert Father Edward to a potential scandal.

FATHER EDWARD PODLASZEWSKI—Priest at Holy Rosary Church from 1917 to 1919. His love affair with his teenage housekeeper and his ambitions to build a new church in Isadore were the catalysts for the revelation of Sister Janina's secret burial. He appeared before a church tribunal and was stripped of his position, title, robes, and duties, and his ability to say public Mass as a result. He was shuffled to churches in Ohio, Kentucky, and New Jersey before eventually returning to Wisconsin and Michigan, then disappearing from church records.

JACOB (JAKE) ROSINSKI JR.—Neighbor of Holy Rosary Church in Isadore. It was to his house Sheriff Kinnucan and his men brought the remains of Sister Janina after they had been exhumed from the cemetery. Jacob Rosinski testified at the trial that he had heard Stella disparage Sister Janina on many occasions.

DR. J. F. SLEPICA—Leland physician and, along with Dr. Fralick, a coroner of Leelanau County in 1919. He conducted an unofficial autopsy of Sister Janina's remains, testified at the trial, and was one of four physicians appointed by Judge Mayne to ascertain whether or not Stella was sane enough to stand trial for the murder of Sister Janina.

SOPHIA TRUSZKOWSKA, BLESSED MARY ANGELA—Founder of the Felician Order.

DETECTIVE MARY TYLICKA, A.K.A. MRS. DOMBROWSKI—Wisconsin-based private detective Sheriff Kinnucan hired to extract a jailhouse confession from Stella. She testified at Stella's trial that Stella did confess the murder to her. She was accused, along with Sheriff Kinnucan, of torturing Stella in the jail.

SOURCES AND RESOURCES

Court Documents

Hearing transcript, *The People of the State of Michigan v. Stanislawa Lipczynska*, Circuit Court for the County of Leelanau, filed April 28, 1919.

Affidavit of Edward Podlaszewski, taken May 9, 1919, and notarized in Cleveland, Ohio.

Intake admission form on case #2575 at the State Pathological Hospital, Ann Arbor, Michigan, dated May 17, 1919.

Official Analysis of Mental State of Stanislawa Lipczynska, authored by Drs. Albert M. Barrett, A. S. Rowley, Joseph F. Slepica, and James A. King, submitted to Leland Circuit Court, July 10, 1919.

State of Michigan Supreme Court transcript, *The People of the State of Michigan, Plaintiff and Appelle v. Stanislawa Lipczynska, Respondent and Appellant*, December 21, 1920.

Parole card for Stanislawa Lipczynska, issued by the Detroit House of Corrections, December 31, 1926.

Books

Archdiocese of Detroit, by Roman Godzak. Arcadia Publishing, 2000.

The Bloodhound: Origin and History, by Hilary Harmar. Publication details unknown.

Butcher's Dozen: 13 Famous Michigan Murders, by Larry Wakefield. Altwerger and Mandel Publishing Company, 1991.

The Catholic Church in the Grand River Valley, 1883–1950, by The Rev. John W. McGee. St. Andrews Cathedral Parish, 1950.

The Catholic Encyclopedia, "Prayers for the Dead," by Patrick Toner, Vol. 4. New York: Robert Appleton Company, 1908.

The Cedar Nun Mystery, by Jack Sweeney. Unpublished, summer 1976.

Encyclopedia of Cleveland History, compiled by David D. VanTassel and John J. Grabowski. http://ech.cwru.edu.

The Errant Nun: Peaceful Peninsula in Turmoil, by Natsolim. MassPac Publishing Company, 1979.

A Golden Treatise on Mental Prayer, edited by G. S. Hollings. A. R. Mowbray and Co. Ltd., 1904.

The Habit: A History of the Clothing of Catholic Nuns, by Elizabeth Kuhns. Doubleday, 2003.

Holy Rosary School Centennial Celebration: 1898–1998, compiled and published by the Holy Rosary School Centennial Committee (Sandy Galla, JoAnn Galla Gauthier, Kathleen Novak Hughes, Judy Weber LaCross, Lucia M. Novak, Leona Novak Witkowski). 1998.

Hymns and Sacred Poems, Charles Wesley. 1879, publication details unknown.

Murder, Mischief, and Mayhem: A Process for Creative Research Papers, by W. Keith Kraus. National Council of Teachers of English, 1978.

The Mystery of the Missing Nun, by Larry Wakefield. Horizon Books, 2000.

The Nun's Rule, by Bishop Richard Poore, Rev. James Morton, and Rev. Francis Aiden Gasquet. The King's Classics, 1905.

Old Polish Traditions in the Kitchen and at the Table, by Maria Lemmis and Henryk Vitry. Hippocrene Books, 1996.

Poles in Michigan, by Dennis Badaczewski. Michigan State University Press, 2002.

Polish Customs, Traditions, and Folklore, by Sophie Hodorowicz Knab. Hippocrene Books, 1993.

Polish Folklore and Myth, edited by Joanne Asala. Penfield Press, 2001.

The Runner Stumbles: A Play with Two Acts, by Milan Stitt. James T. White and Co., 1974.

Sapphic Slashers: Sex, Violence, and American Modernity, by Lisa Duggan. Duke University Press, 2001.

Sisters in Arms: Catholic Nuns through Two Millennia, by Jo Ann Kay McNamara. Harvard University Press, 1996.

Sprague's History of Grand Traverse and Leelanaw Counties, Michigan: A Concise Review of Their Early Settlement, Industrial Development, and Present Conditions, Together with Interesting Reminiscences, edited and compiled by Elvin Sprague. B. F. Bowen, 1903.

These Very Stones Cry Out: Stories on the History of the Diocese of Gaylord, Patrick T. Cawley, editor. Harbor House Publishers, Inc., 1999.

Vintage Views of Leelanau County, M. Christine Byron and Thomas R. Wilson. Huron River Press, 2002.

Unpublished Papers and Personal Accounts

Notes made on the back side of an Eastern Clergy Bureau Coupon by Father Andrew Bieniawski dated 1923, collection of Notre Dame University Archives.

Sbanek family history, written by Stephen Sbanek and dated 1924. Unpublished. From the collection of the Leelanau Historical Society, Leland, Michigan.

Chronology of the legal case drafted by Eduard Adam Skendzel titled "Cedar Nun Murder," undated.

"Disappearance, Discovery, and Death," by Pamela Ann Lieurance. Unpublished college paper, Northwestern Michigan College, November 1, 1998.

"The Mystery of Isadore's Sister Mary Janina," by Lori Priest. Unpublished college paper, Northwestern Michigan College, June 24, 2001.

"Mystery of the Missing Nun of Isadore," by Bernard Bossert Jr. Unpublished college paper, Northwestern Michigan College, March 14, 2002.

"The Church Protects Its Own," by Betty Traines. Unpublished college paper, Northwestern Michigan College, March 13, 2002.

"Was Justice Served?" by Sarah Reincke. Unpublished college paper, Northwestern Michigan College, March 13, 2002.

Article outline on the case of Sister Mary Janina, unpublished and undated, drafted by Gil Kleinknecht, U.S. Marshals Service, retired.

Correspondence

Letter from Father Andrew Bieniawski to Theodore Gruba dated May 5, 1919, collection of Notre Dame University Archives.

Letter from Father Andrew Bieniawski to Mr. S. V. McMahon dated July 8, 1919, collection of Notre Dame University Archives.

Letter from Chancellor A. Fitzpatrick to Father Edward Podlaszewski dated September 8, 1919, collection of Notre Dame University Archives.

Letter from Chancellor A. Fitzpatrick to Father Edward Podlaszewski dated October 28, 1919, collection of Notre Dame University Archives.

Letter from Attorney Charles A. Whitney to Father Andrew Bieniawski dated October 15, 1920, collection of Notre Dame University Archives.

Letter from Attorney Frank Picard to Father Andrew Bieniawski dated December 10, 1920, collection of Notre Dame University Archives.

Letter from Attorney C. A. Whitney to Father Andrew Bieniawski dated December 17, 1920, collection of Notre Dame University Archives.

Letter from Attorney Frank Picard to Father Andrew Bieniawski dated December 31, 1920, collection of Notre Dame University Archives.

Letter from Father Edward Podlaszewski to Bishop Scollard of North Bay, Ontario, dated March 2, 1923, collection of Notre Dame University Archives.

Unsigned letter to Right Reverend Michael J. Gallagher dated December 21, 1926, collection of Notre Dame University Archives.

Letter from Right Reverend Michael J. Gallagher to Governor Alexander Groesbeck dated December 22, 1926, collection of Notre Dame University Archives.

Letter from Father Andrew Bieniawski to Commissioner of Pardons Fred Jeanette, dated December 24, 1926, collection of Notre Dame University Archives.

Letter from Rev. Raymond Baker, Chancellor to Very Reverend A. J. Meunch, rector of St. Francis Seminary in Milwaukee, dated July 3, 1934, collection of Notre Dame University Archives.

Letter from Archbishop Strich of Milwaukee, Wisconsin, to Bishop Pinton dated November 12, 1936, collection of Notre Dame University Archives.

Letter from Father Jos. Koss of St. Stanislawas in Ludington, Michigan, to Bishop Hass dated March 20, 1944, collection of Notre Dame University Archives.

Letter from Rev. Francis Conklin, S.J., to Custodian of the Archives, Archdiocese of Detroit, dated October 21, 1962, collection of Notre Dame University Archives.

Newspaper Articles

"Convent Was Burned Down." *Evening Record,* November 15, 1904.

"Looking for Missing Nun." *Evening Record,* August 27, 1907.

"Nun Disappeared at Traverse City." *Grand Rapids Press,* August 27, 1907.

"Search for Nun Was Fruitless." *Grand Rapids Press,* August 28, 1907.

"Searchers Still Busy." *Evening Record,* August 28, 1907.

"Hunt for Lost Nun." *Grand Rapids Press,* September 1, 1907.

"Sister Mary Is Yet Alive." *Evening Record,* September 3, 1907.

"Singing in Dense Swamp." *Evening Record,* September 4, 1907.

"Convent at Isadore May Be Deserted." *Grand Rapids Press,* September 5, 1907.

"Renew Search for Nun Missing from Isadore." *Grand Rapids Press,* September 7, 1907.

"To Resume Search." *Grand Rapids Press,* September 9, 1907.

"Sister May Have Been Helped Away." *Grand Rapids Press,* September 11, 1907.

"Sister Was Not Found." *Evening Record,* September 11, 1907.

"Officers Find Body of Sister Missing Many Years." *Traverse City Record-Eagle,* February 22, 1919.

"Seek Solution of Murdered Nun." *Traverse City Record-Eagle,* February 22, 1919.

"Chain of Evidence of Slaying of Nun Leads to Manistee." *Manistee News-Advocate,* February 24, 1919.

"Church Lines up Firmly behind a Thorough Probe." *Traverse City Record-Eagle,* February 24, 1919.

"Church to Aid Mystery Quiz." *Detroit News,* February 24, 1919.

"How Isadore Feels." *Traverse City Record-Eagle,* February 24, 1919.

"The Story of Sister Superior Mary Johns." *Traverse City Record-Eagle,* February 24, 1919.

"Arrest in Nun Mystery." *New York Times,* February 25, 1919.

"Arrest Woman for Murder." *Traverse City Record-Eagle,* February 25, 1919.

"Catholic Church Stands Back of State Officials." *Manistee News-Advocate,* February 25, 1919.

"Mrs. Lipcynska Is Arrested for Murder of Nun." *Manistee News-Advocate,* February 25, 1919.

"Where Nun Disappeared." *Grand Rapids Press,* February 25, 1919.

"Nun Mystery Case Snagged." *Detroit News,* February 26, 1919.

"Daughter Will Appear at Murder Hearing of Mother." *Waterloo Times-Tribune,* February 27, 1919.

"Fr. Bieniawski to Investigate Nun Slaying Mystery." *Manistee News-Advocate,* February 27, 1919.

"Mrs. Lipczynska's Daughter Relates Story." *Manistee News-Advocate,* February 27, 1919.

"Search for More Evidence." *Traverse City Record-Eagle,* February 27, 1919.

"Slaying Story Source Sought." *Detroit News,* February 27, 1919.

"Find New Clue under Church." *Detroit News,* February 28, 1919.

"Seek Evidence of Nun Death in Milwaukee." *Sheboygan Press,* February 28, 1919.

"Delay in Hearing Seems Probable." *Traverse City Record-Eagle,* March 1, 1919.

"Judge M. Brown Here to Resume Murder Inquiries." *Manistee News-Advocate,* March 1, 1919.

"Motive Sought in Nun Slaying." *Detroit News,* March 1, 1919.

"Bieniawski Charges a 'Frame-Up' Resulted in Suspicion of Him." *Traverse City Record-Eagle,* March 3, 1919.

"Enemy of Priest Figures in New Slaying Evidence." *Manistee News-Advocate,* March 3, 1919.

"Isadore Priest Revolutionist." *Detroit News,* March 3, 1919.

"Stood Against Vice; Is Hated, Declares Priest." *Manistee News-Advocate,* March 4, 1919.

"To Testify for Her Mother in Murder of Nun." *Hamilton, Ohio Republican News,* March 5, 1919.

"Sheriff Mum on Nun Case Clews." *Grand Rapids Press,* March 6, 1919.

"Local Officers Decide against Holding Inquest." *Traverse City Record-Eagle,* March 8, 1919.

"Examination of Mrs. Lipczynska Thursday at 10." *Traverse City Record-Eagle,* March 24, 1919.

"Examination of Mrs. Lipczynska Occurs Thursday." *Manistee News-Advocate,* March 26, 1919.

"Transfer Order Examination to Court in Leland." *Manistee News-Advocate,* March 27, 1919.

"Fr. Bieniawski on Stand: Important Letter Produced." *Manistee News-Advocate,* March 28, 1919.

"Lipczynska Examination Opens." *Traverse City Record-Eagle,* March 28, 1919.

"Bones Those of a Woman 62" Tall, Say Doctors." *Manistee News-Advocate,* March 29, 1919.

"Calls Woman Slayer of Nun." *Detroit News,* March 29, 1919.

"Mrs. Lipczynska Bound over to May Court Term." *Manistee News-Advocate,* April 10, 1919.

"Woman Charged with Murder May Never Go on Trial for Crime." *Traverse City Record-Eagle,* May 10, 1919.

"Attorneys Leave for Trial of Mrs. Lipczynska." *Manistee News-Advocate,* May 12, 1919.

"Many Wild Stories Veil Actualities in Trial for Slayer." *Traverse City Record-Eagle,* May 12, 1919.

"Court Orders an Examination of Mrs. Lipczynska." *Manistee News-Advocate,* May 13, 1919.

"Court Orders Mrs. Lipczynska Taken to Ann Arbor for Examination." *Traverse City Record-Eagle,* May 13, 1919.

"Tuesday, June 24, Date Set for Continuance." *Traverse City Record-Eagle,*
May 14, 1919.

"Case Depends on Hospital Result." *Traverse City Record-Eagle,* May 19, 1919.

"Needs More Time to Settle Case." *Traverse City Record-Eagle,* June 13, 1919.

"Continue Test of Mrs. Lipczynska." *Manistee News-Advocate,* June 17, 1919.

"Look for Some Startling Developments When Trial for Nun Death Is Resumed." *Traverse City Record-Eagle,* July 5, 1919.

"Expect Startling News in Nun Case." *Manistee News-Advocate,* July 7, 1919.

"Alienists Report on Condition of Mrs. Stanislawa Lipczynska at Leland
Court Today." *Traverse City Record-Eagle,* July 10, 1919.

"Isadore Death Case to Trial." *Detroit News,* July 11, 1919.

"Mrs. Lipczynska Must Answer in Person." *Traverse City Record-Eagle,* July
11, 1919.

"Trial of Nun Confronts Mrs. Lipczynska." *Manistee News-Advocate,* July 11,
1919.

"To Hear Petition for Habeas Writ in Murder Case." *Manistee News-Advocate,*
July 12, 1919.

"Local Attorneys Strongly Defend Mrs. Lipczynska." *Manistee News-Advocate,* July 23, 1919.

"Will Carry Nun Murder Case to Supreme Court." *Manistee News-Advocate,*
July 24, 1919.

"Attorneys to Ask Change of Venue." *Manistee News-Advocate,* July 26, 1919.

"Mrs. Lipczynska Will Stand Trial for Murder of Sister Mary—Asks Change
of Venue." *Traverse City Record-Eagle,* July 29, 1919.

"Mrs. Lipczynska Held for Trial October First." *Manistee News-Advocate,* July
30, 1919.

"Temporary Decision Rests upon Results Apparent When Effort Is Made to
Secure a Jury." *Tranverse City Record-Eagle,* July 30, 1919.

"Mrs. Lipczynska to Go on Trial Next Wednesday." *Manistee News-Advocate,*
September 27, 1919.

"Mrs. Lipczynska Trial Underway Today at Leland." *Manistee News-Advocate,* October 1, 1919.

"Prospective Veniremen in Sister Mary Case Are Asked Whether or Not
They Belong to Catholic Church." *Traverse City Record-Eagle,* October 2,
1919.

"Jury in Lipczynska Case Is Excused until That Time—Canvass Shows
Veniremen Limit Near Reached." *Traverse City Record-Eagle,* October 3,
1919.

"Nun Case Jurors' Religion Probed." *Detroit Free Press,* October 3, 1919.

"Adjourn Trial until Monday." *Manistee News-Advocate,* October 4, 1919.

"Will a Jury Be Secured? That Is All-Absorbing Question Now Looming up in Murder Trial." *Traverse City Record-Eagle,* October 4, 1919.

"Defense Discharges Another Juryman—Examination of the Veniremen Will Continue through Early Week." *Traverse City Record-Eagle,* October 6, 1919.

"Bloodhound Not Bloodthirsty Dog." *Detroit Free Press,* October 7, 1919.

"Defense in Lipczynska Trial Again Asks Change of Venue, Which Judge Mayne Refuses." *Traverse City Record-Eagle,* October 7, 1919.

"Expect to Secure Jury in Nun Case Wed. or Thurs." *Manistee News-Advocate,* October 7, 1919.

"Leelanau County to Try Nun Case." *Detroit Free Press,* October 8, 1919.

"Trial of Mrs. Stanislawa Lipczynska Will Be Underway by Tomorrow Is Indication." *Traverse City Record-Eagle,* October 8, 1919.

"Actual Trial Will Start Monday Afternoon." *Traverse City Record-Eagle,* October 9, 1919.

"Progress Is Made in Lipczynska Case." *Manistee News-Advocate,* October 9, 1919.

"Jury Selected; Murder Trial to Start Monday." *Manistee News-Advocate,* October 10, 1919.

"Nun Case Trial Set for Monday." *Detroit Free Press,* October 10, 1919.

"Mrs. Stanislawa Lipczynska Goes on Trial at Leland—Delay Caused by Late Arrival of Judge Mayne." *Traverse City Record-Eagle,* October 13, 1919.

"Jacob Flees Tells of Digging up the Bones of Sister Mary by Lantern Light." *Traverse City Record-Eagle,* October 14, 1919.

"Nun Was Buried Alive, Charge." *Detroit Free Press,* October 14, 1919.

"State Says Nun Murder Has Been Confessed." *Manistee News-Advocate,* October 14, 1919.

"Avers Bishop Knew Of Grave." *Detroit News,* October 15, 1919.

"Daughter of Mrs. Lipczynska Is Confused in Her Statements, Apparently Contradicting Herself on the Witness Stand Today." *Traverse City Record-Eagle,* October 15, 1919.

"Priest Knew of Nun's Grave." *Detroit Free Press,* October 15, 1919.

"Testimony of Daughter Does Not Correspond." *Manistee News-Advocate,* October 15, 1919.

"Alleged Remains of Sister Mary Janina Are Viewed Today—Mrs. Lipczynska Stoically Glimpses at Nun She Is Charged with Killing." *Traverse City Record-Eagle,* October 16, 1919.

"Mrs. Lipczynska Stares at Skull of Nun; Is Firm." *Manistee News-Advocate,* October 16, 1919.

"Nuns Testify in Death Case." *Detroit News*, October 16, 1919.

"Nun Was Slain, Bishop's Word." *Detroit Free Press*, October 16, 1919.

"Calmly Views Skull of Nun." *Detroit Free Press*, October 17, 1919.

"Nuns Help Solve Mystery." *Traverse City Record-Eagle*, October 17, 1919.

"Nuns Testify at Trial Today of Mrs. Lipczynska." *Manistee News-Advocate*, October 17, 1919.

"Nuns Weep over Bones." *Detroit News*, October 17, 1919.

"An Alleged Confession Introduced." *Sheboygan Wisconsin Press*, October 18, 1919.

"Alleged Confession Is Told." *Traverse City Record-Eagle*, October 18, 1919.

"Avers Nun Was Slain in Grave." *Detroit Free Press*, October 18, 1919.

"Church Officials Knew Nun Lay under Floor." *Fort Wayne News and Sentinel*, October 18, 1919.

"Sister, in Grave, Beaten, Charge." *Detroit News*, October 18, 1919.

"Witness Swears Mrs. Lipczynska Confused." *Manistee News-Advocate*, October 18, 1919.

"Woman Confesses to Murder of Nun." *Nebraska Evening State Journal*, October 18, 1919.

"Admits Bones Those of Nun." *Detroit Free Press*, October 19, 1919.

"Cruelty Basis of Confession." *Detroit Free Press*, October 20, 1919.

"Defense Makes Statement—Charges That Nun's Bones Were Not Buried beneath the Church Immediately after Her Disappearance." *Traverse City Record-Eagle*, October 20, 1919.

"Defense Opens Fight in Nun Murder Trial." *Manistee News-Advocate*, October 20, 1919.

"Accused Says Nun Was Good." *Detroit Free Press*, October 21, 1919.

"Assails Veracity of Nun. Father Andrew Bieniawski Flatly Denies Testimony of Felician Sisters." *Traverse City Record-Eagle*, October 21, 1919.

"Confession of Woman Forced at Trial." *Grand Rapids Press*, October 21, 1919.

"Fr. Bieniawski Impeaches Testimony of Nun." *Manistee News-Advocate*, October 21, 1919.

"Gallagher Nun Case Witness." *Detroit News*, October 21, 1919.

"Local Testimony Barred in Court Action at Leland." *Manistee News-Advocate*, October 21, 1919.

"Principals and Scenes in Nun Trial." *Grand Rapids Press*, October 21, 1919.

"Tells Method of Third Degree." *Sandusky State Journal*, October 21, 1919.

"Confession Lie, Nun Case Plea." *Detroit Free Press*, October 22, 1919.

"Defendant Takes Witness Stand in Nun Murder Trial." *Sheboygan Press*, October 22, 1919.

"Mrs. Lipczynska Tells of Abuse in Leland Jail." *Manistee News-Advocate*, October 22, 1919.

"Respondent on the Stand. Mrs. Lipczynska Makes an Excellent Witness for Herself." *Traverse City Record-Eagle*, October 22, 1919.

"More Bones Are Recovered, Strengthening Contention That Remains Are Those of Missing Nun." *Traverse City Record-Eagle*, October 23, 1919.

"More of Nun's Bones Secured." *Detroit Free Press*, October 23, 1919.

"19 More Bones of Nun Found under Church." *Manistee News-Advocate*, October 23, 1919.

"Nun Case Given to Jury." *Detroit Free Press*, October 24, 1919.

"Nun Murder Case to Go to Jury Later Today." *Manistee News-Advocate*, October 24, 1919.

"Find Woman Guilty of Murdering Nun." *Sandusky State Journal*, October 25, 1919.

"Guilty of Nun's Murder Is Sentenced for Life. Mrs. Lipczynska Hears the Verdict without Emotion." *Traverse City Record-Eagle*, October 25, 1919.

"Mrs. Lipczynska Found Guilty of Nun Murder." *Manistee News-Advocate*, October 25, 1919.

"Nun Case Ends in Conviction." *Detroit News*, October 25, 1919.

"Steps Leading to Solution of Crime." *Manistee News-Advocate*, October 25, 1919.

"Guilty of Nun's Murder." *New York Times*, October 26, 1919.

"Slayer of Nun Gets Life Term." *Detroit Free Press*, October 26, 1919.

"Petition Requests Removal of Priest from Local Parish." *Manistee News-Advocate*, October 27, 1919.

"Murderer of Nun Starts Life Term." *Detroit Free Press*, October 31, 1919.

"Murderess Goes to Pay Penalty." *Traverse City Record-Eagle*, October 31, 1919.

"Tried for Old Crime." *Manitoba Free Press*, October 31, 1919.

"Mrs. Lipczynska Case to Be Argued before High Court Thursday." *Grand Rapids Herald*, October 9, 1920.

"High Court Hears Pleadings for New Lipczynska Trial." *Saginaw Courier*, October 15, 1920.

"Supreme Court Told Mrs. Lipczynska Was Coerced to Confess." *Grand Rapids Herald*, October 15, 1920.

"Mad Moon Days Exemplified in Bird's Suicide." *Traverse City Record-Eagle*, October 20, 1920.

"Woman Claims Being Tricked into Prison." *Bismarck Daily Tribune*, January 3, 1927.

"Northern Michigan's Trial of the Century," by George Meredith. *Northern Express Weekly*, October 28, 1998.

Magazine Articles

"Terrible Crime in Isadore, Mich. Polish Nun Buried Alive." Series of pamphlets published in Polish, by the Pulaski Company of Milwaukee. Date of publication unknown; translated by Paul Brzezinski.

"The Mystery of the Vanishing Nun," by William P. Schramm. *True Detective Mysteries,* March 1930.

"The Felician Sisters of Livonia," by Sister Mary Janice Ziolkowski, CSSF. Harlo Press, Detroit, 1984.

"The Killing of Mary Janina," by Lori Hall Steele. *Traverse City Record-Eagle,* summer magazine, June 12, 1997.

"What Should Janek Learn? Staffing and Curriculum in Polish-American Parochial Schools, 1870–1940," by William J. Galush. *History of Education Quarterly,* vol. 40, no. 4 (Winter, 2000).

"Isadore's Secret," by Elizabeth Edwards. *Traverse, Northern Michigan's Magazine,* March 2001.

"Polish Settlers in Grand Rapids, Michigan," by Edward Symanski. *Polish American Historical Association* magazine, March 2002.

Personal Interviews

Personal interview with Kathy Britten, April 14, 2008.

Personal interview with writer and filmmaker George Meredith, May 28, 2008.

Personal interview with Cedar native Lucia Novak, July 9, 2008.

Telephone interview with writer Jack Sweeney, September 8, 2008.

Brief meeting with writer Jack Sweeney, September 13, 2008.

Personal interview with Cedar native Randy Weber, September 14, 2008.

Interview with Assistant Director, U.S. Marshals Service, retired, Gil Kleinknecht, October 8, 2008.

Personal interviews with Paul Brzezinski, October 28, 2008; December 12, 2008.

Archives

Archives of Michigan, Michigan Historical Society Department of History, Arts and Libraries, Lansing, Michigan.

Congregation of the Sisters of St. Felix of Cantalice's online archives, feliciansisters.org.

Diocese of Gaylord archives, Gaylord, Michigan; Parish Archival Books accessed July 19–20, 1982, by Eduard Adam Skendzel.

Eduard Adam Skendzel Collection (SKZ), University of Notre Dame Archives (UNDA), Notre Dame, Indiana.

Grand Traverse Heritage Center archives, Traverse City, Michigan.

Leelanau County Historical Society archives, Leland, Michigan.

University of Michigan Health System's history of psychiatric care in the state of Michigan, http://www.psych.med.umich.edu/about/history .asp.